LANGUAGE: THE UNKNOWN

European Perspectives
A Series of the Columbia University Press

Other works by Julia Kristeva
published by Columbia

*Desire in Language: A Semiotic Approach
to Literature and Art*

Revolution in Poetic Language

Powers of Horror: An Essay on Abjection

The Kristeva Reader

Tales of Love

In the Beginning Was Love: Psychoanalysis and Faith

Black Sun: Depression and Melancholia

Strangers to Ourselves

LANGUAGE
THE UNKNOWN

An Initiation into Linguistics

JULIA KRISTEVA

Translated by Anne M. Menke

COLUMBIA UNIVERSITY PRESS   NEW YORK

Columbia University Press wishes to express its appreciation of assistance given by the government of France through le Ministère de la Culture in the preparation of this translation.

COLUMBIA UNIVERSITY PRESS
NEW YORK

Library of Congress Cataloging-in-Publication Data

Kristeva, Julia, 1941–
  [Langage, cet inconnu. English]
  Language—the unknown : an initiation into linguistics / Julia
Kristeva ; translated by Anne M. Menke.
    p. cm. —(European perspectives)
  Translation of: Le langage, cet inconnu.
  Bibliography: p.
  Includes index.
  ISBN 0-231-06106-4
  ISBN 0-231-06107-2 (pbk.)
  1. Linguistics. 2. Language and languages. I. Title.
II. Series.
P121.K7413 1989
410—dc19   88-39195
                CIP

CONTENTS

Contents

Where does one start an initiation into linguistics? This book will answer that question, one every student of language, the humanities, and the social sciences has asked himself. This book is more than just a manual; it begins by retracing the history of the study of language as it developed in many different civilizations. The center of interest is the science of language in the West, with an emphasis on today's sciences. Proceeding in this way shows linguistic thought to be closely linked to philosophy and to society. Beyond the technical quarrels among the various schools, linguistic thought appears basically receptive to the adventure of man in his encounter with meaning and societies. If it is true that the era of humanism is followed by— something, as yet unknown, is it not indispensable to approach this unknown through language, which is and will always remain more unknown than man, and coextensive with his being?

This justifies, it seems to me, a new edition of a book written a dozen years ago, for the questions addressed then are still relevant today.

J. K.

LANGUAGE: THE UNKNOWN

PART ONE

INTRODUCTION TO LINGUISTICS

INTRODUCTION

Language at some point was made the privileged object of thought, science, and philosophy. The full import of this gesture has not yet been determined, for while language has been a specific object of thought for many centuries, the science of linguistics appeared only recently. The conception of language as the "key" to man and to social history and as the means of access to the laws of societal functioning constitutes perhaps one of the most striking characteristics of our era, and as such is definitely a new phenomenon. Man has, however, always mastered the use of language—indeed language is so intimately linked to man and society that they are inseparable. Today, more than ever before in history, language is isolated and set apart, as it were. It is grasped as a particular *object of knowledge,* and considered capable of introducing us not only to the laws of its own functioning but also to all that concerns the social realm.

Hence, one can now posit that there have been two stages in the relation between the speaking subject and language. The second stage defines our era.

First, ancient man wanted *knowledge* of what he already knew how to use (language). In this way, myths, beliefs, philosophy, and the sciences of language were created. Second, the scientific knowledge of language was projected onto the whole of social practice, and various manifestations of signifying acts were studied as *languages.* In this way were laid the bases of a scientific approach to the vast realm of human actions.

The first move, that is, setting up language as a specific object of knowledge, implies that language ceased to be an unwitting activity: it began to "speak its own laws." Let us say that "speech began to speak the spoken." This paradoxical turn detached the speaking subject (man) from what constituted him (language), and made him *say how he speaks.* This was a moment fraught with consequences, of which the first was that it no longer allowed man to think of himself as a sovereign entity that could not be broken down into smaller ones. Man had to analyze himself as a speaking system—as *language.* Perhaps we could say that while the Renaissance substituted the cult of Man with a capital M for that of the God of the Middle Ages, our era is bringing about a revolution of no less importance by effacing all cults, since it is replacing the latest cult, that of Man, with language, a *system* amenable to scientific analysis. Considering man as language and putting language in the place of man constitutes the demystifying gesture par excellence. It introduces science into the complex and imprecise zone of human activities where ideologies and religions are (usually) established. *Linguistics* turns out to be the lever of this demystification; it posits language as an object of science, and teaches us the laws of its functioning.

The science of language came into being in the last century. The word *linguistics* was recorded for the first time in 1833, but the term *linguist* could already be found in 1816 in François Raynouard's *Choix des poésies des troubadours* (vol. 1, p. 1). The science has been advancing rapidly, and continues to shed light from new angles on language, a practice we know how to engage in but of which we have no knowledge.

Whoever says *language* says *demarcation, signification,* and *communication.* In this sense, all human practices are kinds of language because they have as their function to *demarcate,* to *signify,* to *communicate.* To exchange goods and women in the social network, to produce objects of art or explanatory discourses such as religions or myths, etc., is to form a sort of *secondary linguistic system* with respect to language, and on the basis of this system to install a communications circuit with subjects, meaning, and signification. To know these systems (these subjects, these meanings, these significations), to study their particularities as types of language, is the second characteristic of modern thinking, which uses linguistics as the basis for its study of man.

WHAT IS LANGUAGE?

Answering this question leads us to the heart of the problematic that has always been at the center of the study of language. Every era or civilization, in conformity with the whole of its knowledge, its beliefs, and its ideology, has responded differently, and has seen language in relation to the matrices which constitute that civilization. Up until the eighteenth century the Christian era had a theological view of language and investigated above all the problem of its origin, or strictly speaking, the universal rules of its logic. The nineteenth century, dominated by historicism, considered language a development, change, or evolution through the ages. Today, views of language as a *system* and the problems of the *functioning* of this system predominate. Therefore, in order to understand language, we must follow the train of thought that, through the ages and even before the constitution of linguistics as a specific science, outlined the different visions of language. The question *"What is language?"* could and should be replaced with another: *"How was it possible to conceive of language?"* By posing the problem in this way, we resist looking for a supposed "essence" of language, and we present linguistic practice through the process that accompanied it: the thought it provoked, and the representation that was made of it.

Some preliminary clarifications are necessary nevertheless to situate the problem of language in its generality, and to facilitate an understanding of the successive representations that mankind has made of it.

1

LANGUAGE, *LA LANGUE,* SPEECH, AND DISCOURSE

At whatever moment one looks at language—in the most remote historical periods, among people said to be savage, or in the modern era—it presents itself as an extremely complex system in which problems of a different order are mingled.[1]

First, and seen from the outside, language takes on a diversified *material* character whose aspects and relationships must be known. Language is a chain of articulated *sounds* but also a network of written *marks* (a writing), or a play of *gestures* (a gesturality). What are the relationships between the voice, writing, and the gesture? Why do these differences exist, and what do they imply? Language poses these problems for us once we broach its manner of being.

This uttered, written, or gestured materiality also produces and expresses (that is, communicates) what is known as a thought. That is to say, language is at once the only manner of being of thought, its reality, and its accomplishment. The question whether language exists without thought or thought without language has been asked too often. Beside the fact that even mute discourse (mute "thought") uses the network of language in its labyrinth and cannot do without it, it seems impossible today to affirm the existence of extralinguistic thought, unless one leaves the realm of materialism. Differences between the use of the language of communication and that, let us say, of dreams or of unconscious or preconscious processes can be noted. Today's

6

science tries not to exclude these "distinctive" phenomena, but instead attempts to broaden the notion of language by allowing it to encompass what at first glance seems to escape its realm. In the same vein, we will be wary of affirming that language is the *instrument* of thought. Such a conception leads one to believe that language *expresses,* as if it were a *tool,* something—an idea?—external to it. But what is this idea? Does it exist other than in the form of language? To claim that it does would amount to an idealism whose metaphysical roots are only too visible. One can thus see how an instrumentalist conception of language, whose basis presupposes the existence of thought or symbolic activity without language, by its philosophical implications leads to theology.

While language is the material of thought, it is also the basis of social communication. There is no society without language, any more than there is society without communication. All language that is produced is produced to be communicated in social exchange. The classic question "What is the primary function of language: to *produce* a thought or to *communicate* it?" has no objective foundation. Language is all that at once, and cannot have one of these functions without the other. All the evidence that archeology offers us of language practices is found in social systems, and consequently is of a communicative nature. "Man speaks" and "man is a social animal" are themselves both tautologies, as well as synonymous propositions. To emphasize the social character of language is not, therefore, to grant the predominance of its *communicative function.* On the contrary, having been used to counter spiritualist conceptions of language, the theory of communication, if given a dominant position in the approach to language, would risk masking any problematic that concerns linguistic formation and production. The formation and production in question are those of the speaking subject and of communicated signification, which are nonanalyzable constants in that theory of communication. Having made this reservation, we can say that language is the process of communicating a *message* between at least two speaking *subjects,* one of whom is the *addresser* or sender, the other, the *addressee* or receiver (figure 1.1).

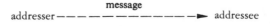

Figure 1.1

However, each speaking subject is both the addresser and the addressee of his own message, since he is capable of emitting a message and deciphering it *at the same time,* and in principle does not emit anything he cannot decipher. In this way, the message intended for the *other* is, in a sense, *first* intended for the one who is speaking: whence it follows that to *speak* is to *speak to oneself* (figure 1.2).

Figure 1.2

By the same token, the addressee-decipherer deciphers only to the extent that he can say what he hears/understands.

One can thus see that the circuit of linguistic communication established in this way leads us into the complex realm of the subject, his constitution in relation to his other, the way in which he internalizes this other and is confused with him, etc.

While language is a practice realized in social communication and by means of it, it constitutes a material reality that, while participating in the material world itself, nonetheless posits the problem of its relation with what is not language, that is, with the *outside*—nature, society, etc.—that exists without language even if it cannot be named without it. What does it mean to "name"? How does "naming" come about, and how are the named universe and the universe that names differentiated from each other? Here is another series of questions which, when clarified, will help us understand the fact of "language."

Finally, what we call language has a history that unfolds in time. From the point of view of this *diachrony,* language is transformed during different eras, and takes different forms among different peoples. For language taken as a system, that is, *synchronically,* has precise operational rules, a given structure, and structural transformations, all of which obey strict laws.

As Ferdinand de Saussure has noted, "Taken as a whole, language is many-sided and heterogeneous; straddling several fields—physical, physiological, and psychological—it belongs both to the individual and to society; we cannot put it into any category of human facts, for we cannot discover its unity."[2] Because of the complexity and diversity of the problems it raises, language calls for an analysis of philosophy, anthropology, psychoanalysis, and sociology, not to mention the various linguistic disciplines.

In order to isolate, from this mass of characteristics bearing a relationship to language, an object that is unified and classifiable, linguistics differentiates *la langue* from language as a whole. According to Saussure, *la langue* is "localized in the limited segment of the speaking-circuit where an auditory-image *(s)* becomes associated with a concept *(c)*." [p. 14]. Saussure diagrammed the circuit as shown in figure 1.3 [p. 12].

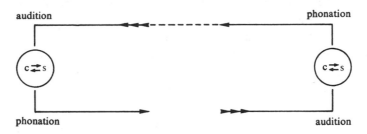

Figure 1.3

La langue is "the social side of language, outside the individual who can never create or modify it by himself; it exists only by virtue of a sort of contract signed by the members of a community" [p. 14]. In this way *la langue* is isolated from the heterogeneous whole of language: it retains only "a system of signs in which the only essential thing is the union of meanings and sound-images" [p. 15].

While *la langue* is, so to speak, an anonymous system made up of *signs* that are combined according to specific laws, and as such cannot exist in what is spoken by any subject, but instead "exists perfectly only within a collectivity" [p. 14], speech *(la parole)* is "always individual, and the individual is always its master" [p. 13]. Speech is, then, according to Saussure's definition, "an individual, willful, and intelligent act" [p. 14]. It is composed of (1) the combination by which the speaking subject uses *la langue*'s code; and (2) the psychophysical mechanism that allows him to externalize these combinations [p. 14]. Speech would be the sum of both the personal, individual combinations introduced by speaking subjects and the acts of phonation necessary for the execution of these combinations.

The language/*langue*/speech distinction has been discussed and often dismissed by certain modern linguists; it serves nevertheless to situate in a general fashion the object of linguistics. For Saussure himself, this distinction led to a division of the study of language into two parts: one that examines *la langue* and is consequently social, independent of the individual, and "entirely psychological"; and one, psychophysical, that observes the individual part of language, speech, including phonation. In fact, the two parts are inseparable. *La langue* is a prerequisite for speech to occur; but at the same time, there is no *langue* in the abstract without the occurrence of speech. Therefore two inseparable linguistics are necessary: a linguistics of *la langue* and a linguistics of speech. The second type of linguistics is still in its infancy.

The introduction into the linguistic field of the notions necessary to *communications theory* has contributed to a reformulation of the *langue*/speech distinction and has given it a new and operant signification. The founder of cybernetics, Norbert Wiener, noted that no fundamental opposition exists between the problems encountered by specialists of communication and those encountered by linguists. Engineers, for example, send a message by means of a *code,* that is, a minimal number of binary decisions. In other words, they use a classification system or, let us say, a diagram representing the invariable and fundamental structures of the message, structures belonging to both the sender and the receiver, with which the receiver himself can reconstruct the message. In the same way, the linguist can find in the complexity of the verbal message distinctive features whose combination furnishes him with the code of that message. As Roman Jakobson has remarked, interlocutors belonging to the same linguistic community can be defined as the actual users of one and the same code; the existence of a common code sets up the communication and makes possible the exchange of messages.

The term *discourse* designates in a rigorous and unambiguous fashion the manifestation of *la langue* in living communication. Clarified by Emile Benveniste, discourse is contrasted with *la langue,* which thence designates language as a collection of formal signs, stratified in successive layers that form systems and structures. Discourse implies first the participation of the subject in his language through his *speech, as an individual.* Using the anonymous structure of *la langue,* the subject forms and transforms himself in the discourse he communicates to the other. *La langue,* common to all, becomes in discourse the vehicle of a *unique* message. The message belongs to the particular structure of a given subject who imprints a specific seal upon the required structure of *la langue.* Without being aware of it, the subject thus makes his mark on *la langue.*

To clarify the outlines of discourse, they can be contrasted with those of *speech* and *history.* According to Benveniste, the locutor of a historical enunciation is excluded from the story he tells: all subjectivity and all autobiographical references are banished from historical enunciations, which are thus constituted as the mode of enunciating the truth. The term "discourse," on the other hand, designates any enunciation that integrates in its structure the locutor and the listener, with the desire of the former to influence the latter. Discourse thus becomes the privileged realm of psychoanalysis. "Its means," Jacques Lacan has said, "are those of speech in so far as speech confers a meaning on the functions of the individual; its domain is that of concrete discourse, in so far as this is the field of the transindividual reality of the subject; its operations are those of history, in so far as history constitutes the emergence of truth in the real."[3]

Hence, it is clear that to study language, to grasp the multiplicity of its aspects and functions, amounts to constructing a stratified science and theory whose different branches have a bearing on the various aspects of language, in order in a time of synthesis to furnish an ever more precise knowledge of man's signifying operation. It will therefore be necessary to know vocal language as well as writing; *la langue* as well as discourse; the internal systematics of utterances and their relationship to the subjects of communication; and, finally, the logic of historical changes and the relation between the linguistic level and the real.[4] In this way the specific laws of the use of symbols can be approached.

2

THE LINGUISTIC SIGN

The idea that the fundamental core of *la langue* resides in the *sign* has belonged to various thinkers and schools of thought, from ancient Greece through the Middle Ages and up to the present time. In fact, every speaker is more or less conscious of the fact that language symbolizes or *represents* real facts by *naming* them. The elements of the spoken chain—for the moment let us call them words—are associated with certain objects or facts that they *signify*.

The sign, or *representamen,* says Charles Sanders Peirce in his *Collected Works,*[1] is that which replaces something for someone. The sign is addressed to someone and evokes for him an object or a fact in the *absence* of this object or fact. And so it is said that the sign signifies "in absentia." "In praesentia," that is to say, with respect to the present object that it re-presents, the sign seems to posit a conventional or contractual relation between the represented material object and the phonic form that represents it. Etymologically, the Greek word σύηβολον comes from the verb συμβάλλειν, which means "to put together"; it was often used to signify an association, a convention, or a contract. For the Greeks, a flag or an ensign was a symbol, just as a theater ticket, a feeling, or a belief is. What unites these phenomena and allows for a common naming is the fact that they all *replace* or *represent*

something that is absent, evoked by an intermediary, and, consequently, included in a system of exchange: in a communication.

In Peirce's theory, the sign is a triadic relation established between
an *object*, its *representamen*, and the *interpretant*. The interpretant, for
Peirce, is a type of *ground* on which the object-sign relationship is
based, and corresponds to the *idea* in the Platonic sense of the term.
For the sign does not represent the entire object but only an idea of it,
or as Sapir would say, the *concept* of that object.

In theory, it can be affirmed that linguistic signs are the "origin" of
all symbolism: that the first act of symbolization was symbolization in
and by means of language. The fact remains that a variety of signs are
presented in the different realms of human practice. On the basis of
the relationship between the representamen and the represented object, Peirce classified signs into three categories:

—The *icon* refers to the object through its similarity with it. An
example of an icon is a design of a tree that represents a real tree by
resembling it.
—The *index* does not necessarily resemble the object but is affected
by it, and in this way, has something in common with it; thus smoke
is an index of fire.
—The *symbol* refers to an object that it designates by a sort of law,
by convention, or by the intermediary of an idea; such are linguistic
signs.

While Peirce elaborated a general theory of signs, it is to Saussure
that we owe the first exhaustive and scientific development of the
linguistic sign in its modern conception. In his *Course in General Linguistics* (1916), Saussure observed that it would be illusory to believe
that the linguistic sign associates a thing and a name; the relation
established by the sign is between a *concept* and a *sound-image*. The
sound-image is not the sound itself, but "the psychological imprint of
the sound, the impression that it makes on our senses" [p. 66]. And
so, for Saussure, the sign is a psychological reality with two sides, the
concept and the sound-image. To take the word "stone" for example,
its sign consists of the sound-image *stone* and the concept "stone"; it is
a convenient envelope that retains what is common to the thousands

of representations we may have of the distinct element "stone" (figure 2.1).

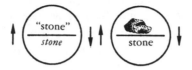

Figure 2.1

These two inseparable sides of the sign, which Saussure describes as two sides of the same piece of paper, are called the *signified* (the concept), and the *signifier* (the sound-image). For Saussure, the linguistic sign is defined by the signifier/signified relation; the object, excluded from this relation, is designated the *referent*. Linguistics is not concerned with the referent; it is interested only in the signifier, the signified, and their relation.

What is the relation between the signifier and the signified?

One of the founding postulates of linguistics is that the sign is arbitrary. That is to say, there is no necessary relation between the signifier and the signified: the same signified "stone" has as it signifier *pier* in French, *kame* in Russian, *stoun* in English, and *shi石* in Chinese. This does not mean that the signifiers are chosen arbitrarily by a single voluntary act, and that consequently they can be changed just as arbitrarily. On the contrary, the "arbitrariness" of the sign is, so to speak, normative, absolute, valid, and obligatory for all subjects speaking the same language. The word "arbitrary" signifies more exactly *unmotivated*, that is to say, there is no natural or real necessity linking the signifier and the signified. The fact that certain onomatopoeias and exclamations seem to *mimic* real phenomena, and like them, seem motivated, does not refute this linguistic postulate, since what is at stake there is clearly of secondary importance.

The theory of the sign does, however, have the advantage of posing the problem of the relation between *la langue* and the reality outside the field of linguistic preoccupations, and of enabling the study of *la langue* as a formal system that submits to laws and is made of ordered and transformational structures. Today, however, this theory is being subjected to criticism that does not completely destroy it but does necessitate certain modifications.

The theory of the sign rests on the reduction of discourse, a complex phonic network, to a *linear chain* in which a minimal element corresponding to the *word* is isolated. However, it is more and more difficult to maintain that the word is the minimal unit of *la langue*. In fact, a word does not achieve its complete signification except in a sentence, that is, by and in a syntactic relation. On the other hand, this same word can be broken down into morphological elements, *morphemes*, which are smaller than it is, and are themselves bearers of signification. The group of morphemes constitutes the signification of the word. In the French words *donner, don, donneur* [to give, gift, giver], the morpheme *don-* can be isolated, which implies the idea of *offer;* the morphemes *-er, -, -eur* attribute various modalities to the root *don-*. The signification of this word can never be complete unless it is studied in *discourse,* while taking into account the enunciation of the speaking subject.

The word, conceived of as an indivisible entity and absolute value, has come to be viewed with suspicion by linguists. In our day, it has ceased to be the foundation of thought on the functioning of language. There is more and more talk of separating it from the science of language. André Martinet was correct in writing that "Semiology [the science of signs], as it is envisioned by recent studies, has no need of the word. And one should not imagine that semiologists are thinking 'word' when they write 'sign.' Some would rather think 'sentence' or 'utterance,' never forgetting, however, that the *-r-* of *paiera* is also a sign."[2] Martinet proposed replacing the notion of word with that of " 'syntagm,' 'a group of several minimal signs' that could be called a *moneme. Au fur et à mesure* [little by little] is one and the same moneme because once *au fur* [little by] is chosen, the speaker cannot refrain from uttering the rest." One can see from this example that linguistics is trying to grasp, beyond immediate appearances, behind the "screen of the word," the truly fundamental features of human language.[3]

Moreover, and doubtless because *la langue* has as its basis the isolated word, the shape the theory of the sign takes is dictated by the *concept* as the model interpretant of the elements of language. There would be no language apart from the *concept,* because the concept as *signified* builds the very structure of the sign. The complete acceptance of this theory would lead us to banish from the realm of language all that is not of the order of the concept—dreams, the unconscious, poetry, etc.—or at least to reduce their specificity to one and the same type of conceptual operation. It would lead to a *normative* vision of the signifying operation, which could not study the multiplicity of signifying practices without relegating them to a pathology to be suppressed. Certain linguists, such as Edward Sapir, note with respect to this that it would be inaccurate to confuse language with conceptual thought such as it now occurs. He goes so far as to affirm that language is above all an "extra-rational" function, which means that its material offers itself up to practices of differentiation and systematization that do not necessarily fall within the province of the subject's reason, the subject being defined as the Cartesian subject.

In the end, a critical examination of the notion of the arbitrariness of the sign has found it lacking. Saussure's reasoning seems to have allowed an error. He did affirm that the substance (the referent) was not a part of the system of *la langue,* but Saussure was in fact thinking about the *real referent* when he stated that *{böf}* and *{oks},* so different with respect to their signifiers, refer to the same idea (to the same signified), and that consequently the signifier/signified relationship was arbitrary. Basically, as Benveniste has noted, it is not the relationship between the signifier *{oks}* and the signified "ox" that is arbitrary. The link *{oks}*-"ox" is necessary: the concept and the sound-image are inseparable and are in an "established symmetry." What is *arbitrary* is the relation between this sign (signifier/signified: *{oks}* / "ox") and the reality it names, in other words, the relation between the language symbol in its totality and the real outside it that it symbolizes. It seems that we have here a contingency for which no philosophical or theoretical explanation can be found in the current state of linguistic science.

What are the theories that have arisen to fill the gap left by the conception of *la langue* as a system of signs?

Linguistics itself, based on the conception (permitted by the theory of the sign) that *la langue* is a formal system, has lost interest in the symbolic aspects of language and studies nothing but its formal order as a "transformational" structure. Such are the later theories of Noam

Chomsky. Early on, he left the level of the *word* in order to tackle the structure of the *sentence,* which became in this way the basic linguistic element capable of being synthesized from syntactic functions. In his second phase, he broke down the fundamental syntactic elements (the *subject* and *predicate*), gave them the "algebraic" notations X and Y, and made them into nouns and verbs in the source of a process said to be "generative." The problems of signification were replaced with a formalization representing the process of synthesis whereby linguistic "universals" (constituents and general rules) can generate sentences that are grammatically—and, consequently, semantically—correct. Instead of trying to discover why *la langue* is constituted as a system of signs, the generative grammar of Chomsky shows the formal, syntactic mechanism of the recursive whole of language, whose *correct* realization results in *signification.*[4] Modern linguistics thus goes further than Saussure; it "desubstantializes" *la langue* and *represents* signification (which it started out by ignoring) as the result of a process of syntactic transformation that generates sentences. This approach recalls that of Leonard Bloomfield, who excluded semantics from the realm of linguistics and assigned it to the realm of psychology.

Another point of view is based on a philosophical critique of the very concept of the sign that links *voice* and *thought* in such a way as to end up erasing the signifier in favor of the signified. Proponents of this view have noted that *writing {écriture},* as a *trace* or [something] traced *{tracé}* (what is called, according to a recent terminology, a *gramme*), veils a "scene" within *la langue* that the sign and its signified cannot see. This scene, instead of instituting a "resemblance" as the sign does, is, on the contrary, the mechanism of "difference." In writing, in fact, something is traced but not represented, and this traced something— this trace—has provided the foundation for a new theoretical science called *grammatology.*[5]

3

THE MATERIALITY OF LANGUAGE

While *la langue* is a network of regulated differences on which signification and communication are based, it is far from being a pure ideality. It is realized by and in *concrete matter* and the *objective laws* of its organization. In other words, while we *know* language by means of a complicated conceptual system, the actual body of language manifests a doubly discernible materiality.

This materiality is found, on the one hand, in the phonic, gestural, or graphic aspects that *la langue* assumes (there is no language without sounds, gestures, or writing).

On the other hand, one can see it in the objectivity of the laws that organize the different subsets of the linguistic whole, and that constitute phonetics, grammar, stylistics, semantics, etc. These laws reflect the objective relations between the speaking subject and external reality; they reflect as well the connections that govern human society, while at the same time overdetermining these relations and connections.

PHONETICS

The linguistic sign, as we have seen, does not contain the material sound: the signifier is the "sound-image," not the concrete noise. However, the signifier does not exist without its material support, the real sound that the human animal produces. This *sound,* the bearer of meaning, must be clearly distinguished from the various cries that serve as the means of communication among animals. The linguistic sound is of a completely different nature, since it is the basis of the system of differentiation, signification, and communication that constitutes *la langue* in the sense we have given it, and that is a characteristic of human society alone.

The linguistic sound is produced by what are improperly called "the organs of speech." As Edward Sapir has noted, "there are, properly speaking, no organs of speech; there are only organs that are incidentally useful in the production of speech sounds."[1] In fact, while certain organs, such as the lungs, the larynx, the palate, the nose, the tongue, the teeth, and the lips participate in the articulation of language, they cannot be considered its instrument. Language is not a biological function like respiration or the capacity to smell or taste, which have as their organs the lungs, the nose, the tongue, etc. Language is a function of differentiation and signification, that is to say, it is a social and not a biological function, although it is made possible by a biological operation.

Nor can it be said that language is biologically localized in the brain. Physiological psychology, it is true, is able to localize the different material manifestations of language in various brain centers: the auditory center commands the hearing of meaning; the motor centers control the movements of the tongue, the lips, the larynx, etc.; and the visual center governs the work of visual recognition necessary for reading, etc. However, all these centers control only the constituent parts of language; they do not in any way provide the basis for the highly synthetic and social function that constitutes the use of *la langue.* In other words, the bodily organs that participate in the material formation of language can provide us with the quantitative and mechanical foundations of linguistic operation, but they cannot explain the *qualitative* leap that the human animal makes when he begins to note differences in a system, which becomes in this way the network of significations through which subjects communicate in society. This network of differences cannot be localized in the brain or anywhere else. It is a social function overdetermined by the complex process of exchange and social tasks, produced by it, and incomprehensible without it.

Having said this, we can describe the organs that offer the mechanical basis for linguistic articulation: the vocal apparatus and its functioning.

Expelled by the lungs, air travels through the respiratory passages and vibrates the glottis, which nonetheless does not imprint any differentiation on sounds. The glottis, formed of two parallel muscles, or vocal cords, that can be brought together or apart, forms the laryngeal sound by bringing the vocal cords together.

This uniform sound can pass through the *oral cavity* or the *nasal cavity,* which particularize the different sounds of *la langue.* The oral cavity is composed of the lips, the tongue, the upper teeth, the palate (with an inert, bony part in the front, and a movable, soft palate or velum in the back), the uvula, and the lower teeth. Through the interplay of these components the oral cavity can expand or contract, while the tongue and lips attribute various values to the laryngeal sound. The oral cavity thus is used both to *produce* sounds and to make the voice *resonate.* When the opening of the glottis is wide, that is, in the absence of laryngeal vibration, the oral cavity produces the sound. When the glottis vibrates, that is, when the cords are close together, the mouth merely modifies the laryngeal sound.

The nasal cavity, unlike the oral one, is completely immobile, and acts only as a resonator.

Several criteria of sound articulation have been determined that permit the establishment of a pertinent classification system of acoustic qualities. Saussure proposed the following factors for distinguishing the characteristics of a sound: expiration, oral articulation, laryngeal vibration, and nasal resonance. "For each phoneme," he stated, "we must determine its oral articulation, whether a laryngeal sound is present . . . or absent. . . . , and whether nasal resonance is present . . . or absent" [*Course,* p. 43]. He consequently distinguished *voiceless* sounds, *voiced* sounds, voiceless nasalized sounds, and voiced nasalized sounds.

Saussure used the type of oral articulation as a basis for establishing
the following systematization of the minimal elements of the spoken
chain or *phonemes* ("a phoneme is the sum of the auditory impressions
and articulatory movements, the unit heard and the unit spoken"
[p. 40]:

The *occlusives:* obtained by complete closure or hermetic, but mo-
mentary, occlusion of the oral cavity:

(a) labials: p, b, m;

(b) dentals: t, d, n;

(c) gutturals: k, g, ɜ.

Nasals: Nasal sounds are voiced nasalized occlusives.

Fricatives or *spirants:* the oral cavity is not completely closed and
allows the passage of air:

(a) labials: f, v;

(b) dentals: s, z, š *(chant)*, ɜ *(génie);*

(c) palatals: x' *(ich,* Ger.), γ' *(liegen,* North Ger.).

(d) gutturals: χ *(Bach,* Ger.), γ *(Tage,* North Ger.)

Liquids: (a) Laterals: the tongue touches the front palate while leaving an opening on both sides; as with the dental *l,* the palatal *l,* and the
guttural *l;*

(b) Vibrants: the tongue is farther from the palate, and vibrates
against it; as with the rolled *r* (produced with the tip of the tongue
applied against the teeth sockets), the fricative Parisian *r* (produced
with the back part of the tongue).

Vowels require an effacement of the oral cavity as producer of
sound: the mouth functions only as a resonator, and the timbre of the
laryngeal sound makes itself clearly heard. Several distinctions can be
made among the vowels:

i, ü can be called *semivowels,* according to Saussure; the lips are
retracted for the pronunciation of *i* and rounded for *ü.* In both cases,
the tongue is lifted toward the palate: these phonemes are called
palatals.

e, o, ö: their pronunciation requires a small separation of the jaws
with respect to the preceding series;

a: is articulated with the mouth open as far as possible.

The description of the phonetic production of vowels as well as of
consonants must take into account, among other things, the fact that

phonemes do not exist in isolation. They are part of a whole, the utterance, and are in a relationship of internal dependency to the utterance. The science of sounds must therefore be a science of *groups of sounds* in order to fully account for the true character of phonation. Thus, depending on whether a sound in a syllable is pronounced in a *closed* or *open* fashion, an *implosion* (>) in the first case, or an *explosion* (<) in the second, can be distinguished, as for example, with appa. These two combined pronunciations give explosive-implosive, and implosive-explosive groups, etc. We thus arrive at the definition of a *dipthong:* it is an "implosive link in which the second phoneme is relatively open, making a specific acoustical impression. We might say that the sonant continues in the second element of the combination" [p. 61]. Saussure cites as an example the groups *uo ia* in certain German dialects *(buob, liab)*.

Linguistic sounds are also distinguished by their *duration,* or *quality.* This property is variable in different languages, and also depends on the position of the sound in the whole of the spoken chain. In French, for example, a long quality exists only in a stressed syllable.

We can therefore see that the interinfluence of sounds in a spoken chain gives way to a *combinatory phonetics* that studies the modalities of influence of vowels and consonants according to their occurrence. These modifications do not always change the fundamental character of sounds. Thus *t* and *d* can become *palatalized* by contact with a palatal vowel *(ti-, di-* don't have the same consonant as *ton, don);* *velarized* by contact with posterior vowels, or *labialized* owing to the rounding of the lips that accompanies the articulation of neighboring labial vowels. There are nevertheless phenomena that bring about greater changes in the sounds.

Assimilation is due to one sound becoming closer to another, depending upon the way it is articulated and its place of articulation. An example is the French verb *entendre,* "to hear/understand"—the *n* is articulated in place of the *t* and the *d.*

Dissimilation is the accentuation of the differences between phonemes. In popular French *colidor* is found instead of *corridor.*

Intervention occurs when phonemes change places, and *metathesis* happens when this change takes place over distance. In this way the proper name Roland has taken the form Orlando in Italian.

Haplology is the disappearance of an element of the spoken chain that should be repeated. The example frequently given is tragicomedy for tragico-comedy.

The spoken chain, constructed in this way of phonemes, cannot, however, be reduced to a line chopped into fragments represented by isolated phonemes. In language use, phonemes are combined into superior units, such as *syllables*. For Grammont and Fouch, whose formulation has been confirmed by acoustical phonetics, the syllable is characterized by an *increasing tension* of the phonatory muscles followed by a *decreasing tension*. At a higher level, the spoken chain consists not of words but of *phonetic groups* constituted by a stress on the last syllable. In "friend of the people," there is a single stress on *peo,* which makes the expression a single phonic group. Beyond phonetic groups, we find the *sentence* determined by the breath that divides the spoken chain.

Let us note finally that these material particularities of linguistic phonemics, of which we have given only a very brief and schematic survey, are specific for each national language and vary according to eras: the phonemics of medieval French is not the same as that of modern French.

THE GRAPHIC AND THE GESTURAL

Despite the numerous studies of the many different types of writing that humanity has produced over the ages, current science has not yet proposed a satisfactory theory of writing, its relation to *la langue,* and the rules of its operation. There has been much debate of a metaphysical nature about whether vocal language or a graphic system was the "origin." Van Ginneken, relying on the work of the Chinese scholar Chang Cheng-Ming, has, in opposition to nearly everyone, maintained the thesis of the anteriority of writing with respect to phonetic language. His basis is the fact that Chinese writing, for example, seems to imitate gestural language, which consequently would be anterior to phonetic language.

This controversy, besides being scientifically impertinent, since we have little of the information needed to judge an "origin" of language, appears outmoded today because of the *theoretical* inconsistency involved in the formulation of the basic question. The problem of the "priority" of the written over the vocal, or vice versa, cannot have any historical sense; it has only a theoretical sense. If one acknowledges, for example, that the trace (the written) is a *mark* of the difference constituting signification, and that as such it is inherent in all language, including vocal speech, then phonetics would consequently *already* be a trace, even if phonetic material has contributed to developing particularities in the system of language that writing would perhaps have indicated differently. In social exchange, phonetics has acquired independence and autonomy. Only in a second time frame has writing come back as a secondary envelope in order to fix vocalism.

Writing endures, is transmitted, and acts in the absence of speaking subjects. It uses *space* in order to indicate itself by defying *time*. While speech takes place in time, language with writing passes through time by acting like a spatial configuration. It designates in this way a type of operation in which the subject differentiates himself from his surroundings: but to the extent that he *marks/indicates* these surroundings, he does not extricate himself from them. He does not fabricate an ideal dimension for himself (the voice, the breath) in order to organize communication, but practices it in the matter and very space of this reality of which he is a part, while differentiating himself from it because he marks/indicates it. Writing is an act of differentiation and of participation with respect to reality; it is language without a beyond, without transcendence. Written "divinities" belong to the same world as the material one that traces and receives them. And we feel that the written trace and the gesture, while constituting an act of differentiation and designation, are not yet *signs* in the sense defined above. The triangle of the sign (referent/signifier/signified) seems to be reduced to a *mark* (in writing) or to a *relation* (in the gesture) between the subject and what is external to him; there is no intermediary of an already constituted and "of itself" "idea" (interpretant, signified). The close relation between the gesture and certain writings system such as those of the Chinese or the North American Indians has been noted. According to J.-G. Février, referring to the work of G. Mallery and of Chang Cheng-Ming, in the winter-count system, "pipe" is written not by representing the object but by tracing the gesture that designates it.

For the Chinese, the hieroglyph for "friend" or "friendship" is a design of the friendly gesture of two interlocking hands: 肀 or 丬 .

A real object or a combination of objects can represent writing, that is to say, language. In this case, the object or group of objects is removed from its practical utility and articulated as a system of differences that become signs for the subjects of the communication. The most striking example of this type of concrete language in which the "sign" has not yet been distinguished from the referent, but, quite simply, is the referent included in a communicated system, is given to us by Herodotus (4:131–32). He relates that when King Darius invaded the country of the Scythians, this people sent him a gift consisting of a bird, a mouse, a frog, and five arrows. The message was to be read in this way: "Unless, O Persians, ye become birds and fly into the air, or become mice and hide yourselves beneath the earth, or become frogs and leap into the lakes, ye shall never return home again, but be stricken by these arrows."[2]

A more appropriate example of a graphic system most resembling writing that is truly traced is furnished by "writings" formed of a "general equivalent," that is to say, a single material whose different presentations serve to indicate different objects. An example of this is the knots used by the Incas to indicate the animals they killed in battle. The Spanish historian Garcilaso de la Vega described these knots in the following way: "For affairs of war, or of government, for tributes or ceremonies, there were various *quipus,* and in each package of these were many knots with threads of red, green, blue, white, etc., attached to them. Just as we create many differences with the twenty-four letters [of the alphabet] by placing them in different ways in order to obtain varied sounds, the Indians obtained as great a number of significations by the various positions of the knots and colors."[3]

As far back in history as the archeological and anthropological sciences go, true writings are already traces, grammes, or complex graphic systems. The most ancient traces have been situated at the end of the Mousterian period, and are especially widespread toward the year 35,000 B.C. during the Chatelperron period. They consist of notches in rock or bone; there are no figurations which would lead to the supposition that the writing was mimetic, that it copied or represented an already existing "image," or, later, a constituted phoneticism. One can cite as an example the Australian churinga writing system that traced in an abstract manner the bodies of ancestors and different environments. Other paleontological findings confirm the thesis that the first writing systems marked the rhythm and not the form of the procedure that engendered symbolization but did not become representation.

Toward the year 20,000 B.C., graphic configuration was common and evolved rapidly. By 15,000 B.C., a technical mastery of engraving and of painting almost equal to that of the modern era could be found. It is striking that representations of humans lost their "realistic" character and became abstract; they were constructed with the help of triangles, squares, lines, and dots, as on the walls of the Lascaux caves. Animals, however, were represented in a realistic manner that tried to reproduce their form in motion.

Language (spoken and written) and *figurative art* consequently became confused in what André Leroi-Gourhan has called "the intellectual couple phonation/written form." For him, a significant part of figurative art derives from "picto-ideography," a synthetic manner of marking that, while representing images (Latin: *pictus,* painted, represented), transmits a "conceptualization," or rather a differentiation and an unrepresentable systematization ("idea"). This type of writing is not a simple transfer of phoneticism, and is perhaps even constituted completely independently of it. However, it still constitutes language. We as subjects belonging to a cultural zone in which writing is phonetic and *literally* reproduces phonetic language find it is difficult to imagine that a type of language—writing—could have existed and still exists today for many peoples that functions independently of the spoken chain, a type of language that is consequently not *linear* (as is the emission of voices), but *spatial,* and so registers a mechanism of differences where each mark's value depends upon its place in the traced whole. Starting with the Lascaux caves, one can note the constant *topographical* relations between the figures of the animals represented there: in the center, a bison and a horse; along the edges, stags and ibex; on the periphery, lions and rhinoceros. According to Leroi-Gourhan, "the symbolic assemblage of figures must have been supported by an oral context with which it was coordinated and whose values it spatially reproduced."

Such spatial mechanisms seem to constitute the graphic-material support, and consequently, the durable and transmissible support, of the entire mythic or cosmic system of a given society. One could say that these graphic systems, half writing, half "artistic" magic, or half religious representation, are mythograms.

The combinatory property of graphic elements also makes it possible to compose scriptural wholes that already mark more complex syntactic or logical formations. Sinologists call these *logical aggregates;* they are made of a juxtaposition of several *graphemes* (graphic elements). Thus, to indicate that during one year there was an "abundance of meat," the winter-count writing system included a circle (= hiding place or heap), which enclosed the head of a buffalo, and a stake or a type of scaffolding (for smoking or drying the meat).

The "multidimensionality" of these graphic systems is seen in a number of nonalphabetic writings, as in Egypt or China, or among the Aztecs or the Mayas. The elements of these writings, as we shall see, can be considered as pictograms or simplified ideograms. Some of these acquired constant phonetic value, which led to an alphabetic phoneticization of writing where each element was associated with a certain phoneme. Scriptural spatialization was reduced and replaced with phonetic linearity. This is true of Egyptian hieroglyphic writing: each *pictogram* has a phonetic import. In contrast, the Chinese *ideogram,* on the one hand, has become far removed from the image-representation (if one admits that Chinese writing had a figurative basis), and, on the other hand, has not led to a phonetic alphabet, even if certain elements have a constant phonetic value and can be used as phonemes.

The science of writing, by systematizing the archeological data relative to various writing systems, has been able to distinguish three types of writing: *pictographic, ideographic* (or hieroglyphic), and *phonetic* (or alphabetic). This traditional typology is currently contested, and one can substitute for it a classification of writing systems into the following five categories.

Phraseograms are inscriptions that transmit entire messages without distinguishing the various words contained within them. The term was proposed by the American scholar Gelb, and is similar to the expression "synthetic writing" proposed by Février. Phraseograms can be divided into two subgroups. The first, *pictograms,* are complex designs or series of designs that fix a content but do not themselves refer to its linguistic form. Such a type of writing has been used by the American Indians, the Eskimos, etc. to illustrate concrete situations. Since it was unstable and conjectural, the pictogram could not develop into a true writing. The second subgroup is that of *conventional signs,* such as totemic signs, taboos, magic signs, signs of different tribes, etc. These were used in isolation without a constant relation to other signs and could not, therefore, form a writing.

Logograms (from the Greek *logos*) are marks of different words. Proposed by Bloomfield, Gelb, Istrine, etc., the term *logogram* replaces the imprecise term *ideogram.* Marcel Cohen uses "sign-word" and Février "word-writing." The word "logogram" is used for ordered writings such as those of the Chinese, the Sumerians, and, in part, the Egyptians, which issued from pictography, and whose elements designate words or, more precisely, semantic units of discourse in the form of words or combinations of words. Compared to pictography, logography represents not only the content but also the syntactic order and sometimes the phonetic aspect of the utterance.

The term "logogram" also has the advantage of indicating that the minimal written element is not an idea or a concept without material support (as the term "ideogram" would have posited) but rather a word, or a unit of language, that is part of a material system of differentiated marks.

One category of logograms, for example, the Chinese "ideographic hieroglyphs," are directly linked to the signification of the word. These logograms evoke the form of the phenomenon they indicate, and can often be read in many ways. The possibility of several readings of a single mark is also found in the system of the ancient Egyptians: "to go" could be read "š-m," s-'b," or "j-w." These logograms are sometimes called *semantic logograms.*

The second type of logograms, of which an example are the "phonetic hieroglyphs" of the Chinese, is immediately linked to the phoneticism of the word. This type is consequently used to designate homonyms, despite the fact that the words in question may have different meanings. These logograms are *polysemous,* that is, they have several meanings. For instance, in old Chinese, the logogram *ma* could signify the word "horse," but also the words "mother" and "to swear," which phonetically resemble the first word. These logograms bear the name of *phonetic logograms.*

Morphemograms, the third type of writing, mark the various parts of the word, the *morphemes.* The history of writing contains hardly any fully developed morphemography, since the breakdown of words into morphemes is in fact an extremely difficult and complex analytical task.

Syllabograms are writings that distinguish different syllables without taking into account whether or not these coincide with morphemes. Three subcategories can be distinguished: either (a) the signs mark syllables of various phonetic constructions (Assyrian-Babylonian writing); (b) the signs indicate only open vowels (as in Cretan Mycenaean writing); or (c) the principal signs designate only isolated vowels in combination with consonants and the vowel *a.*

Finally, *phonograms* are the marks of the minimal phonic elements of the spoken chain, the phonemes. There are *consonantal* phonetic writings, whose principal letters designate consonants (such as the Arabic or Hebrew, etc., alphabets) and *vocalized* phonetic writings (such as Greek, Latin, Slavic alphabets), in which signs mark consonants as well as vowels.

The science of writing, for which we have given only a broad outline (as proposed by Istrine) of the types of writing, remains faithful to a conception of language based upon the model of spoken language. Even if a step forward has been made with respect to the classic distinction pictogram/ideogram/phonogram, this progress only transfers to the field of writing the knowledge we have of spoken language. Writing is considered to be a *representation* of the spoken, its fixative double, and not a particular material whose combinative nature leads one to think of a linguistic operation different from that of phonetics. The science of writing seems therefore the prisoner of a conception that confuses *language* with *spoken language,* which is articulated according to the rules of a certain grammar. A. Meillet, following Saussure, expressed this position in 1919: "No design can suffice to render a language *(langue)* graphically, no matter how simple the structure of this language *{langue}* is. There are a lot of words whose value cannot be clearly expressed by any graphic representation, even by giving the representations the most symbolic value. Above all, the very structure of *la langue* cannot be expressed by designs that represent objects: *la langue* exists only if there is a group of grammatical procedures. The structure of language led necessarily to noticing its sounds; no symbolic notation could suffice."

In our time, under the influence of philosophical research and the knowledge of the logic of the unconscious, some researchers consider the various types of writings as languages that don't necessarily "need" "phonetic expression," as Meillet believed they did. They thus represent particular signifying practices that have disappeared or been transformed in the life of modern man. The science of writing as a new realm (and until our time its specificity has been misunderstood) of linguistic operation; of writing as language, but not as vocal speech or grammatical chain; of writing as a specific signifying practice that enables us to perceive unknown regions in the vast universe of language —this science of writing has yet to be developed.

LINGUISTIC CATEGORIES AND RELATIONS

In the course of describing the phonic, scriptural, and gestural materiality of language, we have already had occasion to mention and even to demonstrate that it is a complicated *system* of elements and relations through which the speaking subject orders what is real; moreover, this system is what the linguist analyzes and conceptualizes. It is important, in this chapter on the "materiality" of language, and to clarify the meaning we will give to the term "materiality," to indicate if only briefly how the different linguistic categories and relations both organize the real and give the speaking subject a knowledge of this real —a knowledge whose truth is confirmed by social practice.

The manner in which different linguistic tendencies and schools have envisaged the forms and constructions of language will appear in the course of this work. The reader will note the multiplicity and often the divergence of opinions and terminologies, owing as much to the theoretical positions of the authors as to the particularities of the different languages for which the theories were devised. We shall limit ourselves here to pointing out, in a general and summary manner, some aspects of linguistic construction and their consequences for the speaker and his relation to the real.

Linguistic science is divided into several branches that study linguistic elements or categories and their relations from various aspects. *Lexicography* describes the dictionary: the life of words, their meanings, their selectivity, and their combinations. *Semantics*—the science of the meaning of words and sentences—is concerned with the particularities of the relations of signification among the elements of an utterance. *Grammar* is conceived of as "the study of forms and constructions." However, in our day, the reshaping and renewal of linguistic science has brought about a blurring of the boundaries of these continents which, more and more, interfere with, are confused with, and melt together into conceptions that are always new and ever-changing. It follows that, if we take as an example a certain stage of the conceptions of *grammar*, for instance, this example involves only its limited field and could not exhaust the complexity of the problem of linguistic categories and relations.

Envisaging *la langue* as a formal system, linguistics currently distinguishes, among linguistic forms, those that are autonomous (they signify notions: *people, to live, red,* etc.) and others that are semi-independent or simply links (they signify relations: *of, to, where, of which,* etc.). The former are called *lexical signs,* the latter *grammatical signs.*

These signs are combined in discursive segments of varying complexity: the *sentence,* the *clause,* the *word,* and the *form* (according to P. Guiraud, in *La Grammaire,* 1967).

Words have *affixes* (suffixes, prefixes, infixes) that serve to form other words (or semantemes) by being juxtaposed to the radical, as in *do-er, do-ing, re-do,* etc. A category of affixes, the *inflections,* "mark the grammatical status of the word in the sentence (case, mood, connecting words)."

Words form *sentences* by being arranged according to strict laws. The relations between words can be marked by their *order.* Order is decisive in *isolating* languages such as French; in contrast, it has only a relative importance in an inflected language such as Latin. Tonic stresses, connections, and especially *agreement, sequence of tenses,* and government *{rection}* indicate the relations between different parts of sentences.

When treating *grammatical categories,* traditional grammar distinguishes *parts of speech, modalities,* and *syntactic relationships.*

Parts of speech vary in different languages. French has eight of them: the substantive, the adjective, the pronoun, the article, the verb, the adverb, the preposition, the conjunction, and the exclamation.

Modalities refer to nouns and verbs, and designate their manner of being. These are number, gender, person, time and space, and mood.

Syntactic relations are the relations into which specific and modalized (with the help of modalities) words enter (as parts of speech) in the sentence. Current science considers the marks of *case* and *modality* as syntactic marks as well: they do not exist "of themselves" or outside relations in the sentence; on the contrary, they take shape and are clarified only in and by means of syntactic relations. In other words, a word is a "noun" or a "verb" because it has a precise syntactic role to play in the sentence, and not because it is the bearer "in and of itself" of a certain meaning that predestines it to be a "noun" or a "verb." This theoretical position, valid for the Indo-European languages, applies even more to languages such as Chinese in which there is no morphology strictly speaking; the word can "become" one part of speech or another ("noun," "verb," etc.) depending on its syntactic function. Thus modern linguistics tends to reduce *morphology* (the study of forms: declension, conjugation, gender, number), *lexicology,* and even *semantics,* to *syntax,* the study of constructions, and tends to formulate every signifying linguistic utterance as a syntactic formalism. Such is the theory developed by Chomsky in his "generative grammar," which we shall discuss again later.

The basic syntactic categories that are traditionally singled out are:

—the *subject* and the *predicate:* "a notion-theme (the subject) to which is attributed a certain character, a certain state or activity (the predicate)";[4]

—the *determinants* of the noun or of the adjective, which, together with the subject, form the *noun phrase* in Chomsky's terminology;

—the *verb complements,* which are added to the verb in order to designate the object or the circumstances of the action. In the terminology of Chomsky, they form with the predicate the *verb phrase.*

The question has been asked: do these categories mark/indicate the elements and relations of a specifically linguistic order, or are they, on the contrary, a simple transfer of logical notions? Grammar has, in fact, long been a prisoner of logical (Aristotelian) notions which, from antiquity to the nominalism of the Middle Ages, and especially during the eighteenth century, have attempted to make grammar and logic equivalencies. Today it is obvious that logical categories, far from being "natural," correspond only to certain very specific languages and even to certain types of utterances, and cannot cover the multiplicity and the particularity of linguistic categories and relationships. One of the most striking works ever to liberate grammar from its dependence on logic was *Des mots à la pensée: Essai de grammaire de la langue française* by J. Damourette and E. Pichon (1911–1940): it restores the subtleness of categories of thought as they are found in discourse, with no concern for logical systematization. The *logical* project has persisted nevertheless, and has given rise to two types of theories.

On the one hand are the psycho-logical grammars, such as that of M.-G. Guillaume (1883–1960). The author distinguishes *la langue,* which he calls "immanence"—a confused, prediscursive zone where speech is organized—from the operation that realizes thought, and, finally, from "discourse" or "transcendence," which is already a construction in linguistic signs. Guillaume studies instead what precedes discourse, and calls his science "psychomechanical" or "psychosystematic." For him, "discourse" or "transcendence" models and orders thinking activity ("immanence") by means of "captures," that is, grammatical forms.

On the other hand are the recent logical theories—mathematical logic, combinatory logic, modal logic, etc.—which furnish linguists with finer procedures for formalizing the relations at work in the system of *la langue;* these do not leave the specific field of linguistics or aspire to a theorization of prelinguistic thought. Certain transformational models, such as that of the Soviets Saumjan and Soboleva, are built on a foundation of logical principles: in this particular case, those exposed by Curry and Feys in their *Combinatory Logic* (1958).

The linguistic categories and relations that different theories and methods isolate inside *la langue* reflect and bring about—the causality is here dialectic—concrete, real situations that science can elucidate starting from an analysis of linguistic data. We will give here as an example the way in which Benveniste, in *Problems in General Linguistics* (1966), was able, by studying the categories of *person* and *tense*, to reconstruct the very system of subjectivity and temporality.

The author envisages subjectivity as "the capacity of the speaker to posit himself as 'subject.' " "Now we hold," writes Benveniste, "that that 'subjectivity,' whether it is placed in phenomenology or in psychology, as one may wish, is only the emergence into being of a fundamental property of language. 'Ego' is he who *says* ego.' "[5] This is the foundation of subjectivity, which is determined by the linguistic status of "person." Only the pronoun and the verb possess the category of person. Person is so inherent to the verbal system that verb conjugation follows the order of persons; this was already the case in India (where grammarians distinguished three persons—*purusha*) and in Greece (where scholars represented verbal forms as πρόσωπα, *persons*). Even languages such as Korean or Chinese, whose verb conjugations do not follow the distinction of persons, possess the personal pronouns and consequently (implicitly or explicitly) add the person to the verb.

There is a double opposition at play inside the system of persons. The first is that between *I/you* on the one hand, and *he* or *it* on the other; *I* and *you* are persons implicated in the discourse, while *he* or *it* are situated outside *I/you* and indicate someone or something about which one speaks, but without necessarily being a specific person. "The consequence must be formulated clearly," writes Benveniste, "the 'third person' is not a 'person'; it is really the verbal form whose function is to express the *non-person*. . . . It suffices to notice . . . the very particular situation of the third person of the verb in most languages. . . ." [p. 198] (An example of this is the impersonal "it" of "It is raining.")

The second opposition is that between *I* and *you*. "I use *I* only when I am speaking to someone who will be a *you* in my address. It is this condition of dialogue that is constitutive of *person,* for whom it implies that reciprocally *I* becomes *you* in the address of the one who in his turn designates himself as *I*. Here we see a principle whose consequences are to spread out in all directions. Language is possible only because each speaker sets himself up as a *subject* by referring to himself as *I* in his discourse. Because of this, *I* posits another person, the one who, being as he is completely exterior to 'me,' becomes my echo to whom I say *you* and who says *you* to me" [pp. 224–25].

If "real" subjectivity and linguistic subjectivity are closely interdependent and overdetermined by the linguistic category of person, the same is true for the category of the verb and the correlations of tense that it marks. Benveniste distinguished two levels of enunciation: *historical* enunciation, which allows the use of the aorist, the imperfect, the pluperfect, and the prospective[6] but which excludes the present, the perfect, and the future; and the enunciation of *discourse,* which allows the use of all tenses and all forms except the aorist. This distinction concerns the category of person as well. "The historian will never say *I*, or *you*, *here* or *now*, because he will never make use of the formal apparatus of discourse, which resides primarily in the relationship of the persons *I:you*. Hence we shall find only the forms of the 'third person' in a historical narrative strictly followed" [pp. 206–7]. Benveniste gives the following example of a historical enunciation [in French]:[7]

Après un tour de galerie, le jeune homme *regarda* tour à tour le ciel et sa montre, *fit* un geste d'impatience, *entra* dans un bureau de tabac, y *alluma* un cigare, *se posa* devant la glace, et *jeta* un regard sur son costume, un peu plus riche que ne le permettent [here the *present* tense is due to the fact that the author is reflecting upon something that escapes the outline of the narrative] en France les lois du goût. Il *rajusta* son col et son gilet de velours noir sur lequel *se croisait* plusieurs fois une de ces grosses chaînes d'or fabriquées à Gênes; puis, après avoir jeté par un seul mouvement sur son épaule gauche son manteau doublé de velours en le drapant avec élégance, il *reprit* sa promenade sans se laisser distraire par les oeillades bourgeoises qu'il *recevait*. Quand les boutiques *commencèrent* à s'illuminer et que la nuit *parut* assez noire, il *se dirigea* vers la place du Palasis-Royal en homme qui *craignait* d'être reconnu, car il *côtoya* la place jusqu'à la fontaine, pour gagner à l'abri des fiacres l'entrée de la rue Froidmanteau. . . . (Balzac, *Philosophical and Analytic Studies: Gambara*)

"Discourse," on the contrary, "freely employs all the personal forms of the verb, *I/you* as well as *he* or *it*. Explicitly or not, the relationship of person is everywhere present" [p. 209].

We can see how language, with the categories of verbs, tenses, and persons and by their precise combination, at least overdetermines if it does not determine the temporal oppositions *experienced* by speaking subjects. The linguist therefore *objectively* finds in the material of *la langue* an entire problematic (in our example, that of subjectivity and temporality) that is *really* at work in social practice. *La langue* seems to forge by its very categories what has been designated "subjectivity," "subject," "interlocuter," "dialogue," or "tense," "history," "present," etc. Is that to say that *la langue* produces these realities, or, on the contrary, that they are reflected in *la langue?* This is an insoluble, metaphysical problem, to which we can only oppose the principle of the *isomorphism* of the two series (the real/language; the real subject/ the linguistic subject; experienced temporality/linguistic temporality) of which the second, language and its categories, would be both the *attribute* and the *mold* that arranges the first series, extralinguistic reality. It is in this sense also that we can speak of a "materiality" of language by not allowing ourselves to posit language as an ideal system closed in upon itself (such is the "formalist" attitude) or as a mere copy of a regulated world that exists without it (such is the "realistic," mechanistic attitude).

Linguistic categories change with time. Latin grammar is different from that of Old French, which differs from the grammar of modern French. "[Language] runs from our hands every day and since I've been alive has changed by half," wrote Montaigne. Obviously today language is normalized, regularized, and fixed by a stable writing, so that changes in categories do not come about as quickly, even if they do constantly take place. Without affirming that every change in the categories of *la langue* necessarily implies a redistribution of the field in which the speaking subject organizes the real, we must call attention to the fact that these changes are not without importance for the conscious and especially the unconscious functioning of the speaker. Let us take the example given by M. W. von Wartburg in *Problems and Methods in Linguistics,* which was taken up again by P. Guiraud. In Old French, the verb *croire,* "to believe in" requires two constructions, *croire en* and *croire ou {en le},* since proper names were used without an article and common names with an article (believe in God, believe in the beginning, believe in the devil). But, in the course of the evolution of the French language, *ou {en le}* became confused with *au {à le};* as a result, the opposition *croire en / croire en le* has become blurred. Speakers have, however, kept the sense of an opposition but have reinterpreted it semantically in a way that has nothing to do with the initial grammatical opposition: *croire en* henceforth designates a profound belief in a divine being, *croire à,* the belief that something exists. And so von Wartburg writes, "A Catholic believes in *{en}* the Virgin Mary; a Protestant believes in *{à}* the Virgin Mary."[8] [That is, a Catholic believes in (the divinity of) the Virgin Mary; a Protestant believes that she existed (as a person). — Tr.]

On another level, and in the framework of the same grammatical system and the same stage of *la langue,* variations exist that do not cross the threshold of intelligibility of the message but do transgress some of its rules and can be considered agrammatical. They have, however, a specific, *rhetorical* function in particular styles, and are the object of *stylistics.*

We will now tackle another linguistic problem, that of meaning and signification, which we evoked above when discussing the nature of the linguistic sign. *Semantics* studies this problem. Its autonomy as a particular discipline in the analysis of *la langue* is fairly recent. While grammarians of the nineteenth century spoke of *semasiology* (from the Greek term *sēma,* sign), the French linguist Michel Bréal proposed the term semantics and was the first to write a *Semantics (Semantics: Studies in the Science of Meaning,* 1896; English version, 1900). Today semantics is conceived of as the study of the function of words as bearers of meaning.

A distinction has been established between *meaning* and *signification;* meaning is the *static* term for the mental image that results from the psychological *process* designated by the term *signification.* It is generally admitted that linguistics is concerned only with *meaning,* while *signifi-*

cation is reserved for a vaster science, henceforth called *semiotics,* of which semantics is only a particular case. Since it is obvious that meaning does not exist outside signification, and vice versa, the studies defined by these two concepts frequently overlap.

Let us mention some of the numerous problems posed by semantics.

While in general a word in a communication has a single meaning, words themselves frequently have several meanings. Thus, *state* signifies "manner of being, situation," "nation (or group of nations) that is organized, and submits to a government and to common laws," etc.; the French word *carte* can signify "card used for identification," "list of food," "map," etc. To this phenomenon called *polysemy* is added *synonymy,* where several words designate a single concept, as in *work, labor, affair, occupation, mission, task, job, grind,* and *business. Homonymy* designates words that were different in the beginning but which ended up getting confused, as in [the French words] *je, jeu* [I, game].

Every word in a context has a defined and precise meaning, a *contextual meaning,* which often differs from its basic meaning: in French, *livrer des marchandises,* "to deliver the merchandise," and *livrer bataille,* "to begin the battle," show two contextual meanings of the word *livrer,* "to deliver" which are not identical to the basic meaning. To these two meanings are added stylistic values: supplementary meanings that enrich the basic meaning and the contextual meaning. In "The workers occupied the joint," the contextual meaning of "joint" is "factory," but the supplementary stylistic value connotes a popular, familiar, or deprecating intention. It can be seen that stylistic values can be of a sociocultural order as well as a subjective one.

Semantics thus overlaps rhetoric. The study of meaning was confused in antiquity with the study of *"figures" of words,* and today it often intersects the study of *stylistics.*

The classical study of tropes has until today been presented as the foundation of the studies of the *combination,* and even the *change,* of meaning. It is known that the Latins, following the Greeks, designated fourteen types of *tropes:* metaphor, metonomy, synecdoche, antonomasia, catachresis, onomatopoeia, metalepsis, epithet, allegory, enigma, irony, periphrasis, hyperbole, and hyperbaton. The semanticians of today single out the logical relations that underlie these tropes, and derive from them the basic operations for changes in meaning.

S. Ullmann, for example (*The Principles of Semantics,* 1951), distinguishes changes due to *linguistic conservatism* from those due to *linguistic innovation.* The latter class has several subcategories:

1. Transfer of name: (a) by similarity of meaning; (b) by contiguity of meaning.

2. Transfer of meaning: (a) by similarity of name; (b) by contiguity of name.

An example of *spatial contiguity* of meaning (lb) is the French term *bureau,* "desk," which comes from *bure;* the bure cloth was used to cover the piece of furniture and bequeathed it its name.

Such are the mechanisms of changes in meaning; the causes of these changes are either *historical* (scientific, economic, or political changes that affect the meaning of words), *linguistic* (phonetic, morphological, syntactic, contagion, folk etymology, etc.) *social* (limitation or extension of the semantic zone of a word following its specialization or its generalization), and finally *psychological* (expressiveness, taboo, euphemisms, etc.).

Semantics, like structural linguistics, has become structural. Saussure was already putting each word at the center of a constellation of associations (either by meaning or by form), and was giving the schema shown in figure 3.1.

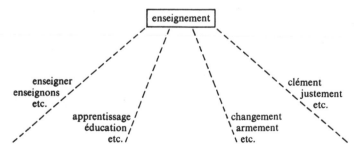

Figure 3.1

In our day structural semantics uses the concept *morphosemantic fields* (Guiraud) to indicate "the complex of relations of forms and meanings formed by a collection of words" (see P. Guiraud, *La Sémantique,* "Que sais-je?" 1969).

In his *Structural Semantics* (1966; English version, 1983), A. J. Greimas proposed isolating in each word the *semes,* the minimal elements of signification whose combination produces the *sememe* (or the word as a complex of meaning). Semes are divided up according to the semic axes in binary opposition. Moreover, a sememe is composed of a *semic kernel* (the basic meaning) and *contextual semes.*

The complex problems of signification, which structural semantics is far from having resolved, are also being tackled by philosophical semantics, logic, psychosociology, etc. All these theories are completely in flux, which makes any attempt to summarize them impossible.

Without claiming to have compiled a history of linguistic theories, a task that will not be possible until a general theory of history has been elaborated, we are going to try to penetrate further into the root of the problematic of language by rapidly reviewing the multiple systems used by various societies to think about their languages. We will then proceed to a description of linguistic representations and theories through the ages.

PART TWO

LANGUAGE IN HISTORY

INTRODUCTION

From myths to the most elaborate philosophical speculations, the positing of the problem of the beginnings of language—its appearance, its first steps—has not stopped. Even if linguistics as a science refuses to consider and even less to envision it (this problem was declared outside the field of interest of the Linguistic Society of Paris), the question exists and its permanence is a chronic ideological symptom.

Beliefs and religions attribute the origin of language to a divine force, to animals, and to fantastic beings that man supposedly imitated. Scholars have also wished to find the *original language* spoken by the first men, from which all other languages would have issued. Thus Herodotus (2:2) reports the experience of Psammetichus, King of Egypt, who supposedly raised two children from birth without contact with any language whatsoever; the children's first word was *bekos* ("bread" in Phrygian, which led the king to conclude that Phrygian was more ancient than Egyptian).

Thinkers have also tried to gain access to the "origin" of language by observing how the deaf and dumb learn linguistic practice. Others have observed children as they learn language. Still others have attempted to discover the primordial laws of language by observing the speaking habits of bilingual polyglot peoples, taking as their hypothesis that polyglotism is a historical moment prior to monoglotism (that is to say, prior to the unification of a language by a given community). No matter how interesting all this information is, it reveals only the process by which an *already constituted* language is *learned* by subjects in a given society, and can inform us only about the psychosociological particularities of the subjects speaking or learning a particular language. But it can shed no light on the historical process of the formation of language, and even less on its "origin."

When modern researchers try to resolve the question of the "prehistory" of language, they understand this to mean above all the most ancient stages known—those either recorded by documents or reconstructed by comparative studies—which enable the formation of hypotheses about the earlier stages for which we have no witnesses. Among the basic information available for reconstructing the linguistic past, the following sources have proved the most useful: the deciphering of the Egyptian hieroglyphs, the cuneiform inscriptions, the epigraphs of the peoples of Asia Minor or of the Etruscans, the Germanic runes, the oghamic monuments, etc. From this written evidence, deductions can be made not only about linguistic practice but about the social life in general of various populations. For its part, comparative linguistics, by following the life of words in different languages—their migration and transformation—can deduce certain linguistic laws that allow us to reconstruct the distant past of language. To these studies can be added the discoveries due to the deciphering of archeological material, such as epigraphs, the names of gods, places, personae, etc., whose consistency and duration in history are a reliable clue granting access to the distant past of language.

Several theories/hypotheses have been proposed to explain the "origin" and prehistory of language; these audacious hypotheses have been quickly refuted and destroyed by propositions inspired by other ideological principles. For instance, the Soviet N. Marr formulated a *stage* theory of language, and divided languages into four types corresponding to the stages of society: (1) Chinese and various African languages; (2) Finno-Hungarian and Turko-Mongolian; (3) Japhethic and Hamitic, characterizing feudalism; and (4) Indo-European and Semitic languages, characterizing capitalist society. [According to Marr,] a universal language should represent communist society. This theory was vigorously criticized by Stalin, who affirmed that a language is not a superstructure and consequently does not faithfully follow the historical transformations of social structures.

A theory of linguistic prehistory in six stages, which traces the trajectory leading from animal communication to highly developed human language, was proposed by G. Révész in *The Origins and Prehistory of Language* (1946; English version, 1956). In the prehistoric and historic stages, according to the author, one can observe a reduction of language to the *imperative, indicative,* and *interrogative* modes, and a decline in the importance of gestures. As for the system of communication of primitive man, deictics,[1] cries, and gestures occupy a dominant place. This language, still according to Révész, is limited to the *imperative,* the *vocative,* and the *locative* modes.

Abandoning the ambition of constructing general theories such as these for which no scientific proof can be furnished, linguistics currently limits itself, as A. Tovar has noted, to "establishing an archaic stage of languages having the same characteristics." This work was done, as far as phonetics is concerned, by W. Schmidt. Van Ginneken, for his part, has proposed a type of language that he considers to be as primitive and as old as writing. This "language" is a system of lateral or "click" consonants (obtained by lateral tongue movements); vowels are absent. Van Ginneken finds an example of this phonetic system in the Caucasian language and among the Hottentots.

With the decisive help of archeologists and paleontologists, linguistics is trying to establish, if not how language appeared, at least how long man has been speaking. The hypotheses are hesitant. For Böklen, language appeared during the Mousterian period. Leroi-Gourhan shares that opinion. He believes that the graphic symbol is the truly exclusively human leap, and that consequently there is human language wherever there are graphic symbols: "One can say that while in the technique and language of Anthropians as a whole, motor functions condition expression, in the figurative language of the most recent Anthropians, thinking determines the graphic system. The most ancient traces date from the end of the Mousterian period and become abundant near 35,000 B.C., during the Chatelperron period. They appear at the same time as coloring materials (ochre and manganese) and objects of adornment."

Can one consider that language underwent a period of development, of slow and laborious progression during the course of which it became the complex system of signification and communication that it is today, and that history finds as far back as it goes into the past? Or should one admit, with Sapir, that from the "beginning" language was "formally complete" and that once there was man there was language as a complete system in charge of all the functions it has today? In this second hypothesis, there would be no "prehistory" of language, but simply language, with no doubt differences in the organizational mode of the system (phonetic, morphological, syntactic, etc. differences) that give way to different languages.

The hypothesis of the sudden appearance of language was defended by Claude Lévi-Strauss. He considered all culture as "a collection of symbolic systems with language, matrimonial rules, economic relations, art, science, and religion placed in the highest rank." Renouncing the search for a sociological theory to explain symbolism, Lévi-Strauss, on the contrary, looked for the symbolic origin of society. For the vast collection of signification systems that make up the social, functions, just as language does, in an unconscious fashion. It is, just like language, founded on exchange (communication). It would follow from this parallelism that social phenomena could be assimilated (from this point of view) to language, and that starting from linguistic functioning one could gain access to the laws of the social system. However, Lévi-Strauss wrote, "no matter what the moment and the circumstances of its appearance in the animal scale were, language could only have been born in a single stroke. Objects couldn't just start to signify progressively. After a transformation whose study is a matter not for the social sciences, but for biology and physiology as well, a passage was effected from a stage where nothing made sense to another where everything did." Nevertheless Lévi-Strauss clearly distinguished the sudden appearance of *signification* from the slow acquisition of the knowledge that "this signifies." "The two categories of the signifier and the signified were simultaneously and solidarily constituted, like two complementary blocks; in contrast, knowledge, that is, the intelligible procedure that permits the identification, by their relation with respect to each other, of certain aspects of the signifier and certain aspects of the signified . . . , got started only very slowly. The universe signified well before man began to know what it was signifying."

In a similar vision, eliminating the problem of a prehistory of language by studying instead the question of the specific structure of the linguistic system and of each signifying system, a theory of *linguistic relativity* was posited. It consists of the hypothesis that every language with a particular oganization different from others signifies the real in a different way; there would therefore be as many types of signifying organizations of the universe as there are linguistic structures. This idea, which dates from Wilhelm von Humboldt and was taken up again by L. Weisgerber, was reinvented by Sapir and developed above all by Benjamin Lee Whorf, principally in his studies on the language of the Hopi Indians, a language he contrasted with the "average normal European language." The Hopi language has nine verbal voices, nine aspects, etc., which for Whorf constitute so many ways of signifying, and indicate the Hopis' particular ways of thinking about space and time. Whorf forgets that in other languages the same "particularities" can be obtained by different linguistic means (a "voice" can be indicated and replaced by an adverb, a preposition, etc.); he also forgets that the set of signifying systems in a society is a complex and complementary structure, in which the spoken language, categorized by a certain theory, is far from exhausting the diversity of signifying practices. This does not mean that science will not be able to find in the system of *la langue* the "specificities" that it is currently in the process of discovering in extralinguistic signifying systems; it only means that it would be too audacious to deduce the "mental" character of a society from the remarks, historically and ideologically limited, that one can make about *la langue*.

Considering with prudence the theory of linguistic relativity, anthropology and anthropological linguistics are studying languages and linguistic theories of so-called primitive societies, not to reach in this way the "initial" point of language, but to construct a vast overview of the different modes of representation that have accompanied linguistic practice.

4

ANTHROPOLOGY AND LINGUISTICS: THE KNOWLEDGE OF LANGUAGE IN SO-CALLED PRIMITIVE SOCIETIES

In looking for an object that could be scientifically studied and could supposedly provide access to the culture of "primitive" society, anthropology found language. By analyzing the different forms under which language presents itself, and its internal rules, as well as the awareness various peoples have of it (in their myths and religions), anthropology established and broadened its knowledge of so-called savage societies.

The first studies that opened the path to this "linguistic anthropology" were those of Edward Tylor (*Primitive Culture*, 1871, and *Anthropology*, 1881), but he had an English predecessor, R. G. Latham. Malinowsky in 1920 developed the thesis that the linguistic structure revealed the social structure, and confirmed it in his study *Meaning in Primitive Languages*. This tendency was pursued by other scholars such as Hocard, Haddon, and J. R. Firth. In Europe, anthropology drew inspiration from the work of Saussure and de Meillet, and found a linguistic orientation in the research of Durkheim and de Mauss. Among American scholars, the principal debt is to Franz Boas for the most decisive and committed formulations in this field. After having studied the language and writing of the American Indians and Eskimos, and the relation of their language and writing to their cultural and social organization, Boas affirmed that "the study of language must be considered as one of the most important branches of ethnological study."[1] He felt

4 8

that if the phenomena of language had become by means of ethnology and anthropology, objects in and of themselves, it was "largely due to the fact that the laws of language remain entirely unknown to the speakers, and that linguistic phenomena never rise into the consciousness of primitive man,[2] while all other ethnological phenomena are more or less clearly subject to conscious thought" [p. 59]. Boas did not, however, agree with the theory of linguistic relativity. "It does not seem likely that there is any *direct* relation between the culture of a tribe and the language they speak, except in so far as the form of the language will be molded by the state of culture, but not in so far as a certain state of culture is conditioned by the morphological traits of the language" [p. 63].

Because it studies "primitive" language in a social and cultural context, in light of this context and with respect to it, anthropology is often opposed to a purely formal, deductive, and abstract approach to linguistic facts. Like Malinowski, it pleads for an approach that would put living discourse within its contemporary context of social situations where the linguistic fact is produced; only in this way would this "fact" become the principal object of linguistic science.

The vision of language proposed by *sociological linguistics* is similar to this one and can be added to it. With J. R. Firth, this science notes that the linguistic categories elaborated by classical phonetics—morphology, syntax, etc.—do not take into account the different *social roles* played by the principal types of statements used by man. "The multiplicity of social roles we have to play as members of a race, a nation, a class, a family, a club, as sons, brothers, lovers, fathers, workers, etc., demands a certain degree of linguistic specialization." It is precisely these social functions of language, such as they are presented in the very structure of *la langue,* that sociolinguistics studies in order to grasp the supplementary information needed to clarify the unconscious mechanism of the social functions themselves.

While linguists, anthropologists, and sociologists try to draw from the linguistic data of "primitive" peoples conclusions about the laws that silently govern their society, these peoples themselves have elaborated representations and theories, rites and magical practices linked to their language, which constitute for us an *example* not only of the first steps of what was to become in our day "linguistics" but also of the place and role that language could have had in civilizations quite different from our own.

What first strikes "modern" man—experienced in today's theory and linguistic science, and for whom language is exterior to the real, a fine film whose only substance is conventional, fictitious, and "symbolic"—is that in societies that are "primitive," or as they say, "without history" or "prehistoric," language is a *substance* and a *material force.* While primitive man *speaks, symbolizes,* and *communicates,* that is to say, establishes a distance between himself (as subject) and the outside (the real) in order to signify it in a system of differences (language), he does not *know* this act to be an act of idealization or of abstraction, but knows it instead as *participation* in the surrounding universe. While the practice of language really presupposes for primitive man a *distance* with respect to things, language is not conceived of as a mental elsewhere, or as an abstract thought process. It participates as a cosmic element of the body and nature, and is joined with the motor force of the body and nature. Its link with corporal and natural reality is not abstract or conventional, but real and material. Primitive man does not clearly conceive of any dichotomy between matter and spirit, the real and language, or consequently between "referent" and "linguistic sign," much less between "signifier" and "signified": for him, they all partake in the same way of *one* differentiated world.

Complex *magical systems,* such as that of Assyrian magic, rely on an attentive treatment of speech conceived of as a real force. It is known that in the Akkadian language, "to be" and "to name" are synonyms. In Akkadian, "whatever is" is expressed by the locution "all that bears a name." This synonymy is symptomatic of the equivalency generally admitted between words and things that underlies verbal magical practices. It also appears in exorcisms linked to the prohibition of pronouncing such-and-such a name or word, and to incantations that must be recited in a low voice, etc.

Various myths, practices, and beliefs reveal this vision of language among primitives. Frazer (*The Golden Bough,* 1890) noted that in several primitive tribes the *name,* for example, is considered a reality and not an artificial convention, so that "magic may be wrought on a man just as easily through his name as through his hair, his nails, or any other material part of his person."[3] For the North American Indian, according to this same author, his name is not a label but a distinct part of his body, like his eyes, teeth, etc., and consequently mistreating his name would wound him just like a physical wound. To safeguard a name, it is entered into a system of *prohibitions* or *taboos*. The name must not be pronounced, for the act of its pronunciation/materialization can reveal/materialize the real properties of the person who bears it, and thus render him vulnerable to his enemies' glance. Eskimos used to take new names when they grew old; Celts considered the name a synonym for the soul and the "breath." Among the Yuins of New South Wales in Australia and among other peoples, still according to Frazer, the father reveals his name to his child at the moment of initiation, but few others know his name. In Australia, names are forgotten, people are called "brother," "cousin," or "nephew." The Egyptians had two names; the little name was good and was made public, while the great name was considered bad and had to be concealed. Such beliefs about the proper name are found among the Krus of Western Africa, among the peoples of the Slave coast, the Wolofs of Senegambia, in the Philippine Islands (the Bagobos of Mindanao), the Bourrous Islands (the West Indies), the island of Chiloe in the open sea along the south coast of Chile, etc. The Egyptian god Ra, bitten by a snake, reportedly lamented: "I am he of many names and forms. . . . My father and my mother gave me my name, and it remained hidden in my body since my birth, that no magician might have magic power over me" [p. 303]. But in the end he revealed his name to Isis and she became all powerful. Taboos are also imposed on words that designate degrees of kinship.

Among the Caffres, women are forbidden to pronounce the name of the husband and the father-in-law, as well as any words resembling them. This brings about a modification of the women's speech; they speak, in fact, a distinct language. Frazer recalls on this subject that in antiquity Ionian women never called a husband by his name, and that no one was supposed to name a father or daughter while the rites of Ceres were being observed at Rome. Among certain tribes west of Victoria, taboos require men and women to speak to each other in their own languages even though they understand each other's language; in addition, one is permitted to marry only someone who speaks a foreign language.

The names of the dead are also subject to the laws of taboo. Such customs were observed by the Albanians of the Caucasus, and Frazer noticed them as well among the Australian aborigines. In the language of the Abipones of Paraguay, new words were introduced each year, for they abolished by proclamation all words resembling the names of the dead, and replaced them with others. Such proceedings obviously preclude the possibility of a narrative or a history: the language is no longer a depository of the past; it changes with the real passage of time.

Taboos also concern the names of kings, sacred persons, and gods, and also a large number of common names. This is also true with the names of plants and animals considered dangerous; pronouncing them would amount to invoking the danger itself. Thus in the Slavic languages the word signifying "bear" was replaced with a word plus an "anodyne" whose root is "honey"; this gives, for instance, *med'ved* in Russian (from *med,* "honey"). The evil bear is replaced by something euphoric—by the inoffensive nourishment of the food of that species; the name by metonymy replaces the dangerous word.

These prohibitions were not consciously motivated. They seem to go without saying, to be natural "impossibilities," and can be lifted or expiated only by certain ceremonies. Several magical practices are founded on the belief that words possess a concrete and active reality, and it suffices to pronounce them for their action to occur. This is the basis of various prayers or magical formulas that "bring" healing, rain to the fields, an abundant harvest, etc.

Sigmund Freud, who attentively examined the data reported by Frazer, was able to explain the taboo on certain words or the prohibition on certain discursive situations (wife-husband, mother-son, father-daughter) as being part of the prohibition on incest. He noted a striking resemblance on four points between the obsessional neuroses and taboos: (1) the absence of motivation of the prohibitions; (2) their fixation by virtue of an internal necessity; (3) their ability to be displaced and to contaminate the prohibited objects; (4) the existence of ceremonial rules deriving from the prohibitions (see *Totem and Taboo*).[4]

As Freud himself noted, "It would obviously be hasty and unprofitable to infer the existence of any internal relationship [between obsessional neurosis and taboos] from such points of agreement as these, which merely derive from the operation of the same mechanical causes" [p. 26]. We must emphasize this remark, for, while the two structures resemble one another, nothing requires us to think that taboos are "due" to "obsessions." Psychoanalytic notions are elaborated and function in the realm of modern society, and categorize in a more or less rigorous fashion the psychical structures in that society. To transport them into other societies where the very notion of "I" (of subject, of individual) is not clearly differentiated is doubtless an act that denatures the specificity of the societies being studied. One can, on the contrary, suppose that acts such as taboos, and maybe in general the very practice of language as a reality that acts (one that is not abstract, ideal, or sublimated), are exactly what prevent "neuroses," including obsessional neurosis, from being formed as the structure of a subject.

Other evidence proves that "primitive" man not only refuses to separate the *referent* from the *sign,* but that he also hesitates to split the *signifier* from the *signified.* The "phonic-image" has for him the same real weight as the "idea," and is moreover confused with it. He perceives the network of language as *solid matter,* so that phonic resemblances are for him the indicator of the resemblances between signifieds, and consequently, referents. Boas reported examples such as these among the Pawnees in America; several of their religious beliefs are prompted by linguistic similarities. A striking case is furnished by Chinook mythology: the hero comes upon a man who is trying in vain to catch a fish while dancing, and informs the man that he needs to fish with a net. This story is organized around two words that are phonetically identical (on the level of the signifier) but have different meanings (divergent on the level of the signified): the words *to dance* and *to fish with a net* are pronounced in the same way in Chinook. This example proves with what refinement "primitive" man distinguishes the various levels of language and even ends up playing with them. It's as if he were suggesting with subtle humor that he is perfectly capable of manipulating the signified without, however, forgetting that he is anchored in the signifier that carries him, and that he—a speaker attentive to the materiality of his language—always hears and understands.

Certain peoples possess well-developed theories about the functioning of language. These theories are unfurled as veritable cosmogonies, and as a result, when the modern ethnologist translates by "speech" the cosmic and corporal force "primitives" thought about, the discrepancy between it and our conception of this term is such that a doubt persists: is it really a matter of "language" as this word is understood by modern men? What the Western scholar translates as "speech" or "language" at times turns out to be the work of the body itself, desire, the sexual function, or the verb, of course, and all that at once.

Geneviève Calame-Griaule in her study on the Dogons (*Words and the Dogon World*, 1965; English version, 1979),[5] a population that lives southwest of the loop of the Niger, remarks that for this people the term "sɔ̀," which designates language, signifies at the same time: the faculty that distinguishes men from animals; *la langue* in the Saussurian sense of the term; the language of one human group as opposed to that of another; the word itself; and discourse and its modalities: subject, question, discussion, decision, judgment, narrative, etc. [p. 4]. But also, to the extent that every social act presupposes a speaking exchange, and to the extent that every individual act is itself a means of expressing oneself, "speech" is sometimes a synonym for "undertaking" or "doing." Current expressions attest to this meaning: *sɔ̀: vomo yoà:,* "his words have gone inside," he has succeeded in his undertaking (by persuading his interlocutor); and *nɛ̀ yògo so y,* "it has now become tomorrow's speech," we put off until tomorrow the pursuit of work [p. 5]. The Dogons call *speech* the result of the act, the work, or the material creation that remains: the wrought hoe and the woven cloth are so many "words" [p. 5]. Since the world is impregnated with speech, and speech is the world, the Dogons have constructed their theory of language as an immense architecture of correspondences between the variations of individual discourse and the events of social life. There are 48 modes of "speech" broken down into two times 24, the key number of the universe. Thus Calame-Griaule observes, "each 'speech' within this system corresponds to a technique or institution, a plant (as well as a specific part of the plant), an animal (and one of its organs), and an organ in the human body" [p. 109]. For example, "the speech of the navel," *bɔ̀gu sɔ̀*, designates deceit or false appearance, for when one takes care of the wound of the newborn, it is often infected even if it appears from the outside to be healed. Any false promise or theft would consequently be called *bɔ̀gu sɔ̀*, as is pillage in the technical order, the thieving mouse among animals, the groundnut which is not a real food, etc. [p. 142]. At the same time, these "speeches" are systematized according to "mythical accounts that explain their psychological and social value, as well as their numerical position in the symbolic order of classification" [p. 109].

Such immersions of speech in the real world are not isolated phenomena. The Sudanese Bambaras, according to Dominique Zahan (*La Dialectique du verbe chez les Bambaras*, 1963), consider language a physical element. While they distinguish a first not-yet-expressed speech, one that is part of the primordial word of God, called *ko*, they also isolate the material substrate of speech, the *phoneme* in general, by giving it the name *kuma*. This last word has an affinity with the word *ku*, which signifies "tail." A Bambara maxim, by the way, has it that "Man has no tail, he has no mane; the 'holding' point of man is the speech from his mouth." If one were to listen analytically one would easily discover in these comparisons the extent to which the Bambara conception of speech is *sexualized* and seemingly indistinct from the sexual function. This observation is confirmed by the Bambaras' representation of the organs of speech. They are the head and the heart; the bladder, the sexual organs, the intestines, the kidneys; the lungs and liver; the trachea, the throat, and the mouth (tongue, teeth, lips, saliva). Each of these organs *forms* speech: the liver, for example, judges speech and either allows it to pass or stops it; the kidneys render the meaning precise or confer a certain amount of ambiguity on it—"speech is deprived of all agreeableness if the humidity of the bladder does not enter into its composition"; finally, "the sexual organs, by means of movements that are a simplification of the gestures accomplished during coitus, give the verb the pleasure and taste of life." The whole body—eyes, ears, hands, feet, and posture—participates in the articulation of speech. Thus, for the Bambaras, to speak is to bring out an element of one's body: to speak is *to give birth*. Let us point out that the Dogons also attribute functions such as this to the organs of the body in producing speech.

The linguistic element is just as material as the body that produces it. On the one hand, the primordial sounds of speech are related to the four cosmic elements: earth, air, fire, and water. On the other hand, since speech is material, the organs of its passage must be prepared to receive it. Hence the tatooing of the mouth, or the filing down of the teeth, which are the symbols of day and night and, once filed, are identified with the path of light. These rites of preparing the mouth for wise speech, intended primarily for women, coincide with the rites of incision or are identified with them. Here then is a supplementary proof of the fact that for the Bambaras a mastery of speech is a mastery of the body, that language is not an abstraction but instead participates in the entire ritual system of the society. Language is so corporal that flagellation rites, for example, symbolizing the body's endurance of pain, are supposed to represent the mastery of the organ of speech. We cannot here elucidate all the consequences that such a theory of language implies for the speaking subject's relation to his sexuality, knowledge in general, and his inclusion in the real.

The Melanesians, who live in eastern New Guinea and the principal achipelagos that run parallel to the Australian coast, also have a corporal representation of the functioning of language. M. Leenhardt (*Do Kamo: Person and Myth in the Melanesian World,* 1947; English version, 1979)[6] relates the following Melanesian legend about the origin of speech: "The God Gomawe was out walking when he met two people who could not answer the questions he asked, nor did they say anything at all. Judging their bodies to be empty, he left, caught two rats and scooped out their bowels. He went back to the two men, opened up their bellies and filled the cavities with the rats' organs—intestines, heart, and liver. As soon as the incisions were closed, the men spoke, ate, and were able to gain strength" [p. 6]. The conviction that it is the body that "speaks" is clearly attested in expressions such as "What is your belly?" for "What is your opinion?"; or "distressed bowels" for "to be sorry"; or "bowels running sidewise" for "to hesitate" [p. 7]. The mind or the head are not the emitting center of the language-idea. On the contrary, to compliment a speaker is to call him a "hollow head," which implies without a doubt that the rigor of his discourse is due to the fact that he is a product of his stomach, of his entrails [p. 8].

For the Dogons, Calame-Griaule writes, "the various elements that compose speech are found in a diffuse state in the body, particularly in the form of water. When man speaks, the verb comes out in the form of vapor, the *water* of speech is 'heated by the heart' " [p. 53]. The *air,* as well as the *earth,* which gives the word its signification (its weight) and corresponds in this way to the skeleton in the body, and *fire*, which determines the psychological conditions of the speaking subject, are so many components of language for the Dogons. Their relation to sex is also clearly posited: speech is sexed. There are male (low and descending) and female (high and rising) tones, but the various modalities of speech and even different languages and dialects can be considered to belong to one or the other category. Male speech contains more wind and fire, female more water and earth. The complex theory of speech among the Dogons also includes a notion that puts discursive use in close relation to what can be called the psyche: the notion of *kikinu* designates "the tone in which it [speech] is expressed, and this is associated directly with the speaker's psyche" [p. 35].

Such corporal conceptions of language do not mean that no particular attention is paid to its formal construction. According to the Bambaras, language is generated in several stages—gestures, grunts, and sounds; they believe that aphonic man goes back to the golden age of humanity. Primitive language for them is composed of monosyllabic words made up of a consonant and a vowel. The different phonemes are specified and in charge of particular sexual and social functions; they are combined with *numbers* and various elements or parts of the body, and form in this way a regulated cosmic combinative. Thus Zahan notes that "E" for the Bambaras is the first sound that "names me and the other; it is the 'I' and the 'you,' the analogue of correlative desire, and analogous to the number 1, to the name, and in harmony with the little finger." [The letter] 'I' is the nerve of language, it marks insistence, pursuit, research. Even among the Melanesians, language is a complex and differentiated milieu. It is represented as a container, a functioning enclosure; or, as we would say today, a working system. Leenhardt confirms that this people names "thought" by the words *nexai* or *nege*, which designate a visceral container (the visceral bags, stomach, bladder, womb, heart, woven fibers of a basket). Today the word *tanexai* is used, meaning "to be there together," "fibers," or "contour"; *tavinena* means "to be there," "bowels" [p. 9].

Certain tribes, not satisfied with a classification of speech, possess an extremely refined and detailed theory of the *graphic* correlatives of these types of speech. If what Meillet has written is true, that "the men who invented and perfected writing were great linguists and that they are the ones who created linguistics," we find in ancient civilizations that later vanished graphic systems that bear witness to subtle thinking, if not to a "science" of language. Certain of these types of writing, such as that of the Mayas, have not yet been deciphered. Others, such as the writing system of Easter Island which A. Métraux considers a memory-aid for cantors, have provoked numerous and sometimes irreconcilable commentaries. Barthel was able to note that, having 120 signs, this scriptural system can produce 1,500 to 2,000 combinations. These signs represent people, heads, arms, gestures, animals, objects, and plants, as well as geometric designs, and function as ideograms that can have several significations. For instance, the same ideogram signifies *star, sun,* and *fire.* Some signs are images (woman is represented by a flower) or metaphors ("a person eating" represents a poetry recital). Finally, certain signs acquire a phonetic value; this phenomenon is favored by the fact that homonyms abound in Polynesian languages. But this writing, which testifies to an advanced state of the "science" of language, does not seem to be able to mark/indicate sentences. Despite the effort of several scholars, it cannot yet be considered completely deciphered.

Figure 4.1. An example of the combination of a hieroglyphic text (top) with number signs (a dot = one; a hyphen = five) and a pictogram (bottom) in Mayan writing (Dresden manuscript, p. xvi). The illustration is borrowed from V. Istrine, *Origine et développement de l'écriture.*

Mayan writing—one of the most interesting and most secret monuments of ancient civilizations—remains to this day undeciphered (see figure 4.1). Research is being carried out in two directions: by postulating that Mayan signs are phonetic, or by imagining that they are pictograms and ideograms. It seems more and more to be a question of a combination of the two types, but the deciphering process is far from finished.

If the Mayan population inherited the ethnic and cultural tradition of its predecessors, the Olmecs, who inhabited the Mexican territory a thousand years before our era, then the archeological monuments, their writing, and the manuscripts probably date all the way from the first years of our era until the prohibition of this writing by the Spanish colonizers and their destruction of the greater part of the manuscripts. Since the use of writing was an attribute of priests and linked to religious cults, it disappeared when the Mayan religion did; the population did not know its secret. Mayan texts generally represent historical texts woven with dates and numbers. It is supposed that they reflect a cyclical conception of time according to which events recur; consequently, registering their succession allows the future to be predicted. The rhythm of time, the "symphony of time," is what J. E. Thompson saw in Mayan writing (*Maya Hieroglyphic Writing,* Washington, 1950).

An interesting theory of Mayan writing was proposed by the Soviet researcher Yuri B. Knorosov (*The Writing of the Mayan Indians,* Moscow-Leningrad, 1963). Abandoning the hieroglyphic hypothesis, he returned to the alphabetic hypothesis of Diego de Landa, the first decipherer of the Mayas. Knorosov considered Mayan writing to be composed of "graphic complexes" each of which was composed of several (1–5) graphemes; the graphic elements were linked in a square or circle, and made of signs such as the heads of men, animals, birds, plants, or other objects. This writing would resemble Egyptian writing of the Old Kingdom where pictograms seem to be the indications of the hieroglyphic text they accompany.

In an earlier phase, Knorosov proposed deciphering signs as *syllabic* signs combined with phonetic and semantic logograms (see figure 4.2). Since 1963, Knorosov's hypothesis has been that these signs are instead *morphemic.* What is remarkable about this hypothesis is that if it is well-founded, in history there would have been only two occurrences of independent *morphemographic* writing: Mayan writing and Chinese writing. Certain specialists, such as Istrine, consider this hypothesis unlikely, given the long development of ancient Chinese writing, and also given the difference between the monosyllabic Chinese language, which favors morphemography, and the Mayan language, in which 60 percent of the words are composed of three or four morphemes. Under such conditions, the existence of morphographic writing would therefore require a complex and difficult analysis of lan-

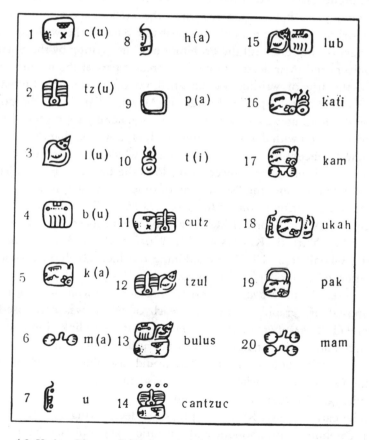

Figure 4.2. Various Mayan syllabic signs, deciphered by Knorosov (1–10) and examples of their use in phonetic writing (11–20)—according to the author's hypothesis formulated in 1950. [Yuri B. Knorosov, *The Writing of the Mayan Indians*, Moscow-Leningrad, 1963]

guage. This, however, is not impossible in a civilization as extraordinary as that of the Mayas, especially since Mayan civilization can elicit certain resemblances to Chinese cosmogonic conceptions: one instance of such a resemblance is the inclusion and pulverization of the signifying "subject" in a divided and ordered cosmos, which would be perfectly reflected in the fabric of meaning disseminated beneath the syllables of a morphemic scriptural system.

Dogon writing presents particularities that are interesting in a different way. It includes four stages of which each is successively more complex and more perfect than the one before. The first stage is called "trace" or *bumɔ* (from *bumɔ*, "to crawl") and evokes the track left on the ground by the movement of an object. It is a vague design, sometimes of unconnected line segments that nonetheless outline the final form. The second stage is called "mark" or *yàla;* it is more detailed than the trace, and sometimes stippled, to remind one, Calame-Griaule writes, that Amma [the creator of speech] first made the "seeds" of things. The third one, the "diagram" or *toʒu ,* is a general representation of the object. And finally there is the completed "design," the *t'oȳ* [pp. 212–13]. This four-stage procedure, which is not true writing— the Dogons could not mark sentences—does not apply solely to the

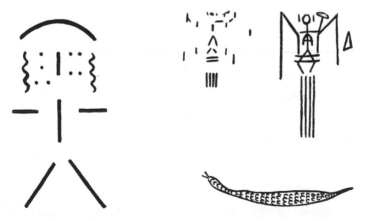

Figure 4.3. Examples of Dogon writing: On the left, naming children (first stage of the design). Top right, first and last stage of the "speech of weaving." Bottom, "the speech of Lebe-Seru's law," symbolized by the snake. From G. Calame-Griaule, *Words and the Dogon World* (Philadelphia: Institute for the Study of Human Issues, 1968), pp. 225–27.

design itself, or to *la langue* as a system of signification and communication. Like the word "speech" itself, it is concerned with various aspects of real life: "Speech for Giving Birth to Children" [p. 153], as well as "Speech of the Forces Within Amma's Creation" [p. 137], "Speech for Naming Children" [p. 120], etc. (see figure 4.3). It can be seen, consequently, that writing marks the *formation* of words (or of signification) but also of things; *written* words and things are found to be intimately mingled, to be joined to a same reality in the process of differentiation and classification. The universe, along with speech, is organized like an immense combinatory, like a universal calculus laden with mythological , moral, and social values; speech, however, does not isolate the act of signifying—its verb—in a mental elsewhere. The participation of language in the world, in nature, in the body, in society —from which it is nevertheless practically differentiated—and in their complex systematization, constitutes perhaps the fundamental trait of the conception of language in so-called "primitive" societies.

5

THE EGYPTIANS: THEIR WRITING

Egyptian texts deal little with the problems of language. But the importance they attribute to writing and the magisterial role it played in Egyptian society are the most solid proof of the Egyptian conception of the system of *la langue.*

Writing, like all the languages in the world, was invented, according to the ancient Egyptians, by the god Thoth, the Ibis. Scribes were represented as writing while squatting in front of an image of Thoth's sacred animal, the baboon. On several documents one sees the god himself writing, assisted by an ancient goddess, Seshat, whose name means "she who writes." Writing, a deified object venerated on all sides, was the sacred occupation of the cast of scribes, who occupied the high ranks of Egyptian society. Certain statues even show great lords who had themselves represented in the position of scribes. The Lausing papyrus thus praises the incomparable qualities of the scribes compared to whom all other professions seem to have no importance: "Spend the entire day writing with your fingers, and at night, read. Take as your friends the papyrus roll and the palette, for it is more agreeable than one can imagine. Writing, for those who know it, is more adventurous than any other occupation, more agreeable than bread and beer, than clothes and unguents. Yes, it is more precious than an inheritance in Egypt or a tomb in the West."

This cast of scribes designed, engraved, or painted a large number of hieroglyphs; today archeology, ethnology, and linguistics are reconstituting the history of the language of ancient Egypt on the basis of these hieroglyphs. Today, the appearance of hieroglyphic writing is situated toward the end of the second Neolithic[1] civilization (Negada II, Gerzean), but it developed above all under the first dynasty. There were approximately 730 signs under the Middle Kingdom (2160–1580 B.C.) and the eighth dynasty (1580–1314 B.C.), but only 220 were commonly used; and of these 80 were in use for everyday writing.

The deciphering of these hieroglyphs, which were unavailable to Western science for a long time, is due to Jean-François Champollion (1790–1832). Before him, several scholars had tried in vain to penetrate the rules of this writing. From 1650 to 1654, the Jesuit Athanasius Kircher edited in Rome a study in four volumes in which he proposed translations of the hieroglyphs; his genius and intuition, while often penetrating, did not enable him to correctly decipher a single sign. The starting point for Champollion's work was the stone known as the Rosetta stone. It was covered with three kinds of writing: 14 lines of Egyptian hieroglyphs, 32 lines of demotic writing, and 54 lines of Greek writing. Champollion had the idea not only to compare the comprehensible writing (the Greek) with the one that wasn't (the Egyptian) but also to find a sure axis of correspondence between the two texts. This axis was the proper names *Ptolemy* and *Cleopatra;* these could be distinguished in the hieroglyphic text, since they were isolated in a cartouche (see figure 5.1). This method enabled Champollion to establish the first correspondences between Egyptian signs and phonemes. After a long process of deciphering the texts written on the monuments of Dendera, Thebes, Esna, Edfu, Ambas, and Philae, Champollion was able to establish the complexity of the Egyptian scriptural system, which was not only phonetic. In his book *Précis du système hiéroglyphique des anciens Egyptiens* (1824), Champollion distinguished three types of writing: *hieroglyphic* writing, *hieratic* writing—

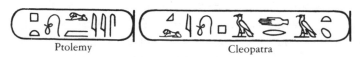

Ptolemy   Cleopatra

Figure 5.1

which he called "a veritable *tachygraphy* of the hieroglyphs; it is the writing of the nonhieroglyphic papyrus found on mummies"—and finally *demotic* or *epistolographic* writing, "that of the intermediary inscription of the Rosetta," and distinct from true hieroglyphic writing.

According to Champollion, the alphabet of the phonetic characters is "the key to hieroglyphic writing"; "this alphabet is the result of a series of phonetic proper names, engraved both on the monuments of Egypt over an interval of almost five centuries and on various places in the land. Phonetic writing was therefore used by all classes of the Egyptian nation, and for a long time was required as an auxiliary to the three hieroglyphic methods."

The ancient Egyptians therefore distinguished sounds and were moving toward phonetic writing. Nevertheless, their "signs" were far from being an alphabet. They were used in three different ways.

1. The sign might designate at the same time the word and the concept; it was then called a "sign-word" or *logogram.*

2. The sign might convey only sounds; it was then called a *phonogram* and was used to write not only the name of its model but also the consonants that formed this name. For instance, *peri* signified "house" in ancient Egyptian. As a phonogram, this sign for house was used to transcribe all words whose consonants were *p, r,* and *i.*

3. Finally, the image could invoke a notion without referring to a precise word and without being pronounceable; it was then called a *determinative.* As a *determinative,* the sign "house" was not pronounced but was added to words designating edifices. The *determinative* played a distinctive role: it prevented words with the same consonants from being confused by relating them to precise classes.

As images, these signs were stylized: they reproduced the general contour or an essential detail. On the other hand, as part of a mural or sepulchral design, these images corresponded to the angle of the designer's vision—some were frontal, others in profile, viewed from above, or viewed from the side.

Although it was relatively stable, Egyptian writing underwent modifications, especially during the Greco-Roman epoch, by being simplified and diversified. Generally one observes a phoneticization of ancient signs, which therefore acquired a phonetic value, essentially the value of the first consonant they had previously noted.

All these remarks relate to hieroglyphy, the monumental writing that Champollion already distinguished from *cursive* writing, of which the most ancient is *hieratic* writing. This form of writing came into play when the scribes transferred monumental writing to paper, schematized the signs, and lightened the details. The principal modifications were the lengthening and the thinning of the sign-word, the introduction of diacritical elements outside the signs, and the appearance of ligatures. In this way one obtained a rapid, almost uninterrupted trace, which was made from right to left.

Toward the seventh century B.C., a second variation of cursive writing appeared, the *demotic,* which was intended in principle for administration; it was later called "popular," demotic writing. It quickly became a writing form for common use, and some literary or religious texts were written in demotic (*The Book of the Dead,* for example).

How could these Egyptian writing forms, so elaborate and so appropriate to various social needs, have disappeared? The question has elicited numerous commentaries and hypotheses. The fact that Christianity replaced the Egyptian religion is perhaps one of the reasons for the decline of the priest-scribe caste, and consequently for that of their discourse and their hieroglyphic writing. Reasons arising from the development and rules of this type of writing itself have doubtless played a no less important role in its disappearance. Demotic writing was preserved until the fifth century B.C. Since it was reserved for administration, it was not supplanted for religious reasons. Today it is supposed that the phoneticization of this writing rendered it too difficult and inefficient compared to the Greek alphabet, whose simplicity had already seduced the Egyptians.

Egyptian writing remains today the indispensable monument to decipher for anyone who wants to know ancient Egypt. It testifies to a conception of *la langue* in which the concept and the sound, the signifier and the signified, forming one body, seemed to blend with the stylistic inscription-reproduction of the real. In the functioning of logograms, the linguistic unit was not distinguished from the conceptual unit, and seemed to objectify a single body. On the other hand, Egyptian phonograms prove, as R. Weil has written, that "the notion of the syllable was completely absent." The vowel was not transcribed. The Egyptians indicated only "the skeleton" of words, the "consonantal skeleton" according to Cohen, as if the vowel network of a word were as stylized as its design, reduced to its carcass, to its most marked differential elements, the consonants. Within vocalism, the Egyptians continued to write, that is, to sort out and to systematize. After all, the use of determinatives that were not pronounced does indicate a logical process of systematization of linguistic signs into various categories, an outline of grammatical reasoning.

The role of voice seems reduced in Egyptian writing; voice counts less than logical and traced relations. It can be deduced that this writing was constituted more as a reflection on the modes of signifying than as a transcription system for vocalism (as phonetic writing is). In Egypt, therefore, writing was, in this sense, distinct from the verb, from vocal exchange; it was therefore social, and necessarily had to disappear when economic conditions changed: when exchange (commercial society) was installed as the dominant principle, when the Greek civilization invaded the Mediterranean basin.

6

MESOPOTAMIAN CIVILIZATION: THE SUMERIANS AND AKKADIANS

Mesopotamian civilization elaborated the writing called *cuneiform,* on whose basis we can today construct certain aspects of that civilization's conception of the functioning of language. Living in the ancient Near East, the Sumerians and the Akkadians used a writing system composed of groups of wedges engraved on clay tablets, whose material no doubt influenced the form of the signs. There were 550 signs of which 250 to 300 were commonly used. Certain signs functioned as logograms, others had a phonetic value representing either a vowel *(a, e, i, u)*, a bilettered syllable *(ab, ur; ba, ru)* or a trilettered syllable *(sul, dir)*.

As a result, some polyphones (each sign having several phonetic values: the same sign marks "water" and "arm"), and some homophones (there are 17 signs read as *si*) were produced. To remedy this confusion, *silent* signs were added that played the role of *determinatives* (they classified signs into categories, thereby clearing up the ambiguity) and *phonetic complements* (which clarified the initial and final [signs] of the word). This system underwent profound change, going from ideography to alphabetism. In a first phrase, signs were purely ideograhic; later, several notions (or words) were represented by the same sign-logogram; homophony began. Finally, grammatical signs representing a suffix or an infix were introduced. Thus, the sign of plurality or duality was joined to the logogram to indicate a plural or a dual, but was not pronounced.

Sumerian was a living language from the fourth to the second millennium B.C., and persisted as the secret language of the Akkadians. A Sumero-Akkadian bilingualism followed that necessitated a truly scientific study of Sumerian. Syllabaries and lexicons were made for this purpose, which attest to the foundations of a systematization of language. Several collections of this type existed, which resemble the dictionaries of today. For instance, starting in 2600 B.C., lexicographic indexes were found; they were called "a science of lists"—table-diagrams of salaries, of deliveries, etc.—and were at the same time enumerations and classifications of *polysemantic* signs (for instance, the sign for "mouth" was identical to the one for "tooth," "speech," "to speak," "to yell") and *complex representations* (for instance, an egg near a bird signified "to give birth"). Signs were classified according to the number of strokes: there were signs of 1, 2, $3n$ horizontal strokes, of 1, 2, $3n$ vertical strokes, and of 1, 2, $3n$ oblique strokes. Remarkably, these catalogues constituted classes in which were grouped, for example, all words containing the same *seme* (minimal trait of signification)—*kus* (of leather), *za* (of stone), *bur* (vases)—or instead all words deriving from the same sign—*rat, fish,* etc. These classifications involved nouns only, and did not give adjectives or verbs. Bilingual dictionaries were made on this principle, and even a quadrilingual dictionary was found in the library of Rap-anu.

Mesopotamian writing and linguistic science (philology and lexicography) developed, therefore, in a linked fashion: the practice of writing demanded of scribes a true science. This practice implied not only a perfect knowledge of inscription procedures but also a systematization of the language into semantic categories that were at the same time the categories for the entire cosmos and social universe. To catalogue the language was to catalogue the real. The use of writing also had a magical and religious application. However, far from serving only priests, writing played a perfectly secular economic and social role. This, however, did not diminish the respect and veneration in which writing and those who used it were held: "He who excels in the science of writing will shine like the Sun," a scribe wrote. The scribe was highly appreciated in Sumerian society; certain scribes became high government dignitaries. For instance, Anam, King of Uruk, who was first an archivist, had his name followed by the hybrid title "writer-perator" [writer-king]. The Akkadians shared this esteem for writing, which they attributed to the most secret of sciences: "I have learned," Ashurbanipal said, "what Adapa the sage brought to men, the precious hidden knowledge of all written science. I have been initiated into the [books of the] omens of heaven and earth. I have devoted myself to them in the company of scholars. I am able to discuss *lecomancie;* I solve muddled divisions and multiplications that defy understanding. I have succeeded in reading ingenious Sumerian and obscure Akkadian, languages that are difficult to understand well. I am capable of deciphering word for word the stones inscribed before the deluge, which are hermetic, silent, and muddled."

This highly praised writing was invented circa 3500 B.C. Its procedure, used until the Christian era, became an international graphic system and was used by all the peoples of earlier Asia. It was adopted for transcribing languages such as Hittite, Hurrian, Urartian, Persian, Elamite, etc.

Cuneiform writing originated from pictograms. The first signs reproduced objects vertically on monuments, and were read in columns from right to left. Cohen remarks in *La Grande invention de l'écriture* (1958) that when clay palettes began to be used for writing, writing became partially horizontal and was read from left to right. "Represented objects were no longer in their natural position (for instance, legs, jars, and vegetables were prone). From then on, there were no more sign-things, but instead sign-words or even phonograms (transferred sign-words, or signs-parts of words)."

The evolution of this system toward phonetics in the Akkadian period proves that an awareness of an alphabetization of language began to form: there was a distinction of phonemes in the spoken chain. In contrast to Egyptian writing, cuneiform writing marked the vowels *a, e, i,* and *u,* and also systematized the syllables: *mu, ma, mi; ku, ka, ki; ur, ar, ir.* Therefore a distinction between vowels and consonants must already have existed. Even before the Akkadian contribution, which some consider decisive for the phoneticization of cuneiform writing, ancient Sumerian writing was phonographic to a certain extent, according to Cohen, because it used "the translation rebus." Thus, *gi(n),* "to be stable," was written with the sign for "reed," and was pronounced *gi.* When the Akkadians encountered a writing that did not correspond to their language, they used it to indicate sounds instead of word-entities, notions, objects, etc. For the Sumerians, "water" was written ⁓ and pronounced *a.* The Akkadians took the sign for *a,* but no longer related it to "water," for "water" in Akkadian was pronounced *m.* The value of the sign was thus detached from its materiality: from the real it marked, and from the graphic system that marked it. The signifier was separated from the signified, and this separation led at the same time to a signifier/graphic system separation. The Sumerian sign⁓, "water"/*a,* was replaced in Akkadian by 𐎅 in cuneiform, which was pronounced as *a* but whose meaning no longer had anything to do with water. This hypothesis explains the change to phonetic if not alphabetic writing as being the result of a process of mentalization and breakup of the intimate relation referent/signifier/signified, proper to the pictogram and ideogram.

The complex cuneiform writing never became an alphabetic writing, however, and despite its apparent clumsiness, was never abandoned in favor of the alphabetic scriptural systems known to the populations of the Akkadian provinces, such as the alphabet of the Canaanites (fourteenth century B.C.

The knowledge of the functioning of *la langue* that we find in Mesopotamian dictionaries on the one hand, and in cuneiform writing on the other, was already moving toward abstraction. This removed the signifying chain from its entrenchment in a real cosmogony and articulated it as an object autonomous of internal dependencies (shown in the markings of different phonemes in writing, or the lexicographic classifications of dictionaries), although this remained implicit in scriptural and philological practices. Explicitly, the Akkadian's theory of language was mythic and religious. Writing, just like science, the arts, and the construction of cities and temples, was taught by a man-amphibian, Oannes, who, before returning to the water, left behind a book about the origin of the world and civilization. A text of Sardanpalus attributes the origin of writing to the god Nabu, son of the great god Marduk and the goddess Tashmetum.

7

CHINA: WRITING AS SCIENCE

The functioning of the Chinese language is so closely linked to Chinese writing, and at the same time, vocal speech is so distinct from it, that even if modern linguistics wanted to separate the spoken from the written, it would be difficult to understand one without the other. It is indeed a unique example in history, where in general phoneticism and writing form two independent registers, for *la langue* to be extricated at the crossroads of the two. As a result, knowledge of language in China constitutes knowledge of writing: there is almost no Chinese linguistics in the form of thought on vocal speech, although there are theories about graphic emblems, and classifications of these emblems.

The Chinese phonetic system is particularly complex. In current Chinese, every syllable can be pronounced in four tones (eight in the archaic language) that modify its value. The language is monosyllabic and abounds in homophones: for instance, *shi* pronounced in the second tone can signify *ten, time/weather, food, eclipse, to remove, stone,* etc. It is moreover isolating, that is to say, nonagglutinative. This phonetic polyvalence is also found at the syntactic and morphological level. The Chinese word can be used as a noun, verb, or adjective, without changing its form. Only its context—the function of the word in the whole of the discourse—attributes a precise value to the precise occurrence of the concrete word. Demiéville made these remarks about this particularity of the Chinese language:

> Parts of speech do not exist in Chinese from a semantic point of view. There is no Chinese word that always and necessarily designates a thing, a process, or a quality. Nor do parts of speech exist, with certain reservations, from a morphological point of view. They exist only from a functional point of view. While it can be said that, in such-and-such a syntactic context, such-and-such a Chinese word is used here as a noun, there as a verb or an adjective, it is exclusively in this sense that it functions as a subject, attribute, or object, as a predicate, or as a determinant. This seems quite simple, but in fact, we experience a world of difficulty when we try to isolate ourselves from a semantic point of view. That one and the same word can signify, with one and the same form, sometimes a state of being or a modality of becoming, elsewhere a quality, a circumstance, and all the rest, this goes against convictions we have inherited from Aristotle and the Greco-Latin rhetoricians, and have held throughout centuries of scholasticism, and which, if I may say so, grip our very soul. There is something scandalous and revolting in it for us; and for this reason one constantly sees parts of speech, after they have been evicted on principle, make their way back into Chinese grammar by some back door. This is true for even the most recent Western authors or contemporary Chinese specialists. For if the latter have undertaken a grammatical study of their language, it is due to an impulse that comes from the West. They experience even more difficulty than we do in liberating themselves, in this study, from the shackles of European categories. It is a rare scholar who shows enough firmness of judgment to maintain on every occasion, as Henri Maspero has not ceased to do, that parts of speech in Chinese are a mirage that we must get rid of once and for all. The grammatical polyvalence of words is an absolute fact in Chinese.

Several conclusions can be drawn from this description of the Chinese language, for the relationships among language/meaning/real as well as for the internal (morphological, semantic, syntactic) organization of the language.

In the Chinese language, the relations normally established among the referent/signifier/signified are modified. It is as if these three terms become confused if they are not organized hierarchically; meaning/sound/thing, fused into a single traced mark—into an ideogram—arrange themselves like functional actors in a spatial theater. For, as Granet has written (*La Pensée chinoise*, 1934), the Chinese word "is something very different from a sign used to note a concept. It does not correspond to a notion whose degree of abstraction and generality we want to fix in as definite a way as possible. It evokes by first making apparent the most active images of an undefined complex of particular images." *Since it is not a sign*, the Chinese word, for Granet, is instead an *emblem* "that is given life only with the help of grammatical or syntactic devices."

Even though it becomes the *representamen* of the *thing*, the Chinese word doesn't lose the thing; it only transfers the thing to a plane where it becomes ordered with others in a regulated system. In this way *la langue* and "the real" are one and the same thing. Guillaume, in his psycho-systematic terminology, indicated this fact as follows:

> Anything particular that is introduced into the Chinese word is submitted, as soon as it is apprehended, to a singularizing tension whose effect is a *growing closeness between the pronounced word and the thing it evokes*. When this closing-in effect nears its maximum, the word is not far from satisfying the equation word-thing. . . . The word, having thus become the thing itself in the mind of the speaker, through a subjective but irresistible impression of identity, takes away with it all the reality as well as all the efficiency.

This welding of the *concept*, the *sound*, and the *thing* in the Chinese language, which causes *la langue* and the real to construct a whole without coming face to face like an object (the world, the real) and its mirror (the subject, *la langue*), is materialized by and in Chinese writing. This ideographic writing is more than three thousand years old, and it is the only one that hasn't evolved toward alphabetization (as Egyptian and cuneiform writing both did). The specificity of this writing, which prevents the abstraction of an idea and a sound outside the real traced mark that first unifies them and then distributes their marks in a logical calculus, was defined in this way by Meillet:

> The signs are phonetic [?] in that each one represents not the idea itself but the idea as it is expressed by a definite phonetic whole [this must be rectified: graphic].[1] They are ideographic in that what is expressed is not the sound considered in and of itself but the word, that is to say, the association of a meaning with a sound. Signs are—in part at least—ancient representations or ancient symbols, but which do not for the most part have any recognizable connection to the ideas indicated by the words they represent.

How did Chinese writing arrive at the state, described by Meillet, that we now know it to have?

The oldest Chinese writing was generally *pictographic;* it represented objects—plants, animals, body movements, instruments, etc.—in a schematic, stylized, and conventional manner. Later, *indirect symbols* (in Haloun's terminology) or *indicative symbols* (Karlgren's terminology), formed by substitution, were added to these pictograms. For instance, the word *fu,* "full," is derived from the old ideogram for "jar." During a third period of time, combinations of two or more pictograms produced complex signs called *logical* or *associative compounds.* For instance, *hao,* the verb "to love" and the adjective "good," is a combination of the signs for "woman" and "child" or "female" and "male." The sounds corresponding to the two compounds disappeared and gave way to a third sound, that of the written term, by juxtaposing the two component ideograms.[2] Finally, a fourth category of ideograms is called *mutually interpretative symbols.* For instance, Joseph Needham has explained that *"khao* 老 'examination,' was said to be derived from *lao* 耂 'old' because naturally the young are examined by the old. But in fact these two characters originally meant exactly the same thing, namely, 'elder,' and later there was a bifurcation or specialisation of meaning and sound" [pp. 29–30].

Two thousand ideograms, belonging to the categories we have mentioned, are currently used in modern writing. But from the second millennium on, owing to the homophony of the Chinese language, some signs had to be borrowed. "There was a tendency to use one character with the sense which properly belonged to another of the same sound but different form" [p. 30]. For instance, the third personal pronoun *chhi* 其 originally signified "basket" and was marked 𠀒. This type of character is designated by the name *loan character*.

The last category are the *determinative-phonetic characters*. They are radicals that are added to a phonetic element to indicate the semantic category it belongs to. For instance, *thung* 同 "with, together," is always a phonetic element but can be combined with several silent radicals that function as semantic determinants:

> *chin* 金 (metal) + 同 *thung* = *thung*, copper, bronze.
> *hsin* 心 (heart) + 同 *thung* = *thung*, moaning, dissatisfied.

And so on [p. 30].

Other determinatives are not pronounced, and function only as semantic determinative radicals. For instance, *shui* 水 "water," when combined with pronounceable words, designates that they have a seme in common with water:

> *shui* 水 *(water)* + *mo* 末 branches = *mo* 沫 foam
> *shui* 水 *(water)* + *lau* 闌 late, end = *lan* 瀾 waves
> *shui* 水 *(water)* + *mei* 每 each = *hai* 海 the sea

Etc. [p. 31].

Composed in this way, Chinese characters testify to a semanticological way of thinking that is objectified in the very constitution of the characters. The marks are joined together and produce meanings according to their mode and combination without trying to transcribe pronunciation, which, as a result, acquires perfect autonomy. Leibniz compared the functioning of Chinese writing—a writing that is a true logical analysis of signifying units—to that of an algebraic system: "If there were [in Chinese writing] a certain number of fundamental characters of which the others were only combinations," this writing or linguistic systematization "would brave some analogies with the analysis of thoughts." Needham compared the way in which Chinese characters function by combining to how molecules and atoms combine.

The characters may be considered molecules composed of the permu-
tations and combinations of 214 atoms. Indeed, all the phonetic elements can be reduced to radicals, or even better, to the marks of
semes, whose application produces the molecule-semanteme (the word).
Seven "atoms" at the most can be found in one "molecule," and an
"atom" may repeat at most three times—as if forming a crystal structure—in the same semanteme [p. 31].

Translated into modern linguistic language, this particularity of Chinese
writing means that it is difficult, if not impossible, to attribute the
element-characters of the Chinese writing-language to categories of
discourse with fixed signification. Each word is "syntaxed": it has a
specific construction, and therefore its own syntax whose components
acquire one value or another depending upon their syntactic role. That
is, Chinese writing (which, Meillet would suggest, is, like all writing,
first a *science of language*) puts *syntax* in the place of morphology. On
the level of larger constructions, such as the sentence, the role of
context—or, in other words, the *syntactic* relations of the constitutive
elements—is even more decisiive. It is the syntactic context that attributes a precise and concrete signification to each semanteme, and its
grammatical value as a noun, verb, adjective, etc. A *distributional*
analysis that itemizes the concrete syntactic occurrences of each semanteme could also serve as the starting point for a Chinese grammar. The
very structure of the language seems to suggest such an approach, to
the extent that it emphasizes the importance of syntactic order in its
organization. For instance, *full* words with grammatical polyvalence can
be distinguished from *empty* words with a reduced distribution, appear-
ing at fixed locations like "the fixed stars of a moving firmament"
(Dobson). Starting from this distinction and a distributional analysis, it
can be established that the Chinese sentence is composed of "words"
(one character), "composite words" (two characters in habitual alliance), and "syntagms" (any other combination including those with
certain empty words).

In this way writing has established the laws specific to the Chinese
language. But we find *explicit theory* about this in the philosophical
thought and scientific classifications that the Chinese have elaborated
over the course of time.

The linguistic-scriptural element corresponds to the real element it indicates (see figure 7.1). The invention of writing was attributed to Li Ssu, the minister of the first sovereign, Huang-Ti. Li Ssu apparently got his inspiration from the tracks birds leave on the soil. It is also supposed that before truly graphic writing there was a marking system based on knotted ropes. In any case, the beginning of writing is closely tied to magical rites. Writings are talismans, and represent man's mastery over the universe. However, *and this is a particularity of the Chinese conception of written language,* while writing has something to do with magic, it is far from laying claim to a saintly quality, or from acquiring a sacred value. On the contrary, writing is *synonymous* with *political and governmental power* and is confused with the political function. The prince-governor had as his primordial mission to *arrange* things by *designating* them correctly; it is by means of writing that he accomplished this mission.

The relation between the object and the graphic element is often considered one of *designation* in Chinese theories. Thus Confucius felt that the sign for "dog" 犬 was a perfect design of the animal. One can see that it is not a question of a *realistic resemblance* between the ideogram and the object. The "sign" is a stripped-down figuration that indicates the object it refers to but does not reproduce it. The relation of *indication* rather than of *resemblance* between the grapheme and the

Figure 7.1. These designs, borrowed from the grammarian Chang Yee, attest to the analogy between Chinese ideograms and figurative representations. From Jacques Gernet, *L'Ecriture et la psychologie des peuples* (Centre International de Synthèse. Paris: Armand Colin, 1963).

referent is clearly expressed by the term *chih* 指 "finger, toe, digit," translated by European linguists as "sign," "signifier," or "signified." This is imprudent, in our opinion. We find it in a text *On the Finger and the Object* by Kung-sun Lung, a Chinese philosopher of the "Sophist" school, which existed during the fourth and third centuries B.C.

> Every object [*wu*] is a finger [*chih*, "signified"?] but the finger ["signifier"?] is not the finger ["signified"?]—if no finger ["signifier"?] exists in the world, no object can be called an object.
>
> I say that the finger is not the finger; if no object exists in the world, can we speak of a finger? . . . Besides the finger is what plays a common role in the world. . . .
>
> If no relation [thing/finger: *wu/chih*] exists in the world, who would speak of a non-finger ["non-sign"?] If in the world there is no object, who would speak of a finger ["sign"?]? If there is no object in the world and no relation, who would speak of a non-finger? Who will say that *every object is a finger?*[3]

Perhaps we could get closer to the meaning of these thoughts if, instead of "sign," "signifier," and "signified," we translate "de-signation," "de-signator," and "de-signated."

In the same line of thinking, that is, by considering *la langue* as the designation of the real, a hypothesis was developed stating that Chinese ideograms were not designations of objects, but designations of designations, that is, designs of *gestures*. This thesis was defended by Chang Cheng-Ming (*Chinese Writing and Human Gesture*, 1932).

The first attempt at considering and systematizing the linguistic-scriptural group as a specific object was presented to us by Chinese dictionaries. The first among them, *Shuo Wen Chieh Tzu*, recognized 514 radicals. During the Ming and Ching dynasties, the number was reduced first to 360, then to 214, where it has remained until our time. The six classes of characters, which we mentioned initially, were defined by Chinese scholars themselves, notably by Liu Hsin and Hsü Shen of the Han dynasty. The six writings *(liu shu)* gave their names to dictionaries such as the *Liu Shu Ku* (1237–1275). Here is the classification of characters it proposed:

1. imaged forms (pictograms);
2. designations of situations (indirect symbols);
3. meetings of ideas (associative complexes);
4. transferable significations (mutually interpretative symbols);
5. borrowed (borrowed phonetic characters);
6. image and sound (determinative-phonetics) [*Science,* p. 32].

An evolution of pictograms (predominant around the fifteenth and fourteenth centuries B.C.) toward determinative phonetics (more developed during the twelfth to eleventh centuries B.C.) should be noted. Since the phoneticization of characters led to confusion about this monosyllabic and homophonic language, Chinese linguists proceeded to analyze sound and characters according to the "cutting and joining," or *fan-chhieh* principle. For instance, the pronunciation of a character like *kan* is explained as being composed of *k(uo)* + *(h)an.* The method appeared around 270 B.C. with Sun Yan, and Needham, following Nagasawa, believes it is due to the influence of Sanskrit scholars [p. 34]. An important dictionary, *Chhieh Yün* by Lu Fa-Yen, published in 601, applied this method.

Since the Chinese language became simplified over the centuries, by the eleventh century A.D., this type of dictionary was no longer in use. At that time, in 1067, Ssuma Kuang composed a series of *tables* that reorganized the ancient system and adapted it to the new system of pronunciation. It was his *Lei Phien* dictionary that Needham considered the typical example of these tabulation systems, which were originally linguistic, historical, and philosophical, and which formed the basis of coordinate geometry [p. 34]. In other words, this type of linguistic systematization gave birth to a large part of Chinese mathematics. To this category of dictionary-tables belong the *Thung Chih Lüeh* of Chêng Chhiao (1150) and the *Chung Yuan Yin Yün* of Chou Tê-Chhing (1250).

European thinking had access to the linguistic and/or scriptural system of the Chinese at a very late date, and the same is true for their theory and science of language. Louis Lecomte's book *Nouveaux mémoires sur l'état présent de la Chine* (1696) is considered the starting point for European sinology. The establishment of the Jesuits in China in the seventeenth century was the most important channel for knowledge of the Chinese language. At that time, Europe was seduced by nonalphabetic writing, and most of all by the Egyptian hieroglyphs known before Chinese writing. Several works even "demonstrated" the Egyptian origins of Chinese writing: Athanasius Kircher (*China Illustrata*, 1667); John Webb, Joseph de Guignes (*Mémoires dans lequel on prouve que les Chinois sont une colonie égyptienne*, 1760), etc. De Pauw dissipated this illusion several years later, but real modern sinology did not begin until the nineteenth century, with the teachings of J.-P. Abel Rémusat at the Collège de France in 1815.

8

INDIAN LINGUISTICS

In India, the organization of language and of the thinking about it took a completely different direction from those of the previously mentioned civilizations, and perhaps constitutes the most ancient basis of modern abstract thought on linguistics.

First of all, in other cultures writing was indissoluble from language, to the point that its functioning even dispensed with a specifically linguistic theory of signification. Writing played only a secondary role, however, for the Indians. We know very little of the most ancient writing of these regions, that of Mohenjo-Daro (3000 B.C.). Brahmi writing (300 B.C.) was syllabic, but in contrast to Egyptian, and in part Sumerian writing, it divided the syllables themselves and marked the consonants that composed them.

The near-absence of writing in the beginning, with the memorization this no doubt entailed, and, at the end, the late phoneticization of writing, are quite symptomatic of the fact that language tended to become removed from the reality from which it was hardly distinguished by other civilizations, and that linguistic operation became "mentalized" as a *signifying* operation, with a subject as the place of meaning. Man and his language were thus placed like a mirror that reflected an outside. Very elaborate theories of meaning, symbolism, and the subject were thus developed; from these the modern science of language slowly found its starting point.

A third particularity of the conception of language in India consists in the fact that Indian theories were constructed from Sanskrit, the language of Vedic *literature*. The first examples of this language, said to be "perfect," date from more than one thousand years B.C. This language stopped being spoken during the third century B.C. and was replaced with Prakrits. This meant that the poetic (mythic or religious) texts of a dead language had to be translated. This deciphering of a poetry that was no longer spoken gave rise to Panini's grammar and to all of Indian linguistics. This linguistics found in the texts it deciphered a conception of speech, meaning, and the subject that had already been elaborated in the *Rig-veda*. Thus, linguistics drew its inspiration from the texts it deciphered, and this nascent science made itself the interpreter of an already existing theory that had been recorded by sacred texts. Indian phonetics and grammar were therefore organized in strict relation to Vedic religion and ritual, and represent the linguistic "strata" of that religion.

Speech *(vac)* occupies a privileged place in Vedic hymns which reveal (10:71) that under the aegis of Brhaspati, the "master of sacred speech," "names were imparted to things." The Sages imposed speech on thinking "just as grains are sifted through a screen." Obtaining and using speech were considered a *sacrament (samskrta)* and/or an act related to the sexual act: to some "speech has opened its body just as a woman in her finery opens hers to her husband."

But Vedic texts were already conducting a "scientific" systematization of speech. Hymn 1:164 of the *Rig-veda* (v. 45) says that discourse "measures four parts" of which "three are kept secret, they are not set in motion"; only the fourth one is known, which is the language of men. Louis Renou *(Etudes védiques et paniniennes)*, commenting on this paragraph, thought, as do Geldner and Strauss, that it is a question of "the transcendent part of speech, that which at a later date will be called the *brahman*, and of which is said, as of the *vac*, that man's condition enables him to know only a minimal part." We have here the first splitting of the linguistic process (signifier) whose aim is to grasp the act of signification; modern Western realism tried to find it again by following various paths: the "unconscious" (in psychoanalysis), or the "deep structure" (in transformational grammar). In India, the *brahman*, "sacred speech, magic word" was split into (1) a material word *(sabda brahman)* of which the *atman* is a manifestation; and (2) a transcendent word *(parabrahman)*. This opposition reverberates in the theories of the philosophers of language and produces the distinction *dhvani/sphota* to which we will return. Let us again emphasize that linguistic thinking depended directly on the religious conception evidenced in the religious texts, and was itself part of these texts, at least in its beginning. These texts were largely devoted to language and signification; they closely linked them to the cycles of sexuality and reproduction, and in this way constructed a concept of man as an infinite process of cosmic differentiation. In this systematized universe, where every element acquired a symbolic value, language—the first symbolism—was given the place of honor. Its science, grammar, was called "the supreme science, the purifier of all sciences," "the royal road free of detours," which "aims at realizing man's supreme object."

Among the best-known grammars, the famous grammar of Panini, which is believed to date from approximately four centuries B.C., must be mentioned. It is a work of eight volumes *(astadhvahyi)*, comprised of four thousand *sutras* or maxims. This relatively recent text collected the mass of previous linguistic theories, which had been orally transmitted. The grammar was translated in Europe by Böhtlingk (1815–1840); Renou was responsible for the French edition. The grammar is striking for the precision of its formulations about both *phonic* organization and the *morphology* of the *Sanskrit* language.

Let us first note, with Renou, the close relation of *grammar* to *ritual* in Sanskrit. For instance, the grammatical cases bear no special names, but are marked by numerical signs, or *prathama*. This type of indication seems to come from a ritual where various notions (days, rites, musical modes, etc.) were evoked by ordinal numbers. In contrast, the functions of cases with respect to the verbal process, the *karaka* (that is, anything that causes the verbal action to be executed), are indicated by names of a greatly individualized aspect, among which predominates a group of derivatives of the root *kr-, karman,* which means "action, rite." Several other examples could be given to support this thesis of the direct dependence of grammar on ritual, and of the ritualistic origin of Indian linguistics, which is difficult to isolate from the religious whole.

In its unceasing relation to the liturgical recitation of sacred texts, Indian grammar presented a complex theory of the *phonic* matter of the language: sounds, their articulation, and their link to signification. The terminology of this level indicates that sound was conceived of as matter that assured the reality of the vibration that is the meaning of speech. For instance, *aksara,* "syllable," comes from the religious text *naksarati,* "that which does not leak" or rather "the imperishable basis of discourse." The phoneme, *varna,* had in the beginning the sense of "coloration." Phonic elements were classified according to the mode and point of consonantal articulation, followed by that of vowels and dipthongs; they formed five series of correlations called *vargas.* It was a subtle theory of articulation, one linked to religious signification and to a complex theory of the human body that distinguished different movements of the lips (opening, closing), of the tongue against the teeth (constriction), of the glottis, of the lungs, of nasal resonance, etc., as the producers of phonemes, which already bore (owing to their bodily production) a well-defined meaning.

The theory of the sphota, constructed from such bases, is first found in Patanjali, who lived at the beginning of the Christian era and who wrote commentaries on the *sutras* of Panini, as well as on the *vartika* of Katyayana. This theory, which to our way of thinking is extremely subtle and unusual, troubles contemporary scholars. Certain philosophers and grammarians think that the term *sphota* designates a prototype of the word that the word itself intrinsically contains. For others, it is a question of the word's sonority in its totality and as bearer of meaning, independent of the combination of letters. The sphota would not be exactly the sounds of a word in the order of its letters, but the sounds, or something corresponding to them, recast into an indivisible whole. Thus, when pronounced, the sounds come one by one, but the sphota appears only at the end of the articulation of all the word's sounds, at the moment when the sounds of the morphological totality are emitted along with the meaning inherent in it. Etymologically, sphota signifies "bursting, popping," and consequently wherein meaning bursts forth, spreads out, germinates, and gives birth to itself.

Panini distinguished the sounds of discourse, the *dhvani,* from the sphota, which he instead conceived of as a *matrix* of letters with long and short vowels. For Patanjali, the sphota seemed fundamentally to be a structure, a series of consonants and long and short vowels, or as we say today, and as J. Brough has interpreted it, "a succession of phonematic units" (the sphota can also, by the way, be represented by a single letter).

Bhartrhari was a linguist who lived after Panini and Patanjali. His works, the result of thinking about the Paninian school, were produced near the fifth century. In them, the theory of the sphota is developed and appreciably changed. It has been noted that in Bhartrhari the sphota became "the ontological foundation of language." In fact, the sphota can no longer be pronounced; it is what underlies the pronunciation and the sound of speech. We might call this its conceptual or signifying overdeterminant, if this theory were not so completely submerged in reality and if it did not insist to such an extent upon the real materiality that linguistic practice takes part in and manifests. Bhartrhari was not a substantialist—he did not even ask if the sphota was a voiced substance or not. His theory emerged from thinking about the real in movement, and the sphota became the *minimal unity* of this infinitely divisible, and because of that, transformable universe. Let us cite a long passage that testifies to this transforming realism:

> There are three views among those who hold the theory that words are manifested: (1) the sounds act upon the sense-faculty; or (2) they act upon the word or (3) they act upon both. (The first theory would be analogous to the theory of sight-perception which held that) only the sense-faculty (of sight) is acted upon, namely, by attention and application of ointment; (the second theory would be analogous to a theory of smell-perception which held that) only the thing (for instance, the earth) is acted upon in order that its smell might be received. (According to the third theory) where however, the eye effects the reception of a cognition, it is clear that both the object and the sense-faculty are acted upon by the light; and speech-sounds operate in the same form. Certain theorists maintain that reception of the sound takes place without any

separation of it from the form of the Word (sphota); others
hold that the sound is not perceptible. According to yet others
it is an independent manifesting agent.[1]

The sound/signification (sound/speech) split and the close dependence of the two in the same *process, act,* or *movement* of which the
sphota is like a seed or an atom, an atom of both phonic and significa-
tive mobility, are expressed in this way:

the form of a word is apprehended (as a unity) when the word
is revealed by the sound through the agency of causal factors
which are appropriate to the cognition (of the word), but
which are not themselves (as such) apprehended (i.e., the
hearer is not aware of the separate sense-data). Simultaneously
with the last sound, the word is apprehended by the mind *in
which the seed has been sown by the (physical) sounds,* and in
which ripening (of the speech) has been brought about by the
telling over (of the sounds). As far as the *non-existent forms,*
which (a hearer) considers as existing in the interval (before
the complete word has been pronounced) are concerned, this
is merely incapacity on the part of the hearer; they are, in fact,
only means to the apprehension (of the complete word). There
is the semblance of distinctions in cognition; (similarly) the
attributing of distinctions in words is always seen. The word
appears to be produced in stages and cognition seems to be
dependent on the cognised. Just as earlier numbers (in a series) should be apprehended for the apprehension of subsequent ones, although the latter are different from the former,
so is the apprehension of parts in a unit of speech (an aid to
the apprehension of the whole). When in reality revealing
units in the syllable, word and sentence function independently of each other, they appear to function in combination,
although they are entirely different. Just as on looking from a
distance or in the dark, one at first misunderstands an object,
and (later on) understands it otherwise (i.e., in its true nature),
similarly during the manifestation of the sentence by its causes
(namely, the smaller units like letters and words), the mind first
functions as comprehending the component units (as real units).

Just as there is a (fixed) sequence (in the stages) of the transformation of milk (into curds) and the seed (into the tree),
similarly there is *a fixed sequence* in the series of the hearer's
perceptions (of the intervening words, phrases, etc.). And when
they (i.e., sentences, words, etc.) are made up of real parts,
the difference in form is really due to the (difference in the)
sequence of their sounds. And where words, etc., are considered
as not made up of (real) parts, *the fancying of parts* is a means
(to the realisation of the total unit). [1:83–92; italics added]

Several important points can be found in the thinking of this Indian
grammarian.

1. For him, the sound ("the signifier") is not merely the exteriority
of meaning ("the signified"), but the product in *embryo.* Modern linguistics is only beginning to ponder the role of the signifier in the constitution of meaning.

2. Signification is a *process.*

3. Consequently, morphology (the "forms . . . existing in the interval," Bhartrhari says) does not exist; "the fancying of parts" [of dis-
course] is a false appearance.

4. Signification is an ordered syntax, "a fixed sequence."

Let us first emphasize the *analytical* care given to the division and
systematization of the act of speech, which is nevertheless accompanied by a theoretical tendency to *synthesize.* The linguist was trying to
find the conceptual support corresponding to both the analytical thought
process that breaks down the system of the language and to the theoretical principle that sees in this language a *process,* on the order of the
real process of the universe. The *dhvani* are the successive elements of
the voiced chain. They follow each other according to a strict order, so
as to manifest the sphota, which is not of the same nature as the *dhvani.*
While the *dhvani* are of the order of "parts," the sphota is that which
repartition enables knowledge of, that is, *action.* "The inner principle
called speech which exists egg-like, evolving into speech-activity, assumes sequence through its parts" [1:51].[2]

This signifying action is, for Bhartrhari, infinitely divisible. Its minimal elements are not *phonemes.* Indian linguistics went further than our
European phonology (even taking into account our notion of "mer-

isms," the distinctive trait of phonemes, which arranges them into classes) and declared that we cannot stop the division of the voiced chain into ever-smaller elements of which the last would be so minute that we could call them the "indescribables," *anupakhyeya*. The atomization of linguistic matter has no end.

> If these words (which are abstracted by analysis) exist as real entities in a sentence and letters similarly exist in words then letters themselves should be capable of division, just as atoms are (according to some schools of thought divisible). Since the identification of (self-sufficient) parts is not, any way, possible (in a letter) there would be neither letter nor (as a consequence) the word. And when neither letter nor word can be established {*avyapadesya*}, how can anything else (i.e., meaning) be conveyed? [2:28–29]

Precisely in order to remedy the "metaphysical fading" (we would say today) of reality and especially of linguistic reality, which this division ad infinitum of the linguistic whole (sentence, word, sound) would have produced, Bhartrhari posited the sphota, which is something other than this discontinuity all the while being revealed by it. The sphota for him is what gives a coexistence to discursive atoms, what assures their unity in the word and in the sentence. In language, the sphota is the unit—both voiced and signifying—of the infinitely differentiated. Notice the dialectic at work by and in this term, which, by the same token, becomes the pivot through which language, hereafter conceived of as movement, rejoins the real as a mutation. That amounts to saying that with the sphota, language becomes not only a process, but also an act, a movement, and that the signifier slides under the signified in order to form, in action, meaning. What's more, this mobility is given as a reflection of the mobility of the real world. Signification, refusing to be isolated, follows at a distance the continuous-discontinuous-and-in-constant-change real.

The theory of the sphota found its counterpart in the theory of the *sentence*. Before Bhartrhari, Indian grammar had proposed a classification of the parts of speech, by distinguishing between the *noun* and the *verb*. Various discussions between grammarians and philosophers were ongoing with regard to the pertinence of this distinction. Two points of view can be discerned: the morphological point of view, maintaining distinction, and the theoretical, or, rather, the syntactic point of view, maintaining in principle the nondistinction of these categories. The difference between these categories would appear depending only upon their *function* inside the utterance. For his part, and still with a morphological vision, Patanjali distinguished four categories of words. "For words," he wrote, "the mode of application—*pravrtti*—is fourfold. There are words that [are applied] to a class-*jatisabda;* those [applied] to a quality—*gunasabda;* those to an action—*kriyasabda;* and, in the fourth place, those [applied] to chance—*yadrcchasabda.*"

Bhartrhari abandoned this morphological point of view and outlined a theory of the sentence, which, being a process, was the only complete reality of meaning. Words do not signify outside the sentence's syntax. In other words, syntax is not a simple transposition of morphology: "terms" do not exist before and without the "relations" in the uttered whole. Syntax confers reality on meaning. Bhartrhari's theory of syntax characterizes a synthetic approach that extends, beyond the sphota, to the large units of discourse. He was thus opposed to the noun/verb distinction: every sentence for him was both a noun and a verb, even if both categories were not manifest.

> Since a fact is conveyed either as existent or as non-existent, only a sentence is used to convey it. Word-meaning, whether positive, or negative, is not in practice understood without its being associated with a verb. Therefore it does not (in reality) exist. The statement 'existence' *{sat}* (which is a one-word-sentence) is not understood in the form 'there was existence' 'there is existence' or 'there is no existence' except through its association to the mention of a verb. When the meaning-expressed-by-a-verb is connected with nominal accessories, its expectancy is not satisfied without the mention of the 'existence-idea' (i.e., the meaning of the nominal accessories). *The action-part of the meaning of a sentence is first picked out because of its primacy.* The nominal accessories used to effect the objective-to-be-accomplished (i.e., the verbal action) are (therefore) secondary. However, the effect which the action (itself) brings about is its (own) result. [2:423–27]

In this reasoning, in which it is difficult to sort out what refers to language from what is generally philosophical, one grasps that the action in question is another name for *signification:* the term denotes meaning as process; the act of speech is like [the act of] begetting meaning. We see being sketched out here a conception of signification whose foundation is not in isolated words (nouns, verbs, etc.), that is, in *parts* (for Bhartrhari, "parts are fanciful"), but is instead in the transformation of these parts into a complete utterance, in the process of the generation of this utterance which is constructed like a true "transformational tree" (we are barely modernizing here) and not like a whole divided into parts. Continuing to modernize Indian theories, we can say that Sabara's conception (criticized by Bhartrhari) is a "structuralist" theory: "Action is nothing, speech expresses only things that have been put into a relation." Bhartrhari's conception is, however, an analytical-synthetic, "transformational" one (see chapter 19). This latter conception relies once again on the distinction we called attention to in the beginning, between (1) a pre-meaning operation where the elements are joined together in a nonsuccessive way and give birth to a process that results in (2) an ordered, successive, linear, and communicated spoken word, which alone possesses meaning. "Listeners get the meaning of the sentence through the clear utterance of (all) the words in it. This Speech is described as indistinct, sequential or as uttered in a low voice. The non-sequential appears as being stretched out (i.e., having sequence) when the mind dwells on it," Bhartrhari concluded [2:18b–19].

Finally, in its theory of signification, Indian linguistics approached what we today call a *theory of the enunciation.* It posited as the indispensable elements for engendering meaning the function of the speaking subject, his addressee, the speaking situation, the spatiotemporal position of the subject, etc. "The meanings of words are determined from (their) syntactical connection (in the sentence), situation-context, the meaning of another word, propriety, place and time, and not from their mere form," Bhartrhari remarked [2:314]. We can see that Indian grammar is far from being a simple systematization of an object that is closed, and "in itself"—language; it goes well beyond its enclosures and thinks of its object as a relation of the subject and his outside that is likely to clarify signification.

With whatever use (in view) *{vivaksita}* a meaning is sought to
be conveyed by the speaker, the meaning is established like
that (in that context), because a meaning has several capacities.
Sometimes a connection (of contact) is said to exist between
things which exist far from each other; and sometimes things
in contact appear as being apart. The separation of the (really)
united, the union of the (really) separated, the unity of the
(really) diverse and the diversity of the (really) single,—(in
this way) things are established (as existing in contrary forms),
either because they have many forms or have no forms. The
only binding factor (in the determination of what is meant
whenever reference is made to them) is the word because it
has its capacity fixed. [2:430–33]

We have only outlined here a few aspects of the complex science of
signification that developed in India, in which the problem of language
took up a key position, a pivotal place. Let us indicate in passing that
Indian *logic,* in studies of considerable importance, also tackled the
rules of linguistic construction; this resulted in conclusions that have
been elucidated in our time by J. F. Stall, and that are different from
those of Aristotelian logic.

9

THE PHOENICIAN ALPHABET

Faithful to an evolutionist and Eurocentric attitude, certain linguists feel that the alphabetic writing used today by almost all countries, except some in the Far East, is the result of an "intellectual development" or an indispensable evolution that nonalphabetic [peoples] were unable to attain. Such a concept, taking as its starting point the linguistic consciousness bequeathed to us by the Greeks, is the prisoner of a fairly late approach to language; it has been erected as a norm and excludes in this way any other conception of the signifying operation. It seems more rigorous to us, without talking about an "evolution" of writing and/or of the concept of language, to posit a principle of *difference* between the types of conceptions of language that are marked in the types of writing, as well as in explicit theories themselves.

It is indeed obvious that ideographic writing translates a concept of language for which and in which the thing, the notion, and the term are a whole welded by the mark of the "character." But in this system, the phoneme constitutes a separate register, leaving graphemes the freedom to reconstitute a logicosemantic systematization in which an entire cosmogony is reflected. It is as if, through this *langue*-writing, a communion were being firmly established between the outside and the distance of language, a *sacer*—a sacrament of man/writing and real/cosmos. One could say that ideographic and hieroglyphic writings practice language without *hearing/understanding* it: without hearing/understanding its ideal and phonetic autonomy as separate from what it designates. Is this therefore *la langue* that is being practiced, in the current sense of this word? Or is it an ordering of the cosmos in which what we call *la langue,* if it were isolated from fundamental syncretism, would be nothing but an actor in the "sacrament"?

On the other hand, a completely different practice of *la langue* dissociates the spoken chain from what it expresses, and conceives of it as relieved of its semantic and cosmic-classificatory opacity, and *hears/understands* it as an object in itself in order to analyze the elements of this object—the phonemes—which, by themselves, do not apply to any object or real phenomenon. This results, therefore, in the isolation of the *phoneme,* which is then denoted by an appropriate and constant sign: the *letter* will no longer designate a meaning or an object; it will not even have the function of recalling the signifying process indicated by the Indian sphota; it will simply be an element of the voiced chain.

How can these differences in the conception of the signifying operation, objectified by the difference between the letter and the ideogram, be explained? Egyptian writing, as we saw, outlined an evolution that brought it close to an analysis-marking of the phonic substance of *la langue,* which was nearly independent of the referent and the signified; it did not, however, produce alphabetical writing. Chinese writing remained even further from this procedure. It is in the Syrian-Palestinian world, and more particularly, among the Phoenicians, that a purely phonetic notation of languages was produced using a limited number of signs, no doubt syllabic, which later furnished the model for the alphabet that marks every phoneme. We can suppose, with Cohen, that this phoneticization of writing that resulted in an alphabet "could also have corresponded to a social state that concurrently permitted a certain autonomy" for individuals, a weakening of the centralized States, and an emancipation of the individual "with respect to priests and kings," which led to the formation of an individual consciousness. Such a sociohistorical explanation, which relates the emancipation of the individual to the emancipation of the signifier, and consequently the atom-subject to the atom-letter, has been formulated by Needham. Without affirming that it is a question of cause and effect, we can in fact observe that the ideogrammatical type of writing was often accompanied by a mode of production said to be "Asian" (large productive and interdependent collectives, managed by a central organization, without isolated, urban and "democratic"—in the Greek sense of the term—units); on the level of scientific thinking these societies developed a correlative, dialectical logic, one that is antisubstantial (such as the logic of Chinese science). On the contrary, the Greek alphabetical system had as its correlate, on the sociological level, units of production that were isolated and closed in on themselves, a development of individual consciousness in ideology, and a logic of noncontradiction in science (Aristotelian logic).

Phoenician writing is generally considered to be the ancestor of modern alphabetical systems. In this writing, an *archaic Phoenician alphabet* and a Phoenician writing that is noticeably different from the former can be distinguished. The oldest documents to attest to the archaic Phoenician alphabet date from the thirteenth to the eleventh centuries B.C., and were found in the inscriptions of the city of Byblos, which was the meeting place for many populations and a bridge between Syria and Egypt. Without being able to give the exact date of the appearance of this writing, one can note that it was not ideogrammatical and that it possessed no determinative characters. It did mark the voiced chain, which it broke down into minimal elements. The whole question debated by scholars revolves around knowing whether these minimal elements were *syllables* or *sounds,* that is, *consonants* that suggested more or less approximatively the preceding vowel. According to Meillet, Pedersen, and even Weil, Phoenician writing was *syllabic:* it limited itself to "noting the syllable, that is, a reality that was always able to be pronounced and easy to isolate," even if "of the syllable it noted only the consonant, the essential element for indicating the meaning, and let the reader supply the vowel" (Meillet).

Février went even further by claiming that Phoenician did not separate only the syllables; it also isolated *consonants* and was thus constituted as a "true consonantal alphabet." Nevertheless, Février did clarify that this Phoenician alphabet "is not what we're used to calling an alphabet, that is, a writing that analyzes each word in its consecutive phonetic elements, consonants and vowels, and allocates a special sign to each of these elements, to the vowels as well as to the consonants."

The Phoenician alphabet indeed only isolated "the consonantal skeleton of the word"; it never became fully alphabetized, as did the Greek
one, and that seemingly all at once and spontaneously. While he does
acknowledge that Phoenician writing was phonetic, Février has remarked that it was "incompletely phonetic": "It is a writing that has
banished ideograms, but which, at its core, remains ideographic to a
certain degree since it only notes the root, without taking into account
the vocalization it could receive." This remark can be explained in the
light of the particularities of Semitic languages, which have preserved
to this day a consonantal alphabet. In these languages the root of a
word, that is, the constant element that carries the global sense and
does not depend upon the syntactic function, is represented by the
word's consonants. The root QTL, bearer of the seme "to kill" in
Hebrew, can be pronounced QeTól, "to kill," QôTél, "killing," QâTúl,
"killed," or QâTaLun, "we have killed." It can thus be understood how
a writing can function efficiently and without confusion by marking
only the consonantal root, broken down into its composite elements.
This type of writing, which marks the word's key, seems on the other
hand, Février wrote, "closer to primitive ideography than does the
syllabism toward which the various cuneiform writings tended."

Several branches of Semitic writing developed out of the Phoenician
"alphabet," which spread among the surrounding peoples: the ancient
Hebrew alphabet, Samaritan writing, etc. The Mediterranean basin—
Greece, Cyprus, Malta, Sardinia, and North Africa—having been col-
onized by the Phoenicians, was subject to the influence of their writing
(one of the results is the Punic writing of Carthage).

One last question about the Phoenician alphabet attracts the attention of specialists: where did the form of the characters, their name,
and their order in the alphabetical classification come from? It is supposed that the arrangement of the characters into an alphabet was for
pedagogical reasons, and that it was "the graphic similarity of the
characters that determined the order assigned to them" (Février). As
to the form of the consonant-"letters," it evoked the image of the
object whose name began with the sound marked by the letter. For
instance, *alef* ⅄ signifies "ox" in Hebrew, and its oldest form, found
on the inscriptions of Ahiram, seems to reproduce the ox's head and
horns. The letter could therefore have been borrowed from an ideo-

graphic writing, and its designation is perhaps, according to Gardiner's hypothesis, due to an *acrophonic* method: "The Semitic peoples gave the borrowed ideogram the designation that corresponded to it in their language, and kept the first sound of this designation for the henceforth alphabetical value of the sign."

10

THE HEBREWS: THE BIBLE AND THE CABALA

Hebraic antiquity did not develop a theory, much less a science of language that can be compared to those of India or China. But the presence of language is perceptible in the pages of the Bible; it is mingled with the most decisive moments of the history of Israel, and seems at times to furnish the background for the religious and historical events that are its manifestations.

The *Creation,* as it is described in the Bible, is accompanied by a verbal act, if not identified with it: "And the earth was without form, and void; and darkness was upon the face of the deep. . . . And God *said,* Let there be light: and there was light. . . . And God *called* the light Day, and the darkness he *called* Night" (Genesis 1:2–5).[1] To *name* is a divine, arbitrary, but necessary *(nom véritable)* and obligatory act for man: "And out of the ground the Lord God formed every beast of the field, and every fowl of the air; and brought them unto Adam to see what he would call them: and whatsoever Adam called every living creature, that was the name thereof *{nom véritable}.* And Adam gave names to all cattle, and to the fowl of the air, and to every beast of the field" (Genesis 2:19–20).

The interest of Hebrew thinking in language is also manifested by the search for the *motivation* of names: it is found in a supposed *etymology.* For instance, "she shall be called Woman, because she was

taken out of Man" (Genesis 2:23), and, "And she called his name
Moses: and she said, Because I drew him out of the water" (Exodus
2:10).

La langue, conceived of as the common, unitary, unifying, and creative core, is distinguished from *languages,* whose plurality is portrayed
as a punishment. This theme of a *universal language {langue}* and multiple languages *{langues}* that manifest it but also occult it and muddle
its purity—a theme that certain tendencies in linguistic science even in
our day never cease to laicize, embellish, and clarify—is magnificently
represented by the mythical sequence of the tower of Babel. After the
Deluge and before being separated from one another, the children of
Noah decided to build a city and a tower; their ambition was to "reach
unto heaven" and to "make themselves a name." God could not allow
this discourse, which strove to be beyond time and place, and which
would permit man to become the equal of the divine power. "And the
Lord came down to see the city and the tower, which the children of
men builded. And the Lord said, behold, the people is one, and they
have all one language; and this they begin to do: and now nothing will
be restrained from them, which they have imagined to do. Go to, let
us go down, and there confound their language, that they may not
understand one another's speech. So the Lord scattered them abroad
from thence upon the face of all the earth: and they left off to build
the city. Therefore is the name of it called Babel; because the Lord did
there confound the language of all the earth: and from thence did the
Lord scatter them abroad upon the face of all the earth" (Genesis
11:5–9).

Another biblical myth, this one concerning *writing,* is linked to the
name of Moses. In order for Moses to help his people, he needed
linguistic power: the Bible seems to consider the possession of language
as a spiritual and state-controlled power. Now Moses, by his own
admission, "was not eloquent," and it is in particular God's presence
that constituted the major obstacle to his speech: ". . . I am not eloquent, neither heretofore, nor since thou hast spoken unto thy servant:
but I am slow of speech, and of a slow tongue" (Exodus 4:10). To help
his servant recover the use of *la langue,* which is equated to the practice
of power, the Lord twice intervened.

First, he gave Moses a miraculous rod "That they may believe that the Lord God of their fathers . . . hath appeared unto thee" (Exodus 4:5).[2] Later, to seal the alliance between the Israelites and the Lord, Moses "wrote all the words of the Lord" (Exodus 24:4). But it was God Himself who ended up writing His laws. "And he gave unto Moses, when he had made an end of communing with him upon mount Sinai, two tables of testimony, tables of stone, written with the finger of God" (Exodus 31:18). The biblical text makes explicit that "these tables were the work of God, and the writing was the writing of God, graven upon the tables" (Exodus 32:16).[3]

These stories conceal a precise concept of language and writing. *La langue* seems to represent to Judaic thinking a sur-real, extrasubjective, powerful, and active essence, whose status equals that of God. An agency of authority and inhibition for the speaking subject (Moses), this *langue* renders the practice of *speech* difficult for the subject. Speech unfolds on the inaccessible ground of the divine essence of language. There are two ways to break through this barrier and to accede to a knowledge of *la langue,* to a mastery of its practice, and by that means to *real* (earthly, social) power. The first is by triggering a symbolic chain, that is, a juxtaposition of verbal elements (words) that designate, by a kind of taboo, a single referent whose reality is thus censored and unnamed, and consequently takes on, finally, the name of God. Such is perhaps the meaning of the "miracle" of the *rod* that "is transformed" into a *serpent* which, in its turn, when taken by its *tail,* again becomes a *rod.* (Let us insist upon the sexual, phallic implication of this linking of symbols.) The second means, which displaces the subject from speech and makes him glimpse the operation of [His] internal ["divine"] laws, is the change of speech into writing. This writing is only a transcription of the divine word, or even writing from the finger of God, but in any case it is a copy, a double of a spoken word that already exists without the writing, itself doubled on the two tables and their two faces as if to indicate its character as carbon copy, as repetition. Its function is to make God's word stable, durable, and obligatory, to be His law.

Appropriating writing is the equivalent of *incarnating* language, in the strict sense of the word, that is, it is the equivalent of giving a body to divine language by having the human body absorb it, by introjecting it into the flesh. Writing in the Bible is swallowed and eaten; in order to become *law,* it has to be inscribed in the flesh, and assimilated by the human [social] body:

> But thou, son of man, hear what I say unto thee; Be not thou rebellious like that rebellious house: open thy mouth, and eat that I give thee. And when I looked, behold, an hand *was* sent unto me; and, lo, a roll of a book *was* therein; And he spread it before me; and it *was* written within and without: and *there was* written therein lamentations, and mourning and woe. Moreover he said unto me, Son of man, eat that thou findest; eat this roll, and go speak unto the house of Israel. So I opened my mouth, and he caused me to eat that roll. And he said unto me, Son of man, cause thy belly to eat, and fill thy bowels with this roll that I give thee. Then did I eat *it;* and it was in my mouth as honey for sweetness. [Ezekiel 2:8–3:1]

Writing's relation to the real, as well as to the phonic and morphological reality of language, is not considered. It seems to be cut off, and is reintroduced a posteriori as a relationship of domination of the real by writing. For writing is above all the exercise of a law-giving, paternal, authoritarian essence, conceived of as a *model* to which the real must conform [God's *orders*], and by which it is formed. It is under the influence of this law-model of God's language, and in place of the missing real, that it becomes possible to unfurl the phantasmatical[4] series of signifying (nonreal) links, such as the "miracle" of the rod; the same is true for setting writing up as a law, rule, or copy of God and His absence; writing thus becomes the explanation for the divine absence and compensation for it. Here we are face to face with a monotheistic, theological concept of language.

Several centuries later, a current of Jewish mysticism was able to more profoundly link its experience with language and its inscription: the Cabala. It was widespread, principally in the south of France and in Spain between 1200 and the beginning of the fourteenth century, and was more amply expressed in the *Zohar* as well in the book *Bahir,* which consists of a series of pronouncements on the verses of the Bible. At the crossroads of Christian thinking and the Arab and Indian religions, the Cabala made of the *letters* of the Hebrew alphabet a privileged object of meditation and concentration that opened toward ecstasy, freeing the subject and allowing him to communicate with God. The letters in themselves had no precise signification. Noncorporal, abstract, caught in a formal logic and play, linked to one another like the notes of some kind of music, the letters possessed *numerical* value. The science of this value is called *gematria* in French. Each letter could be linked to a limb of the body, so that an attack on the letter could result in a deformation of the limb in question. The prophetic Cabalist comes close to the practices of Indian yogis, to their breath techniques, to their mastery of the body, all of which were linked to a sacred pronunciation of various phonemes. One can read in the book of the Cabalist Abulafia, *The Doors of Justice,* that "it is the letters that have penetrated his thinking and his imagination, that influence him by their movement, and that concentrate his thinking on different themes, even though he isn't aware of it."

In the European linguistic theories of the sixteenth and eighteenth centuries, which were strongly influenced by theology and its derivatives, Hebrew was the fascinating language, the common origin, and the universal number. One finds in Fabre d'Olivet the apotheosis of this defense of the Hebrew language, of which a true reading would allow, according to the author, an authentic comprehension of the Bible, which he translates by the title *Sepher ou la cosmogonie de Moïse* (see *La Langue hébraïque restituée et le véritable sens des mots hébreux,* 1815). He believed that, if Hebrew was not the mother tongue of humanity, as many of his predecessors, inspired by the biblical story, had believed, then at least its grammatical principles could "lead most surely to the origin [of speech] and uncover its mysteries." In opposition to the thesis of William Jones, who distinguished three fundamental types of languages—Tatar, Indian, and Arabic—Fabre d'Olivet proposed the trichotomy Chinese-Indian-Hebrew. And, in the comparativist spirit of his century, here is how he described the merits of Hebrew:

> I have said that Chinese, isolated from its birth and starting out from the most simple sense-perceptions, had arrived, going from development to development, at the highest conceptions of intelligence; this is exactly the opposite of Hebrew. This

idiom, formed of a language that had already achieved its highest perfection, composed entirely of abstract, intelligible, universal expressions, and delivered in this condition to a robust but ignorant people, fell in these hands from degeneracy to degeneracy, and from restriction to restriction, up to and including its most material elements; all that was spirit became substance; all that was intelligible became perceptible; all that was universal became particular.

These reflections, in which the scientific pretense covers up an ideological speculation that has often been grafted onto the study of language, are quite typical, especially as far as the languages of the great religions are concerned.

11

LOGICAL GREECE

By positing the bases of modern reasoning, Greek philosophy also provided the fundamental principles that have enabled language to be thought about up to our day. In fact, while the linguistics of the last few years, and the theory of signification in general, are growing further and further away from the traditional notions that have dominated classical thinking on language, this is only a very recent, uncertain phenomenon. For centuries, the principles perfected by the Greeks have guided theories and linguistic systematizations in Europe. And even if each period and tendency has deciphered in its own way the models bequeathed to it by the Greeks, the fundamental conceptualizations of language, as well as the basic classifications of it, have remained constant.

The Greeks were the first—after the Phoenicians, whom they considered their masters in this matter—to have used *alphabetical* writing. By borrowing from the Phoenicians their consonantal alphabet and accommodating it to the characteristics of the Greek language (whose radicals are not consonantal like those of the Semitic languages), they were forced to introduce marks for vowels. Each letter received a name (alpha, beta, gamma), and the letter marked the initial phoneme of its name: $\beta = \beta\epsilon\tau\alpha$.

This analysis of the signifier into its minimal components is not an isolated phenomenon in the course of Greek knowledge.

In their theories of the physical world, the pre-Socratic materialist philosophers infinitely divided the "infinite and primordial substance" in order to isolate the *elements* that were the correlates of the *letters* of language, when they were not explicitly confused with them. Empedocles (fifth century B.C.) called them *elements,* Anaxagoras (500–428 B.C.) *homeomers,* Leucippus and Democritus (fifth century B.C.) *atoms;* they were later called στοιχείόν; they are—in one and the same procedure of knowledge—the material correspondents of the *letters* of the signifying act. Among the pre-Socratics, the infinite division of things led, therefore, to a mass of particles, a *seed* that contained them all in embryo: Anaxogoras spoke about σπέρματα, and Democritus saw the great masses of the universe as a πανσπερμία. These physical theories penetrated the *practice* of language among certain pre-Socratics (only Parmenides and Empedocles among the Greek philosophers were poets; Lucretius' name was later added to this list); the same is true for the *theory* of language, which was still being formulated by the pre-Socratics: Aristotle considered Empedocles the inventor of rhetoric. These Greeks materialists, whose theories were later discussed by Lucretius, clearly regarded letters as phonic atoms, as material elements of the same order as material substances. Democritus was the first to use the letters of the alphabet as examples to illustrate his atomistic demonstrations. In the same way Epicurus (341–270 B.C.) held that things could be broken down into miniscule, invisible elements that were the conditions for birth and death, and were assimilable to the letters of the alphabet. The proof that the idea of the correspondence if not the equivalence of corporal elements (the atoms) and the elements of the spoken chain (letters) was widespread in Greece is given by a remark of Posidonius, claiming that the first atomists were the Phoenicians, the inventors of the alphabet.

However, despite the materialists—the last defenders of the solidarity of language and the real (Heraclitus, 576–480 B.C., held that the qualities of objects were reflected in their phoneticism, while Democritus thought that this correspondence was due to social convention)—the very type of phonetic writing, as well as, no doubt, the economic and ideological needs of Greek society, kept suggesting and finally did impose a conception of language as an ideality that reflected an outside, one whose only link with that outside was conceptual.

Indeed, phonetic writing testifies to an analytical conception of the phonic substance of language. Not only was what was later called the "signifier" distinguished from the referent and the signified; it was also divided into constituent elements (phonemes) that were themselves further subdivided into two categories—vowels and consonants. Greek thinking was therefore very attentive to language as a formal system, distinct from the outside it signified (the real); language constituted its own realm, and, without being confused with its material outside, was a specific object of study. We can see here the completion of the process of the separation of language from the real that we made note of in our review of the linguistic theories of preceding civilizations.

Language was no longer a cosmic force that writing organized by organizing the cosmos *at the same time.* The Greeks refined it from the unified and organized ore within which others had mixed the real, language, and those whose handled it. They conceived of language as autonomous, and, by the same token, of themselves as autonomous subjects. Language was first of all a *sonority.* As has been noted, starting with the Homeric tradition, *to think* was described as *to speak,* and was localized in the heart, and especially in the lungs, φήν, φενός, which were thought of as a diaphragm. Starting with this conception of thinking as a *vocal speech,* the end result was the notion of λόγος as the equivalent of *ratio* (reason) and of *oratio* (oration). While it was a vocalism, language at the same time belonged to a subject: it was a subjective vocal faculty authenticated by the proper name of the individual who was speaking. *The Iliad* (1:250) sings, "Nestor rose: a famous orator he was, gracious in speech, whose voice ran off his tongue sweeter than honey. . . ."[1] A *phonic* system controlled by the *subject,* language was, so to speak, a secondary system that, while not without some influence on the real, was far from being the equal of material force. Greeks thought of themselves as subjects existing outside this language, as adults in possession of a real distinct from that of words, in whose reality only children believed. Take, for example, this sentence spoken by Aeneas to Peleides: "Don't think you will scare me with words, Peleides, as if I were a little child. . . . One of those two houses [their families] will mourn a son this day; for I tell you, childish words will not be enough to part us" (*The Iliad,* 20) [pp. 239–40].

The principal manifestations of the completion of the separation of the real and language are the following: alphabetic writing and Platonic and post-Platonic phonetic theory; the constitution of grammar as "the art of writing well" or the science of language as a formal system; and the discussion and propositions about the relation between language and reality (already known in India, these propositions acquired their most completed form in Greece).

The famous dialogue of Plato (429–327 B.C.), the *Cratylus,*[2] testified to these philosophical discussions, which, taking for granted the real/language separation, attempted to establish the modalities of the relation between these two terms. This dialogue is very different from other things Plato has written, and presents two often-contradictory sides to the Socratic concept of language (one defended before Cratylus, the other maintained before Hermogenes, obviously a disciple of Heraclitus). The *Cratylus* gives us an oscillating conception of language that questions itself and seems incapable of uttering anything at all scientific about *la langue:* as soon as *la langue* was touched upon, one was prey to an irrational "inspiration." Plato seems to be responding to the conceptions of the Sophists, for whom language could not express anything fixed or stable, since it was in full motion itself. Parmenides (sixth century B.C.), for example, maintained that language—an elusive fluidity—appeared at the moment when immutable reality was dissolved, and consequently could not express the real. Plato answered these conceptions with ease in the first part of *Cratylus,* although he admitted that it was hard for him to explain the language of poets such as Homer (392–93) [p. 298]. He had even more trouble when Heraclitus' disciple proposed a theory claiming that the world itself was in full motion and contradiction, and that consequently the motion of *la langue* was only corresponding to real mobility (440a–d) [pp. 392–94].

If the *central problems* in this scarcely lawgiving dialogue form can be isolated, then we shall emphasize two of them. The first is the Platonic position in the polemic on the Θέσει (conventional) or φύσει (natural) character of language: are names given to things by social contract, or, on the contrary, are they a result of the nature of things? The second problem, consequently, is the Platonic systematization of the parts and elements of language.

Plato opted for the φύσει character of language, but gave it a more precise signification than it had had in preceding discussions, where there were four interpretations of it. He reconciled the two theses by postulating that language was indeed a human *creation* (and, in this sense, conventional), which resulted, nevertheless, from the essence of the things it represented (and in this sense this creation was natural); because of this, language became an obligation, a law for society. The *name, νόμος,* signified for Plato *law, custom,* and *common practice.*

To speak was to carefully differentiate things by *expressing* them, by giving them names. *Naming* became the differential *act* that *elicited* speech, because it located this speech (along with its subject) in front of things: "Is it not then a part of speaking to name a thing? For they who name a thing, speak the discourses. . . . Is it not then an action to name a thing? since to speak about things was a certain action?" [p. 290].

The distinct *name* of the thing "is an *instrument* used to instruct and to distinguish reality like a shuttle does to cloth." "He who weaves then will employ a shuttle well; and by well is meant in a weaver-like manner; and he who teaches (will employ) a name well and by well (is meant) in a teacher-like manner" [p. 292].

Language had therefore a *didactic* function, it was an instrument of *knowledge.* The name itself was already knowledge of the thing: "He who knows the names, also knows the things," Cratylus said (435d) [p. 385], and "It is impossible to speak a falsehood" (429d) [p. 374]. But Socrates distinguished this "ready-made knowledge" (μαθεῖν) of things by means of their names from the personal, philosophical search for truth.

The name nonetheless revealed the essence of things, for it resembled them. The name/thing relation is one of *semblance,* even of imitation: "A name then is, as it seems, an imitation by the voice of that, which he who imitates, imitates and nominates by the voice what he imitates" [p. 363]. By means of the *voice,* the name was a simulacrum, but it differed from a simulacrum in sound and color: "in their letters and syllables, a person lays hold of entity, so as to *imitate existence* [the essence]" (424a) [p. 365; italics added]. The name therefore "possesses some *natural propriety,* and it is not for every man to know how to give a name to any thing whatever correctly" (391a) [pp. 296–97; italics added]. In order to demonstrate the natural precision of words, Plato proceeded to study several types of words "etymologically": proper names, words that could be composed or decomposed by Plato, and "primitive" words, which for Plato could not be decomposed. Often doubtful, this etymology demonstrates the Platonic postulate: the word is the expression of the *meaning* that the named object bears.

One realizes that in the Platonic conception, not only was language removed from the real that it named and that it considered to be a separate object *to be created,* but the signified itself was isolated from the signifier, and, what's more, its existence was put *before* that of the signifier. The signified preceded the signifier. It was distinct from the referent, and seemingly forgetting the referent, it spread out over a dominating and privileged realm, that of the *idea.* The creation of words consisted in finding a phonic exterior for an idea that was "already there." *Language was above all a signified that had to be organized logically or grammatically.*

It has been observed that certain modern theories, such as the positions of Cassirer (*Philosphie des symbolischen Formen, vol. 1, Die Sprache,* Berlin, 1923), have followed these Platonic postulates and have continued to privilege *meaning* while omitting the *signifier* in the organization of language. The word, in such theories, is a conceptual symbol. In this context, one can appreciate even more the role of Saussure, who emphasized the *form* of the sign, thus clearing the way for a study of the signifier as well as for a truly syntactic (formal relations) analysis of language.

For Plato, therefore, it was the *legislator* who established the name by knowing the form or the ideal matrix of the thing. "It is not then the province of every man, Hermogenes, to establish a name, but of a certain artificer of names; and this, as it seems, is the custom-introducer [legislator], who is the most rare of artificers among men" (389a) [p. 293]. The name imposed by the legislator was applied not directly to the object but only through an intermediary: its *form* or its *idea.* "It is necessary then, O best (of men) for the custom-introducer to know how to form a name of sounds and syllables; and looking to what is really a name, to frame and establish all names, if he is about to be the master-founder of names" (389b) [p. 294]. And again: "So as long as the founder of names, both here and among the Barbarians, assigns the form of a name accommodated to each thing, in any kind of syllable whatsoever, the founder of names here is not worse than the founder in any other place whatsoever" (390a) [p. 295]. Two restrictions, however, checked the law of the legislator. On the one hand, it was up to the dialectician, that is, the one who knew the art of interrogating and responding, to judge the work of the legislator. On the other hand, however *natural* a word might be, "it is surely necessary that compact [agreement] and custom should contribute to the indication of what we have in mind when pronouncing" (435a) [p. 384].

How did Plato systematize language created in this way?

In the linguistic whole, he distinguished a sonic layer that he divided into elements—στοιχεῖα. Aristotle (384–322 B.C.) later defined the στοιχεῖον in this way: " 'Element' means the primary immanent thing, formally indivisible into another form, of which something is composed. *E.g.,* the elements of a sound are the parts of which that sound is composed and into which it is ultimately divisible, and which are not further divisible into other sounds formally different from themselves. If an element is divided, the parts are formally the same as the whole: *e.g.,* a part of water is water; but it is not so with the syllable" (*Metaphysics* 5:3:1014a 26).[3] ". . . The element of each thing is that which is primarily inherent in each thing" (*Metaphysics* 5:3:1014b 15). The term στοιχεῖον also designated Empedocles' four elements, as well as the terms, axioms, postulates, and hypotheses of geometry, and any mathematical proposition.

Reading the Platonic exposition on the phonic elements makes the modern reader realize that, far from being purely formal, Plato's phonetic theory was a consequence of his theory of meaning, and that it is first of all semantic: "Is it not, since *the imitation of existence* [essence] happens to be by syllables and letters, the most proper to distribute first the elements (στοιχεῖα)? Just as those who put their hands to rhythms, to distribute first *powers* [values] of the *elements,* and afterwards of the syllables, and thus at length come to consider the rhythms themselves, but previously not?" [p. 365].

While Plato acknowledged the existence of meaning before language (the *essence*), he did not completely clarify whether the signifier played a role in the constitution of this meaning. In some places he admitted that "it matters not whether the signification be the same in syllables different in one way or another; nor if a letter be added or taken away, is even this any thing, so long as the existence of the thing is in force, and shown by the name" (393b; see also 394a,b) [p. 302]. In other places he is mindful that by "adding and taking away letters, persons vary so very much the meaning of names that by turning them aside sometimes only a little they cause words to have the very contrary meaning" (417d) [p. 351].

The term *element,* a synonym for letter, corresponds in the *Cratylus* to the notion of the *phoneme:* it is obviously a question of the minimal element of the voiced chain. Plato distinguished vowels, consonants, and a third category, "such as are not indeed vowels yet are not mutes" (424c) [p. 365]. Elements formed *syllables,* and from these the rhythm of the utterance could be found (424b) [p. 365].

While in Plato the concepts of *letter* and *phoneme* are not distinguished, later scholars spoke of a *figura,* the written form of the letter, and of its *potestas* or phonic value (see Diogenes Laertius 7:56; Priscian 1:2, 3.1, 3, 8).

In Plato syllables formed *nouns* and *verbs,* with which were constituted "something great and beautiful and entire, like the animal there (described) by a painter's art; discourse [is constituted] by the name-giving, or rhetorical, or whatever art it may be" (425a) [p. 367].

We see here being expressed *grammar, γραμματιχή,* the art of writing, doubtless of pedagogic origin, and practiced by Socrates as the *study of letters* as the elements of words, and of their phonetic value, but also already as a study of the *parts of speech.* The first grammatical distinction was obviously that of *nouns* and *verbs, ὄνομα* and *ῥῆμα* (see Laertius 3:25). Plato was the first to definitively establish this distinction. As for adjectives, which were generally [considered to be] similar to nouns, Plato considered them to be *ῥῆματα* when they were used as predicates.

In this way the *Platonic theory of discourse* was constituted. It was a philosophical theory that mixed linguistic considerations (about the systematization of linguistic categories) and logical ones (about the laws of meaning and signification), without these distinctions being purely linguistic or purely logical in the clear-cut sense of these terms today (see G. Steinthal, *Geschichte des Sprachwissenschaft bei den Griechen und Römern,* Berlin, 1863).

By separating the real from the symbol, Plato created the area of the Idea, and it is there that his theory moved. Aristotle later defined this theory as being of a *logical nature:* "His distinction of the One and the numbers from ordinary things (in which he differed from the Pythagoreans), and his introduction of the Forms were due to his investigation of logic" (*Metaphysics* 1:6:987b 32). Aristotle was thinking about the definition of the concept that Socrates had been the first to apply: he didn't envisage things from the point of view of facts (ἔργα), but from the point of view of notions and definitions (λόγοι). It was this method of the λόγοι that Plato applied as well to his analysis of language, of discourse, and of λόγος.

The detailed theory of this discourse-logos can be found in another Greek philosopher, Aristotle; it is scattered through the mass of his writing, and concentrated in the *Poetics*. The logos, for Aristotle, was an enunciation, a formula, an explanation, an explicative discourse, or a concept. *Logical* became a synonym for concept, for signification, and for the rules of truth. Any recourse to the substance of language and to the specificities of its formation was omitted: "Language is not envisioned from the point of view of facts," Aristotle said, "but from the point of view of notions and definitions." The logos/thing relation was posited in this way: "Hence essence belongs to all things the account of which is a definition" (*Metaphysics* 7:4:1031a 7). He also stated: "Since a definition is a formula and every formula has parts; and since the formula is related to the thing in the same way as the part of the formula to the part of the thing, the question now arises: Must the formula of the parts be contained in the formula of the whole, or not?" (7:10:1034b 20). Finally: "A false statement (λόγος) is the statement of *what is not,* in so far as the statement is false" (*Metaphysics* 5:29:1024b 26). The logos (here perhaps in the sense of "signifying act") was also the *cause* of things, the motor force, the equivalent of matter: "Now there are four recognized kinds of cause. Of these we hold that one is the essence (οὐσία) or essential nature of the thing (since the 'reason why' of a thing is ultimately reducible to its formula—λόγος—and the ultimate 'reason why' is a cause and principle); another is the matter or substrate; the third is the source of motion; and the fourth is the cause which is opposite to this, namely, the purpose or 'good'; for this is the end of every generative or motive process" (*Metaphysics* 1:3:983 25).

Even if one considers, with Steinthal, that before the Alexandrian period there was in Greek no true grammar, that is, a study of the concrete properties of the specifically linguistic organization, one can note that Aristotle had already formulated several important distinctions of *categories of discourse* and their definition. He separated *nouns* (with three genders) from *verbs*, whose main property was their ability to express *time,* and from the *conjunctions* (σύνδεσμοι). He was the first to establish a difference between the meaning of a word and the meaning of a proposition: the word *replaces* or *designates* something, the proposition *affirms* or *denies* its subject a predicate, or instead says whether the subject exists or not.

Here, as an example, are several Aristotelian reflections on the parts of speech, such as they are presented in *Poetics* [4] (1456b):

> All that concerns Thought may be left to the treatise on Rhetoric, for the subject is more proper to that inquiry. *Under the head of Thought come all the effects to be produced by the language.* Some of these are proof and refutation, the arousing of feelings like pity, fear, anger, and so on, and then again exaggeration and depreciation. . . .
>
> For what would be the use of a speaker, if the required effect were likely to be felt without the aid of the speeches? . . .
>
> *Diction* as a whole is made up of these parts: letter, syllable, conjunction, joint [article], noun, verb, case, phrase (λόγος).
>
> A *letter* is an indivisible sound, not every such sound but one of which an intelligible sound can be formed. Animals utter indivisible sounds but none that I should call a letter (στοιχεῖον). Such sounds may be subdivided into vowel, semivowel, and mute. A vowel is that which without any addition has an audible sound; a semivowel needs the addition of another letter to give it audible sound, for instance Σ and P [these are liquids]; a mute is that which with addition has no sound of its own but becomes audible when combined with some of the letters which have a sound. Examples of mutes are

Γ and Δ. Letters differ according to the shape of the mouth and the place at which they are sounded. . . .

A *syllable* is a sound without meaning, composed of a mute and a letter that has a sound. . . .

A *conjunction* is a sound without meaning, which neither hinders nor causes the formation of a single significant sound or phrase out of several sounds. . . .

A *joint* [article] is a sound without meaning which marks the beginning or end of a phrase or a division in it. . . .

A *noun* is a composite sound with a meaning, not indicative of time, no part of which has a meaning by itself. . . .

A *verb* is a composite sound with a meaning, indicative of time, no part of which has a meaning by itself—just as in nouns. . . .

A *case* (or inflection) of a noun or verb is that which signifies either "of" or "to" a thing and the like; or gives the sense of "one" or "many" *e.g.* men and man; or else it may depend on the delivery, for example question and command. "Walked?" and "Walk!" are verbal "cases" of this kind.

A *phrase* (λόγος) is a composite sound with a meaning, some parts of which mean something by themselves. It is not true to say that every "phrase" is made up of nouns and verbs, *e.g.* the definition of man; but although it is possible to have a "phrase" without verbs, yet some part of it will always have a meaning of its own, for example, Cleon in "Cleon walks." A "phrase" may be a unit in two ways; either it signifies one thing or it is a combination of several "phrases." The unity of the *Iliad,* for instance, is due to such combination, but the definition of man is "one phrase" because it signifies one thing.

Aristotle studied further the types of names, simple or composite, as well as the transfer to one thing of a name that designated another thing: metaphor, metonymy, etc.

It was the Stoics, the disciples of Zeno of Cittium (302–264 B.C.), who elaborated a complete theory of discourse; it was presented as a detailed grammar but was not, for that matter, distinct from philosophy and logic. Reflecting on the symbolic process, the Stoics established the first clear distinction between *signifier* and *signified* (τὸ σῆμαινον /τό σημαινόμενον), signification and form, and interior and exterior. They were especially interested in phonetic problems, and in the relation between phonetics and writing. In analyzing the parts of speech, they named them στοίχεια rather than μέρη (parts), which they found in the physical world as well as in language (see R. H. Robins, *Ancient and Medieval Grammatical Theory in Europe*, 1951). We will not here take on the logic of the Stoics, which occupied an essential place in their theory of language; let us nonetheless indicate several of their purely linguistic systematizations. They distinguished four parts of speech:

1. *Nouns,* which signified qualities (it is known that the Stoics distinguished the following categories: quality, state, relation, substance) and which were divided into *common* names and *proper* names;

2. *Verbs* as predicates (as Plato defined them): the verb was incomplete without a subject; it expressed four tenses: continuous present, completed present, continuous past, completed past;

3. *Conjunctions* (σύνδεσμοι);

4. ἄροpα—which include the personal pronouns as well as the relative ones, and the article.

The Stoics distinguished as well the following modalities (or secondary grammatical categories): *number, gender, voice, mode, tense,* and *case,* of which they were the first to establish the theory (Aristotle, as we have seen, also spoke of *case,* but he understood by this term derivations, verbal inflections, etc.).

It was Alexandria, the center of books and of the deciphering of ancient texts, that witnessed the development of a true *grammar* as a study specialized in and directly oriented toward language as an object with inherent organization; this was done by burning the bridges that attached it to philosophy and logic. Decadent Greece, near its collapse and in the paroxysm of its mentalist refinements, gave birth to the grammarians. They were meticulous scholars even though, according to Wackernagel, they "had no great intellectual stature"; they were conscientious professors who taught the young generations Homer's thereafter difficult idiom; they were assiduous classifiers of *la langue* as an abstract form. Most famous were Philetas of Cos, the teacher of Ptolemy's son; Aristarchus, a Homerian commentator; and Cartes of

Mallos, who, after settling in Rome, taught Romans the science of grammar. The best known of the grammar teachers was Dionysius Thrax (170–90 B.C.). F. Theirot, in his Introduction (1784) to *Hermes or a Philosophical Inquiry Concerning Universal Grammar,* by James Harris (2d edition, 1765), said of Dionysius that he was a "disciple of Aristarchus; having taught grammar at Rhodes, where Theophrastus, nicknamed Tyrannion . . . studied under him, he then went to Rome to give lessons on his art, during the first consulate of Pompey."

For Dionysius Thrax grammar was more an *art:* he defined it as "the empirical knowledge of the language of poets and prose-writers." His phonetics represented a theory of letters and syllables. His *morphology* already distinguished *eight* parts of speech: *nouns, verbs, participles, articles, pronouns, prepositions, adverbs,* and *conjunctions.* His syntax is not extant. It was Apollonius Dsycolus (second century A.D.) who elaborated the first syntax by studying the Greek language: this syntax was presented more like a philosophical than a linguistic study.

Let us summarize. At first indistinct from general atomism and confused in a vast naturalist cosmogony; next isolated—not without ambiguity—as logic, as the theory of notions and definitions, as a systematization of the signified; finally abstracted from philosophy in order to be constituted as grammar, that is, as a normative science of a particular object: by passing through these different stages language was separated from the real, and Greek "linguistics" was constituted. Modern theoreticians have repeated this gesture in order to clarify this thinking even further.

12

ROME: THE TRANSMISSION OF GREEK GRAMMAR

The Alexandrian grammarians, at the time of their sojourn in Rome, transmitted to the Romans the Greek knowledge of *la langue:* theories of a philosophical nature as well as grammar. Thus Suetonius (5:75, 160) can be seen, in his work *De grammaticis et de rhetoribus,* designating the first Latin authors, grammarians, and philosophers as *semigraeci.*

Historians point out above all the contribution of Crates of Mallos (168 B.C.), who, sent to Rome as the ambassador of King Attalos, was a professor of grammar and thus created the school of Roman grammarians among whom the most famous were Varro (first century B.C.), Quintilian (first century B.C.), Donatus (A.D. 350), and Priscian (A.D. 500).

Roman scholars, preoccupied above all with elaborating a rhetoric for the strictly linguistic realm, limited their efforts to transferring Greek theories and classifications in order to meet the needs of the Latin language; they did not try to elaborate original propositions about language. This transfer was at times carried out purely mechanically: since the Greek language was considered the universal model for language in general, it was absolutely essential to discover its categories in the Latin language. It can thus be seen that the predominant idea in the study of language at Rome was that of the universality of logical categories, which had already been established on the basis of the

Greek language and remained unchanged in other languages. A practical result of this was how little interest was shown in foreign languages, which, nevertheless, abounded in the Roman empire. Caesar needed interpreters in Gaul; Ovid wrote a poem in the Gete language; Aelius Stilo undertook a study of the Italic languages; these were, however, only isolated exceptions to Latin custom, which did not cross over the threshold into linguistic doctrine.

Varro was the first of the Latin grammarians to elaborate a complete theory of language; it can be found in his work *De lingua latina,*[1] which was dedicated to Cicero.

As far as the general problems of the relation between language and reality are concerned, Varro took part in the discussion, which had also been transmitted by the Greeks, on the "natural" or "conventional" character of speech. In Rome, this controversy was known as the *Analogists* versus *Anomalists* quarrel. The Analogists felt that the non-linguistic realm was reflected in the grammatical realm, while the Anomalists held the converse theory. For them, there was a clear-cut difference between real categories and grammatical categories. Varro tried to reconcile these two theses. For him, *la langue* expressed the regularity of the world, but it also possessed irregularities of its own. A *normative* theory of language, also inherited from the Greeks, was thus outlined. It was a question of formulating a grammar that would postulate the rules of linguistic use considered *correct* (that is, one that in general conformed to Greek logico-grammatical categories), rather than of making of this grammar a *descriptive* study that would discover the particularities of every new language or style that it came across. Let us recall Caesar's position in this controversy between the Analogists and Anomalists. For the emperor was interested in language, and this fact is without a doubt one of the supplementary proofs of the authority and importance of linguistic studies at Rome. Caesar was the author of an *Analogy* in which he defended the principle of grammatical regularity; he proposed certain modifications of linguistic categories to counter irregular language.

Varro's principal interests were of a *grammatical* nature—he analyzed and systematized first grammar as a study of language, and then linguistic categories themselves. Today we have books 5 to 10 of his work *De lingua latina* (composed 47–45 B.C.) in 25 volumes (according to Saint Jerome), as well as 450 fragments of various treatises. Varro defined grammar in this way: "The alphabet is the source of grammar; the alphabet is represented in the form of letters, and these letters form syllables; when syllables are joined they produce an interpretable voiced group; the interpretable voiced groups are assembled into parts of speech, and by their addition the parts of speech form discourse; it is in discourse that speaking well can flourish; one trains oneself to speak well in order to avoid mistakes."[2] Varro considered grammar to be the basis of every science, and justified this privileged place by an etymology that is completely invented: grammar supposedly comes from *verum boare, to shout out the truth.* By embracing the principles of the Stoics, according to which language is not conventional but natural, and therefore not analogical but anomalic, Varro systematized it by following the acquisitions of the grammarians who preceded him.

The first branch of grammar that Varro distinguished was the one that would search for the connection between *words* and *things.* He called it *etymology* and devoted himself to etymological research, whose scientific value would today seem nonexistent. His aim was to find the "origins of the primitive words" [6:37]; these were the basic, indispensable elements of every language, which corresponded to the four philosophical categories of Pythagoras: the body, place, time, and action. Faithful once again to Greek conceptions of language, the Roman grammarian systematized language according to the coordinates of a system of *ideas* (a philosophical, conceptual system) by subordinating it to this system. In other words, his is a systematization of *signifieds,* according to a certain philosophical doctrine governing linguistic classification; the *signifier* was forgotten. Perhaps it could be said that the Greek and Roman grammarians, having heard/understood the *signifier* (the proof is their phonetic writing), censored it in order to *understand* it as a *signified*—in order to make it the manifestation of an *idea* that transcended it.

Here are two examples of "semantic" analysis in Varro: the first constitutes a "semantic field," and the second is presented as an "etymology":

We shall follow them [the classes of places and things] up wherever the kin of the word under discussion is, even if it has driven its roots beyond its own territory. For often the roots of a tree which is close to the line of the property have gone out under the neighbor's cornfield. Wherefore, when I speak of places, I shall not have gone astray if from *ager* "field" I pass to *agrarius* "agrarian man" and to an *agricola* "farmer". [5:13]

Terra "earth" is—as Aelius writes—named from this fact, that it *teritur* "is trodden"; therefore it is written *tera* in the *Book of Augurs* with one R. From this the place which is left near a town as common property for the farmers, is called the *teritorium* "territory"; it *teritur* "is trodden" most. [5:21]

Sol "sun" is so named either because the Sabines called him thus, or because he *solus* "alone" shines in such a way that from this god *(deus)* there is the daylight *(dies)*. [5:68]

The second part of Varro's grammar dealt with the formation and inflection of words: their *morphology*. He distinguished *fruitful {variable}* words from *barren {invariable}* ones, and classified them into four categories: *nouns, verbs, participles,* and *conjunctions* and *adverbs.* He also studied the inflections of nouns, and posited *secondary categories* in order to examine the other parts of speech. Thus for the *verb,* [he studied] *voice and tense* (past, present, and future). When applying the system of Greek cases to the Latin language, Varro translated the Greek terms that designated those cases. One of them, αιτιατιχή, signified the case for the thing one acts upon, or the object; but Varro believed that the Greek word was αἰτιάομαι, which signified *to accuse,* and translated it by *casus accusativus* [8:16]. Here is how Varro partitioned the parts of speech:

nominatus
1. *vocabula* (common names)
2. *nomina* (proper names)

articuli
3. *provocabula* (interrogative and indefinite pronouns and adjectives)
4. *pronomina* (other pronouns)

5. *dicandi* or *pars quae habet tempora* (verbs)
6. *adminiculandi* or *pars quae habet neutrum* (invariables)
7. *inugendi* or *pars in qua est utrumque* (participles).

Finally, the third part of the study of language was *syntax,* which dealt with the relation of words in the sentence. This part has not come down to us.

Another Latin grammarian, Quintilian, who lived in the first century and was the author of the *Institutio oratoria* (we'll come back to this later), has remained famous for having examined the category of the *case.* In place of the six Greek cases, he proposed seven Latin cases, thus taking into account the difference in meaning between the *ablative* and the *dative* in Latin. It was his estimate that the difference in meaning between the cases could correspond to a difference in "structure" between the languages in question. Quintilian, however, seems to have made an error that was later corrected by Priscian: he reduced the case to only one of these meanings while forgetting that a case can have several of them and that it can thus express variations in modalities without having to introduce a new case.

Along with these strictly linguistic constructions, Rome was familiar with the greatest materialist survey of antiquity, a collection of all the materialist philosophies bequeathed by Greece. This was the *De natura rerum* of Lucretius [3] (91–57 B.C.), which, in the form of a poem in the tradition of Empedocles and Epicurus, revived the thinking of Democritus and Epicurus, with the atomistic and, in general, materialistic theories of Leucippus. In this work, of capital importance for our purposes, the Latin poet explicitly developed an *atomistic conception* of the signifying operation. First of all, language for him was not a convention; for Lucretius, as for Epicurus, the factors in the formation of language were *nature* and *need.* Speech was not a merit of the human subject, it was a law of nature that animals after their own fashion possessed as well:

> But the various sounds of the tongue mother nature drove them [men] to utter, and convenience pressed out of them names for things. . . .
> Therefore to suppose that someone then distributed names

amongst things, and from him that men learnt their first words, is folly. For why should he have been able to mark all things with titles and to utter the various sounds of the tongue, and at the same time others not be thought able to have done it? Besides, if others had not also used these terms in their intercourse, whence was that foreknowledge of usefulness implanted, and whence did he first gain such power, as to know what he wanted to do and to see it in his mind's eye? Compel them again he could not, one against many, nor could he master and conquer them, that they should wish to learn the names of things; nor is it easy to teach in any way or to persuade what is necessary to be done, when men are deaf; for they would not have suffered nor endured in any way that he should go on dinning into their ears sounds of the voice which they had never heard, all to no purpose. Lastly, what is so very wonderful in this business, if the human race, having active voices and tongues, could distinguish things by varying sounds to suit varying feelings? seeing that dumb animals, seeing that even wild beasts of all kinds are wont to utter sounds different and varying when they are in fear or pain, and when now joy begins to glow. Indeed you may learn this from plain facts. (5:1028–58)

If language was not in any way a given or a convention susceptible to superstitious interpretations, which Lucretius fought, but was on the contrary a *natural* property that obeyed the *needs* of a human community, then its composition reflected the atomistic composition of matter. The only difference was that the atoms that made up things were much more numerous, and that for the formation of words *order* was of capital importance.

> . . . For the same beginnings constitute sky, sea, earth, rivers, sun, the same make crops, trees, animals, but they move differently mixed with different elements and in different ways. Moreover, all through these very lines of mine you see many elements [letters of the alphabet] common to many words, although you must confess that lines and words differ one from another both in meaning and in the sound of their sound-

ings. So much can elements do, when nothing is changed but order; but the elements that are the beginnings of things can bring with them more kinds of variety, from which all the various things can be produced. [1:823–29]

It can be seen that thinking about linguistic construction was part of a theory of materialist knowledge according to which language reflected reality, and necessarily had to be composed of elements equivalent to those isolated by the science of nature as the minimal elements of the natural order—atoms. Lucretius explained thought by means of *simulacra* composed of atoms: thought therefore reflected the outside by means of simulacra that were composed of atoms in the same way as this outside itself was. Language was conceived of as voiced materiality. Thus Lucretius envisioned words as an assemblage of real *sound*-atoms about which the materialist need only describe the fashioning by the mouth, the tongue, and the lips, as well as the physical propensity in the space of the community. No analysis of meaning, through the *idea* and the ideal categories that Greece had elaborated with and after Plato, was presented. Lucretius returned to pre-Platonic materialism.

Let us insist above all upon the fact that the adoption of *poetic language* for his theoretical exposition *reveals* Lucretius' conception of language. Detailed studies have been able to demonstrate how the *signifying* organization of the poem became the proof of Lucretius' linguistic theory. We have seen how for him letters were material atoms, and atoms were letters. The poetic function made possible a clear manifestation of the correspondence between the material thing and the phonic substance of language. Thus Lucretius wrote, ". . . The same elements a little changed in their relations create fires and firs {*ignes* and *lignum*}. Even as those same words themselves {*ligna* and *ignis*} consist of elements a little changed, although we mark fires and firs with a distinct name" (1:907–14). Following this principle, Lucretius implicitly demonstrated in his verses the "etymology" of words. For example, *materuum nomen* was composed of the signifying atoms of *mater* and *terra:*

Linguitur ut merito *mater*uum nomen adepta
terra sit, e *terra* quoniam sunt cuncta creata. (5:795)

Quare etiam atque etiam: *materuum* nomen adepta
terra tenet marito, quoniam genus ipsa creavit. (5:821)[4]

There is, therefore, a theory of language *implicit* in the practice of *la langue* in Lucretius, and probably in all of what is called "poetry." He constructed words as if the letters (sounds) were at the same time the atoms of a substance that one only needed to take from a material object in order to create a new assemblage that was at the same time object and name. Words were not entities that could not be broken down (modern science has demonstrated this in its turn; see part 1 of this book) and that were held together by their meaning; they were instead assemblages of signifying, phonic, and scriptural atoms, flying from word to word, creating in this way unsuspected and unconscious connections among the elements of discourse. This establishment of relationships among signifying elements constituted a signifying infrastructure of *la langue* that fused with the elements of the material world in an ordered connection. Grammont has written about such phenomena in poetic language: "It is acknowledged that poets worthy of the name possess a delicate and penetrating feeling for the impressive value of words and of the sounds that compose them. In order to communicate this value to those who read, poets often represent around the principle word the phonemes which characterize it, so that the word becomes in sum the generator of absolutely the entire verse in which it figures ..." (*Traité de phonétique,* 1933; see on this topic Saussure, *Les Anagrammes*).

After this materialist jump in the conception of language, which tried to bring it back to a global materialist cosmogony, the decline of Rome, like the decline of Greece, led to abundant formal speculation on language, which was studied as an object in itself for the purposes of teaching. Several centuries after Lucretius, the study of language basked in a new glory. One of the late Roman grammarians, Donatus (fourth century A.D.), wrote a work that became famous during the Middle Ages, *De partibus orationis Ars Minor.* At that time, Rome, like Alexandria, was decadent and was being shaken up by Christianity. Its citizens began to conduct scholarly studies of Rome's Golden Age authors, such as Cicero and Virgil, favoring in this way grammatical studies whose aims were didactic and pedagogical. Donatus executed a minute description of letters, and this description became a veritable phonetic treatise. He also furnished an enumeration of the common mistakes made by his students, as well as a list of the stylistic turns of the classical authors.

The study of the Latin language was already sufficiently advanced to enable scholars to distinguish it from Greek, after having first assimilated it to Greek. Macrobius (fourth century A.D.) undertook the first comparative study of Greek and Latin.

It was with Priscian *(Institutiones grammaticae)*[5] that Latin grammar reached its apogee. A Latin grammarian from Constantinople, he undertook, at the command of the consul Julian, the adaptation into Latin of the teachings of the Greek grammarians. His goal was only to put into Latin the precepts of Apollonius and Herodian, while benefiting from the experiences of the first Latin grammarians. The result of his work, however, was much more considerable.

The historical importance of Priscian consists in the fact that he was the first in Europe to elaborate a *syntax*. This conception of syntax, presented in books 17 and 18 of his *Institutiones,* was inspired by the logical theories of the Greeks and elaborated from a logical perspective. For Priscian, syntax studied "the arrangement whose aim is to obtain a perfect oration." As J. -Cl. Chevalier (*La Notion de complément chez les grammariens,* 1968) has remarked, his work is a "study of forms and their order from a logical perspective, since the notion of *oratio perfecta* is a logical notion."

In addition to his two books on syntax, Priscian wrote sixteen on morphology. This fact alone proves that Priscian acknowledged a *morphology* that was distinct and independent from syntax: words could therefore have a particular form that sufficed to give them meaning, independent of the relations in which they were found inside the sentence.

Even though he considered the word to be an indivisible unity, Priscian outlined a "syntax" of the word by breaking it down into signifying parts, with the whole being the result of these parts: *vires* = *vir* (see R. H. Robins, *Ancient and Mediaeval Grammatical Theory in Europe*). Robins has pointed out that what Priscian was discussing was in fact a veritable theory of *morphemes.*[6] Following Dionysius Thrax, Priscian distinguished eight parts of speech that were differentiated by their meaning.

In order for the meaning of the whole utterance to be clear, each form had to have a precise (syntactic) function in the context, especially when it was a question of forms (gender, number, case, and tense), which did not acquire their full meaning except in the context (for instance, the personal [pronouns] whose gender was not marked: *me ipsum* and *me ipsam*). In such cases of "different signification, the construction is absolutely necessary to make them clear." For example, *amet* used alone is imperative; accompanied by an adverb *(utinam),* the word is optative; with a conjunction, it is subjunctive. Finally, and, after recognizing its syntactic function, the term had to be related to the study of forms: "Every construction, in fact, that the Greeks call syntax must be brought back to the intellection of the form."

Priscian's idea was thus to use grammatical study to equilibrate the contributions of morphology and syntax, for the true comprehension of the utterance depended as much upon the morphological categories of its parts as on their syntactic function. "Forms have no more importance than words in the distribution of these words, or than their signification [signification here means *role in the sentence*]." Thus, even if the two syntactic books followed the order of the morphological chapters (article, pronoun, noun, verb), the author indicated numerous cases of passage—*substitution*—from one morphological category to another, based on the syntactic function that a supplementary morpheme implicitly attributed to it: "One must know that, in certain parts of speech one can hear/understand other ones: for instance, if I say *Ajax,* I hear 'one' implied from the same leader, thanks to the singular number; if I say *Anchisiades,* I hear the genitive singular of the primitive, and the nominative singular of *filius;* if I say *divinitus,* I hear a noun with the preposition *ex (ex diis);* if I say *fortior,* I hear *magis* and the primitive in the positive. There are innumerable examples, and it would be false to suppose an ellipse as from *filius* to *Anchisiades.*" It will be noted that this analysis by *substitution* is close to the distributional theories of modern American grammarians (see chapter 19).

If morphology is completed by syntax and syntax is only added to morphology, this totality does not hold except to the extent that it is submitted to *logic*. Logic, therefore, welds and determines grammar, and thus obeys the Greek tradition that placed language (and its categories) in the position of expressing transcendent thought (and its categories). Two logical concepts, which remain vague, are necessary to Priscian's linguistic reflection: that of the *perfect oration* (a discourse with full meaning that is self-sufficient) and *imperfect oration* (a collection of words that needs to be completed in order to have a full meaning: "If I say: *accusat, videt, insimulat,* these verbs are imperfect and need to have added to them the oblique cases for the perfection of meaning"); and that of *transitivity* (a construction is *intransitive* when the meaning concerns the person who is speaking, *transitive* when the action occurs to another person, and *absolute* when the verb does not need an oblique case.)

Let us make one final remark about Priscian's theories. As Chevalier has written, Priscian "seems at first to distinguish between the constructions inherent in the category of the governor *{recteur}* word, and the categories inherent in the meaning of the word. He defines in this way two types of relations." Such conceptions of Priscian enable him to be seen as the precursor to certain modern theories of language, such as the distributional and generative proposals. We will give here the "generative" example cited by Chevalier: "The nominative is joined to the genitive when it expresses something that is possessed, and a possessor: we would put the thing that is possessed in the nominative, and the possessor in the genitive, as in *Hector filius Priami. . . .* One can 'interpret' this turn by adding a verb that signifies possession; the thing that is possessed then trades its nominative for an accusative, and the possessor its genitive for a nominative, under the pressure of the nature of the verb, since intransitively it requires the nominative and transitively the accusative: 'Quid est enim filius Priami?'; using the method of 'interpretation,' we would say: 'Hoc est Hectorem filium priamus possidet.' "

On the one hand, this "interpretation" makes us think that Priscian —all the while accepting as incontestable the thesis of *la langue* as a *logical* system—had to have noticed the difference and the unequal status that subsists between logical categories (which always remain the same) and the linguistic construction (which varies). It is exactly in this gap between logical categories and the linguistic construction that

Priscian's interpretation can take place; this "interpretation" is nothing other than a description of the various signifying constituents that correspond to the same signified. But this unequal status does not seem to question the validity of a logical schema for analyzing *la langue,* and it doesn't lead the author to a theory stating that the signifier would in its turn modify the logical signified. On the other hand, it is striking to note to what extent Priscian's principle of interpretation, with its clarity and its limits, evokes modern transformational grammar: indeed, Priscian's models, like those of Chomsky, rest upon the principle of cutting thinking up into stable categories that are likely to take on different linguistic expressions but that can still be used to interpret one another, or can be transformed into one another. The grammar of Port-Royal was the first after Priscian and Sanctius to clearly define the postulates of these logical, relational categories underlying linguistic categories.

The grammar of Priscian became the model for all the grammarians of the Middle Ages. French scholars strove to obey his postulates and to think about the French language according to Priscian's models, which were considered omnivalent, even if time revealed them to be incapable of grasping new languages.

13

ARAB GRAMMAR

Among the great acquisitions of thought on language in the Middle Ages, an important place belongs to Arab grammar. By Arab grammar should be understood the linguistic reflections of the peoples who, during the Middle Ages, remained under the domination of the caliphate.

All specialists of Arab culture agree on acknowledging the importance attributed to *la langue* in the Arab civilization. "The wisdom of the Romans lies in their brain, the wisdom of the Indians in their fantasy, that of the Greeks in their soul, and that of the Arabs in their language," an Arab proverb says. Various Arab thinkers, in every age, have exalted the value of *la langue,* and it truly seems that this exaltation has been conceived of as both a *national* duty and a *religious* requirement. The sacred book of Islam, the Koran, is a written monument of *la langue,* which one must know how to decipher and pronounce correctly in order to gain access to its teachings.

There has often been a desire to interpret Arab linguistic theories as having been borrowed from the Greeks and the Indians, and indeed numerous examples testify to this. We find in the Arabs the same disputes between the partisans of the *natural* and the *conventional* character of language, and the same logical, Aristotelian categories as those we found in the Greeks. Moreover, the division of sounds into

eight groups according to the process of physiological articulation—
the *mahariq*—corresponds to the eight *stana* of Panini. All the same,
it has since been acknowledged that while Arab linguistic theories did
borrow from the Greek or Indian ones, the borrowing in general had
to do with logic; the grammar is totally independent of this practice.

Starting from the second century of Islam, the first Arab linguistic
centers could be found, first at Basra and a little later at Kufa. Abu al-
Aswad al-Du'ali (d. 688 or 718) is considered to be the founder of
Arab grammar.

Arab linguistic theory is distinguished by a subtle reflection on the
phoneticism of *la langue*. Sounds were divided into *sadid* and *rahw* on
the one hand, and *safir, takir,* and *qalquala* on the other. This phonetic
theory was closely linked to a theory of music. The great Halil al-
Farahidi (?718–791) was not only a phonetician and scholarly grammarian, but also an eminent theoretician of music. A term such as
haraka, a movement used in phonetics, comes from music. Moreover
the Arabs, being great anatomists, as was the case with Sibawayhi, were
the first to give precise descriptions of the vocal apparatus, to which
they added physical descriptions of the movement of air. Their analysis
of the linguistic system was so fine that they were already able to
differentiate—and they were no doubt the first to do so—the *signified*
element, the *phonic* element *(hart)* and the *graphic* element *(alama)* of
la langue. By also distinguishing vowels from consonants, they identified the notion of the vowel with that of the *syllable.* Consonants were
considered the *essence* of *la langue,* and vowels were *accidents.* Subtle
subclasses of sounds, placed between the consonants and vowels, completed the phonetic classification of the Arabs, as, for example, in the
huruf-al-qalquala class of light sounds.

This interest in the phonic composition of *la langue* was the corollary, if not the expression, of a marked interest in its scriptural system.
Indeed, a specific trait of Arab civilization was to interrogate religion
in and through written texts. The exegeses of the Koran, the sacred
text of sacred writing, were accompanied by a mystical explanation of
the value of each graphic element—of the letter. The preponderance
accorded to writing in the Arab civilization has been explained by the
fact that the Arab empire found it economically and politically necessary to impose its language, its religion, and its culture on the peoples

it invaded. Without reducing the specificity of a conception of writing to sociological reasons, two interpretations (economic and religious) must no doubt be accepted, and attention must be drawn to the artistic and *ornamental* development of the Arab scriptural system.

Indeed, the first specimens of Arabic writing date from around the fourth century A.D., and are borrowings of graphic signs from neighboring peoples without any ornamental effort. They often noted in a confused way the fundamental sounds of language. The desire to embellish the graphic signs appears to have started with the constitution of the Umayyad state. This writing system, called "Umayyad Kufic," was regular and careful; it had been used to write down the works of sovereigns ever since the caliph Abdal-Malite (see figure 13.1). In societies conquered by the Arab empire, the language began to be learned, and Arabic writing, along with the Koran, came to be regarded as sacred. One no longer wrote only to fix a word. Writing became an exercise linked to the practice of religion, it was an art, and every people put its own ornamental style into the execution of these written forms. Thus, *decorative writings* flourished alongside utilitarian written forms. Alongside calligraphy proper, geometric, floral, zoological, anthropomorphic, etc., additions and continuations have been noted. After a blossoming period, this decorative writing began once again (from the twelfth century on) to become more sober, and disappeared at the end of the Middle Ages with the decline of Islam as a conquering religion. However, the decorative tendencies persist even in modern Arabic writing, and its role remains important in a world where writing materializes the ethnic unity of peoples who speak various dialects.

But let us return to the linguistic theory of the Arabs.

Lexicology was a preponderant branch of it. The studies of Isa as-Saqfi (d. 766) are well known; he was a great reader of the Koran and the author of seventy works in the realm of grammar.

With Halil, phonetic, lexicological, and semantic studies became ordered and thorough in form. He was the inventor of Arabic metrics and its rules. Halil compiled the first Arabic dictionary, the *Ayna Book*, in which words were arranged not in alphabetical order but according to a phonetic-physiological principle that reproduced the order in which Indian grammarians had arranged sounds: guttural, palatal, etc. The classification of the contents followed the Greek principle of the distinction between *theory* and *practice*. The sciences of nature (alchemy, medicine), the mathematical sciences, and the science of God were arranged in the *theory* class. Grammar was placed after Muslim theology and before jurisprudence, poetry, and history.

Halil's student, Sibawayhi, took Arab grammar to its summit. His first work, *Al-Kitab,* was its first great systematization.

The lack of a grammatical theory of the sentence has been noted in the works of these Arab grammarians. While they did distinguish a

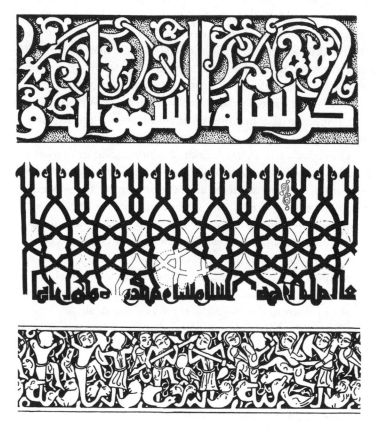

Figure 13.1. The ornamental character of Arabic writing. From top to bottom: Kufic writing being developed on an independent floral decor; Kufic writing with a geometric border; anthropomorphic ornamental writing on a copper object. From Janine Sourdel-Thomine, *L'Ecriture et la psychologie des peuples* (Centre International de Synthèse. Paris: Armand Colin, 1963).

nominal phrase from a verbal one, the concepts of *subject* and *predicate* were missing. In the nominal phrase they indicated what we call a subject by the term *mubtada,* "he with whom one begins," and in the verbal phrase they used the term *fa'il,* "agent." Let us point out that today the term "subject" is still absent from Arabic grammatical terminology. This is one of the numerous symptoms indicating the specificity of Arab grammar. It has held itself apart from Aristotelian logic, has not wanted to subordinate the analysis of *la langue* to its categories, and remains closely linked to Islam's own theories. The concept of *qiyas,* analogy, has enabled Arab grammarians to organize the Arabic language in a harmonious system where everything has motivation. Specialists, nevertheless, cannot but notice that Arab grammar is more empirical than Greek grammar, and more linked to ontological religious considerations. Halil, Sibawayhi, and the entire generation of Arab grammarians that followed, did not work as philosophers, but as readers of the Koran, and as analysts of what, in *la langue,* could correspond to its teaching.

The center of Kufa, after that of Basra, was more clearly devoted to readings of the Koran. The great grammarian of Kufa was al-Farra, the inventor of a new terminology whose original method consisted of organizing grammatical reasoning by citing verses.

The Basra school experienced an illustrious period of development with the generation that succeeded Sibawayhi. The new philologists established themselves in Baghdad.

The Baghdad school, toward the eleventh century, presented a veritable flourishing of theoreticians and grammarians who made considerable progress in the study of language. We can cite only a few names. Al-Mubarrad was able to make Sibawayhi's *Kitab* a fundamental book for any study of *la langue.* The lexicographer Ta'lab was an admirer of great grammatical controversies, etc. An important work on the path to a systematization of the Arabic language was executed by Osman Ibn Qinni (941–1002), the author of the book *Sirr sina at al'i' rab, The Secret of the Art* [of language], in which he defined the essence and function of letters, in themselves and in relation to other letters of a word. He also wrote *Hasa'is (Particularities)* in which he revealed the principles of grammar. The work of Ibn Malik (born in Spain in 1206, died at Damas in 1274) dates from the end of this period. He was the author of *Alfiyya* (published in French by Sylvestre de Sacy as *Alfiyya ou la Quintessence de la grammaire arabe,* 1833); it was a didactic poem composed of 100 verses on grammar. In it Malik revealed a morphological theory that distinguished three parts of speech: the noun, the verb, and the particle. However, his attention was principally directed toward the study of inflections, *israb,* which already constituted an introduction to syntax.

During this time, and with these various grammarians, Spain was becoming one of the important scenes for the elaboration of Arab grammar. After Ibn Qinni, however, the research lacked originality and was satisfied with repeating and orchestrating sources. Let us note that the only object of this research had always been the so-called *authentic* or *desert* Arabic language, such as is recorded in Bedouin poetry and in the Koran, but never in subsequent poetry and prose.

European grammarians, with Raymond Lulle (1235–1309) and also J. C. Scaliger, became interested in the acquisitions of the Arab grammarians. Today it is believed that the notions of *root* and *inflection* were borrowed from the Arab grammarians.

14

MEDIEVAL SPECULATIONS

Two phenomena seem to us to indicate the medieval conception of language.

The first is the awakening of interest in "Barbarian" languages. This interest was manifested by the elaboration of *alphabets* for these languages, as well as of *treatises* pleading for their right to exist, of translations of the scriptures, and even of *grammars* proposing the first laws of their construction.

The second is the development, in the context of Christianity, of the Greco-Latin tradition (Platonic and Neoplatonic) in grammatical theory. The result was a conception of language as a *system of signification*. The modes of signifying became the object of medieval speculation, and thus prepared the way for the logic of Port-Royal and heralded the modern debates on the sign. *La langue* signified the world by using meaning to reflect it (like a mirror; *speculum*). What were the modalities of this "speculation"? that was the theoretical problem of the grammar of the Middle Ages.

Between the second and fourth centuries, the Barbaric peoples began to invent their writings. These were autonomous creations, mixed with borrowings from Latin (or Greek) writing. These graphic systems were *alphabetical;* examples are the oghamic alphabet of the Celts, and the runic of the Germanic peoples.

Runes were characters carved in wood; each one had a vertical notch to which were added horizontal ones. They were divided into three groups of eight letters each in the old Germanic alphabet; the Scandinavian alphabet is a recent variation of this. Runes were closely linked to divinatory practices and religious rites.

In the sixth century the Gothic alphabet appeared, based on Greek and runic writing. Bishop Wulfila (311–384), the translator of the scriptures into the Gothic language, was its creator.

Oghamic writing, widespread in southern Ireland and in the country of the Welsh, probably dates from the fourth century. It consisted of a series of notches of which each group, which was a letter, was differentiated from the others by the number of strokes and their direction.

The Slavs produced their alphabet in the tenth century. It was due to two brothers, Cyrillic (827–869) and Method (d. 885), both Byzantine monks who were given an evangelical mission to Moravia in 864. In order to escape from German and Catholic domination, the Slavs of Moravia had addressed the Byzantine emperor and asked him for an orthodox evangelization in the *Slavic* language. In order to preach in the Slavic language, the two brothers had to translate the scriptures. They used an ancient writing found among the Khazars, as well as the Greek language, to create the Slavic or *Glagolitic* alphabet. *Cyrillic* writing is a later simplification of Glagolitic.

This period of scriptural invention, which spread to all the peoples of Europe, testifies to two important facts that characterize the relation of these peoples to language. First, they began to develop a consciousness of a language as a national attribute, as an expression of an ethnic group, and as the guarantee of its political independence. In this perspective, certain theoreticians of the time even had the audacity to oppose the postulate of the saintliness of the three languages—Hebrew, Greek, and Latin—and to demand the rightful recognition of their own languages. For instance, Khrabe, a Bulgarian writer of the ninth century, wrote in his discourse "On Letters,"

> The Hellenists have no letters for their language, but write their discourse with Phoenician letters. . . . Now Slavic books were created by Saint Constantine, known as Cyrillic, on his own in a few years' time. They [the inventors of the Greek

alphabet] were numerous—seven people took a long time to create their letters, and seventy to translate [the Holy Scriptures from Hebrew into Greek]. Slavic letters are more saintly and honorable, because a saintly man created them, while it was pagan Hellenists who created Greek letters.

If one asks well-read Greeks, "Who created your letters or translated your books, and when did they do it?" it's a rare person who knows. However, if one asks students who are learning the Slavic alphabet, "Who created your alphabet and translated your books?" all of them know and answer, "Saint Constantine the philosopher, known as Cyrillic, created the alphabet and translated the books, along with his brother Method. . . ."

Moreover, and on a purely linguistic level, these alphabets are the proof of a meticulous analysis of the voiced chain into minimal elements. This analysis was sometimes accompanied by an explicit phonetic theory, a forerunner of modern phonology. Snorri Sturluson's (1179–1241) work on Icelandic phoneticism, based on the *Edda,* is an example of this. Pedersen (*The Discovery of Language,* 1924, English translation, 1931) stated that this work was "in the guise of a proposal for spelling reform, an excellent bit of phonetics—a description of Old Norse pronunciation, which is highly significant for us today."[1]

As for the grammatical speculations themselves, they dealt principally with the *Latin* language. Attempts to grammaticize other languages did not begin until the end of the Middle Ages, and it was only during the Renaissance that they were actually completed. Throughout the Middle Ages scholars either commented upon the texts of Donatus and Priscian or deciphered the Vulgate. Among Latin grammars, let us cite that of the Englishman Aelfric, Abbot of Eynsham, which dates from A.D. 1000; the summary in hexameters of Latin grammar by Pierre Hélie (1150) from the Université de Paris, who maintained that there were as many grammatical systems as there were languages; and the famous work of Alexandre de Villedieu, *Doctrinale puerorum* (1200), also written in hexameters.

This last grammar is exemplary to the extent that it adapted grammatical teaching to logical rules, and thus emphasized the path that, from Priscian to Port-Royal, confirmed the subordination of linguistic studies to logical principles. With such a logical perspective, the grammarian in his studies had to privilege the description of *relations* between terms. It was essentially a question of the *order of words,* and the *form of words.* The order determined their logical values. Thus, for example, "The intransitive construction requires the nominative to be the support of the verb." A negation, if there was one, was placed before the verb. While place determined the logical value, invariable forms were nevertheless important. De Villedieu recognized two of these upon which the signification of the sentence relied—the *noun* and the *verb.*

Noun-verb relations, said to be *of government {rection},* gave rise to a description of six cases envisaged on the level of signification and not as grammatical, formal play. A veritable *semantics* was constructed on the basis of this conception of a parallelism between grammar and logic. Syntax was based on the concept of *government {régime};* as Chevalier has remarked, that is the relationship established between the active principle, the governor *{recteur},* and the passive principle, the governed *{régi}.* Syntactic analysis did not envisage larger units than the binary couple noun/verb. De Villedieu's *Doctrinale* remained most influential up until the sixteenth century.

As we have said, the *speculative* grammars of the Middle Ages conceived of language study as a mirror *(speculum)* that reflected the truth of the world, a truth that was not directly accessible. It was therefore through the search for this hidden *senefiance* that these studies later became treatises on the *modi significandi.* One of their principal aims was to define the task of grammar by distinguishing it from that of logic. The difference between the two was established in the following way: logic tends to distinguish what is true from what is false, while grammar grasps the concrete forms that thinking takes on in language, in other words, the semantic relation between content and form. What was the organization of the language system that was supposed to determine the concepts of thought (or to express them)? It was centered on two bases of operation, the *noun* and the *verb;* the former expressed stability, the latter, movement. The verb played the principal, primordial role in the sentence. For Hélie, it was like the troops' general: "The verb governs the sentence. To govern is to carry another word of the discourse along with the verb into a construction in order to perfect this construction." Together the noun and the verb formed the sentence, which was a complex notion, and as such, the object of syntax. Syntax was obviously completely subordinated to morphology. Miming the Aristotelian concept of the *substance* and its *accidents*, logical grammar posited language as a conjunction of declinable words; syntax was only the study of this declension.

The theory of the *modi significandi* strictly speaking postulated the existence of a thing along with its properties *(modi essendi)*, which caused as their effect their own intellection or comprehension *(modi intelligendi)*. Following this last mode, ideal comprehension was covered by a rational envelope, the *sign*, which gave rise to the *modus significandi*. Here is how Siger de Courtrai in *Summa modorum significandi* (1300) defined it: "The active signifying mode is a *ratio*, which is given to the material form by the intellect, so that a particular material form signifies a particular mode of being. The passive signifying mode is the mode of being itself, signified by the material form, thanks to the operation of the active signifying mode, or to the mode of the signified, attributed to the thing itself." The author gave the following example. An object, for example a piece of woodwork, whose color is red, and which is used to decorate a cabaret strikes the intelligence, and man designates it by means of speech "a red panel." The intelligence confers a certain function upon this word, that of designating what it formally aims at; the word *(dictio)* indicates through speech *(vox)* only the point of view of the designator. Signification is indissolubly linked to speech/voice, for the intelligence attributes a meaning to the verbal sign that expresses a part of being. The red color of the panel, in the conditions it is placed in, and thanks to the intervention of the intellect, signifies the vermillion product known as wine. Grammarians called this element of an intentional nature that envelops the word *modus significandi* (see A. Wallerand, *Les Oeuvres de Siger de Courtrai,* Louvain, 1913).

By establishing in this way the voice-concept relationship as the core of speech's signifying mode, Siger de Courtrai founded a theory of the discursive sign.

The signifying mode was divided into (1) *absolutus* and *respectivus,* which established syntax, and (2) *essentialis* (general and special) and *accidentalis*. Parts of speech and their modalities were obtained by combining these.

Medieval theories dealing with the sign and signification are little known and studied today. This lack of information, due in part to the complexity of the texts but perhaps above all to their close link to Christian theology (such as the theses of Saint Augustine), probably deprives us of the richest works the West has produced on the process of signification, before they were censored by the formalism imposed with the rise of the bourgeoisie (see the next chapter).

Today *semiotics* has inherited the scientific linguistic tradition but also the enormous philosophical and theoretical work on the sign and signification that has accumulated over the centuries. It is again taking up and reinterpreting the concepts of *mode of signification,* and of *signifiance*[2] (in the works of Jakobson, Benveniste, Lacan), etc. Detaching these concepts from their theological foundation poses the problem of how to gain access today—after centuries of oblivion or narrow positivism—to this complex zone where signification is elaborated, in order to extract modes, types, and procedures. The *grammatica speculativa* and *modi significandi* books of the Middle Ages, if they are reinterpreted (if not reversed and placed on a materialist base), can be considered precursors in this realm.

Let us mention, among other "modists," Albertus Magnus (1240), Thomas of Erfurt (1350), etc.

The developments of these theoreticians did not radically transform Donatus' and Priscian's proposals on grammar. They only contributed a more profoundly *logical* vision of language, and the *semantics* that resulted from it prepared a path of study of linguistic construction as a formal whole.

Some of the *grammatica speculativa* and *modi significandi* treatises became highly elaborated semantics, such as Lully's semantic combinative, which was taken up later by Leibniz in his *Caractéristique universelle*. As is known, Lulle, before becoming a Franciscan, spent his childhood at the court of Jacques d'Aragon, and seems to have had some contact with Abulafia's cabalistic methods. In any case, his work shows the effects of them, if only by the definition of his art one finds there: *to combine names that express the most general and the most abstract ideas according to mechanical procedures, so that the exactness of proposals may be judged and new truths may be discovered.* His interest in eastern languages and his effort in spreading them are also significant.

We cannot talk about the linguistic theories of the Middle Ages without recalling the philosophical background against which they unfolded, that is, the famous discussion between the *realists* and the *nominalists* that marked that period.

The realists, represented by John Duns Scot (1266–1308), supported Plato and Saint Augustine's thesis of the reality of the infinite being, of which things were only the exteriorization. As for words, they were intrinsically linked to the idea or the concept, and a concept existed as soon as there was a word.

The nominalists, represented by William of Occam (c. 1300–1350), but also by Abelard and Saint Thomas, believed in the real existence of particular things, and felt that the universal existed only in the soul of knowledgeable subjects. On the level of language, they questioned the equivalency of the word and the idea. Words corresponded to individuals. In the sentence "The man is running," neither the word *(suppositio materialis)* nor the human species *(suppositio simplex),* but instead the concrete individual person is running. This supposition is called *suppositio personnalis.* On it Occamism built its doctrine of the role of *words* or *terms* in discourse, whence the name of this doctrine— *nominalism* or *terminalism.*

The end of the Middle Ages was marked as well by a new element in the conception of language. To the defense of national languages, evident since the tenth century, was added the desire to elaborate grammars that suited their specificities. Such was the first French grammar by Walter de Bibbesworth, *L'Aprise de la langue française* of the fourteenth century, and the *Leys d'amour* (1323–1356), the troubador's poetic code, of which one part was a grammar of the *langue d'oc.* The *Donat français,* a complete grammar of the French of the period, was composed in 1400 by several expert clerics. To these facts can be added, as G. Mounin has remarked (*Histoire de la linguistique des origines au XXe siècle,* 1967), a new *historical* conception of language, even though it is far from acquiring the comparativist or philological form it would later have in the nineteenth century. Thus in Dante's (1256–1321) *De vulgari eloquentia,* a defense of the national language was accompanied by an attack against Latin, which was considered an artificial language. On the other hand, the poet noticed the relationship between *Italian, Spanish,* and *Provençal,* and affirmed—he was the first—their common origin. The defense of the vernacular language in Dante is in fact not only a defense of spoken Italian versus Latin but even more a defense of a primitive, logical, natural, or in any case universal linguistic core that future centuries would want to refine and preserve. Here is how Dante himself defined it, and one can already find in these remarks something of the style of the Cartesians and Encyclopedists:

> . . . We say that the Vulgar Tongue is that which we acquire without any rule, by imitating our nurses. We afterwards have another secondary speech, which the Romans called Grammar. And this secondary speech the Greeks also have, as well as others, but not all. Few, however, acquire the use of this secondary speech, because we can only be guided and instructed in it by the expenditure of much time, and by assiduous study. Of these two kinds of speech also, the Vulgar Tongue is the nobler, as well because it was first employed by the human race, as because the whole world makes use of it, though it has been divided into different forms of utterance and words. It is also the nobler as being natural to us. . . .
>
> It was therefore necessary that the human race should have some *rational* and *sensible* sign for the inter-communication of its thoughts: because the sign, having to receive something from the reason of one and to convey it to the reason of another had to be *rational;* and since nothing can be conveyed from one reason to another except through a medium of sense, it had to be *sensible.* . . . Now, this sign is that noble subject itself of which we are speaking; being, as to sound, *sensible* by nature, but *rational* in so far as it carries some meaning. . . .[3]

Thus, at the end of the Middle Ages, the bases of Latin as the mother tongue were shaken, and interest shifted to national languages. The search continued for a common, natural, or universal core in these languages, for a fundamental and vernacular language. At the same time, the teaching of these new languages opened up new perspectives and provoked new linguistic conceptions during the Renaissance.

15

HUMANISTS AND GRAMMARIANS OF THE RENAISSANCE

The Renaissance definitively oriented linguistic interest toward the study of modern languages. Latin continued to serve as a mold for thinking about all other idioms, but it was far from being the only language [studied]. In addition, theory, established on the basis of Latin, underwent considerable modifications so as to correspond to the specificities of vernacular languages.

The study of these vernacular languages was justified, as by Dante, by their origin and their common logical core. Joachim Du Bellay (1521–1560) in his *Défense et illustration de la langue française,* after having attributed the Tower of Babel to human inconstancy, noted that different languages "were not born of themselves in the manner of herbs, roots, and trees: some weak, and feeble in their species, others healthy and robust, and more suited to carrying the weight of human conceptions." He instead declared that "that (it seems to me) is an important reason why one should not thus praise one Language, and reproach another: given that they all come from the same source and origin: the fantasy of men, and were formed from the same judgment, to the same end: to signify among us the conceptions and the intelligence of the mind." This logical vocation of every language justified, therefore, both what Du Bellay wanted to demonstrate, "that the French Language is not as poor as many believe it to be," and his recommendation "to amplify the French language by imitating ancient Greek and Roman authors."

Broadening the linguistic field necessarily led to emphasizing the *historical* conception that had already come to light toward the end of the Middle Ages. And so we find the work of G. Postel, *De originibus seu de Hibraicae linguae et gentis antiquitate, atque variarum linguarum affinitate* (Paris, 1538), and that of G. B. Baliander, *De ratione communi omnium linguarum et litterarum commentarius* (Zurich, 1548), in which the author studied twelve languages in order to find a single common origin—Hebrew. Some fanciful theories were born of this opening-up of the linguistic borders. For example, Giambullari (*Il Gello,* 1546) "proved" that Florentine came from Etruscan, which had been born of Hebrew; Johannes Becanus (*Origines Antwerpinae,* 1569) "demonstrated" that Flemish was the mother tongue of all languages, etc. The goal of some of these linguistic excursions was to demonstrate the value of the vernacular language being discussed by the author, by comparing its merits to those of such unquestionably perfect languages as Greek or Latin. Such is the case, for example, of Henri Estienne (*Traité de la conformité du français avec le grec,* 1569). In a more comparativist perspective, and by establishing typological classifications of his terms, Joseph Justus Scaliger, the son of the grammarian, wrote *Diatriba de europearum linguis* (1599). Moreover, because grammatical study was oriented toward languages such as Hebrew, or toward modern languages, the scholar was confronted with linguistic particularities (absence of cases, the order of words, etc.) whose explanation considerably modified linguistic reasoning itself.

Another specific trait of the Renaissance's linguistic conception was no doubt its interest in *rhetoric* and any original, elaborate, and powerful *practice of language* that could equal classics, or indeed surpass them. In other words, in the humanist tradition language was not considered to be solely a subject of scholarship, but was instead considered to have a life that was real, noisy, and colorful. It thus became the veritable flesh in which Renaissance man's corporal and intellectual liberty was exercised. Let us here recall the laugh of Rabelais (1494–1553), provoked by the scholarly erudition of the "Sorbonnards,"[1] and his fascination for popular language; he disobeyed the rules of the grammarians and offered his stage to dreamlike stories, to puns, farces, plays on words, to fairground speech, and to the laughter of the carnival. Erasmus (1467–1536) in *The Praise of Folly,* and the entire age along with him, were attentive to "mad discourse," and were thus a major symptom of the already affirmed conviction that the functioning of language presented a complexity unsuspected by the codes of logic and medieval scholasticism.

What without a doubt most profoundly marked the *conception* of language, however, was that it became during the Renaissance—and in a generalized fashion—a subject of *teaching.* We have noted that at one period and in certain civilizations, language, which was not differentiated from the body and nature, was the object of a general cosmogony. Afterwards it became a specific object of *study,* distanced from the outside it represented. At the same time, and principally among the Greeks, language began to be *taught,* and its norms instilled in those who used it. In the dialectic of this process between a *subject to be taught* and a *teaching method,* the latter ended up modeling what it had initially proposed to know. The dialectic necessities—namely clarity, systematization, efficiency, etc.—which were themselves dictated by a world in the midst of a bourgeois economic revolution, ended up gaining the upper hand. They checked medieval speculations and overdetermined a reformulation of the Greco-Roman science of language.

The pedagogical needs put forth by Erasmus, who was wary of reasoning and favored *common use* and *formal structures* as the basic principles for teachers, oriented the study of language toward *empiricism.* This approach consisted of devoting oneself to facts and common use, while barely treating theory. "No discipline requires less reason and more observation than grammar," G. Valla wrote. Lebrixa insisted that "one should not give any reason whatsoever." But, by the same token, pedagogical procedures such as tables, inventories, simplifications, etc., introduced a new *formalism* that soon manifested itself.

The beginning of the sixteenth century was marked by a few works of this kind: Vives (1492–1540), a disciple of Erasmus, wrote *De disciplinis libri XII;* Despautère produced *Syntaxis* (1513); Erasmus, *De octo orationis partium constructione* (1521), etc. The French language became the privileged object of grammarians, as is shown by such works as *Principes en françoys, Nature des verbes,* etc. (c. 1500). In 1529,

Simon de Colines and Lefèvre d'Etaples published *Grammatographia;* they described its aim in this way:

> Just as, thanks to those general descriptions of the world called cosmographies, anyone can quickly gain knowledge of the entire world, whereas by going through books one is not sure to succeed at this, even by devoting an enormous amount of time to it, in the same way this *Grammatographia* enables us to see all of grammar in a very short time.

An important characteristic of these empirical grammars of the early sixteenth century is that they were principally *morphologies.* They studied the terms of a clause—noun, verb, etc.—but, as Chevalier has remarked, these words were studied "in their situation," and the grammar carefully established the *formal coordinates* of that situation. The order of words, the relations of government *{rection}* (governed term, governing term, single government, double government) ended up establishing veritable sentence *structures* for which, however, the equivalent in logical relations was immediately sought.

Of course, we cannot here, in the framework of this rapid survey, devote attention to all the important works of the Renaissance grammarians. This task, which is a part of scholarship and is obviously very important for the elaboration of an epistemology of linguistics that has yet to be done, is outside the framework of this book, whose limited aim is to make a general sketch of the principal moments of the changes in the conception of language. So we shall devote our attention to only a few grammarians, whose works, while on the whole not strikingly different, do nonetheless prepare the way for the decisive break in the study of language that the grammar of Port-Royal in the seventeenth century represents. The evolution toward *syntax* of the *morphological* conception of language can be noted in the lines that follow.

Jacques Dubois, known as Sylvius, who was considered a French Donatus, was the author of a grammar called *Isagôge-grammatica latino-gallica.* In this Latin-French work, he devoted himself to transferring the categories of Latin morphology to French. To do this, he cut up utterances not only into words but also into larger segments, and looked for corresponding ones in the other language. One can deduce

from this that Sylvius believed in a core of logical universals common
to every language, and underlying the various constructions of each
language. In the logical schemas he established in this way, Sylvius
applied the Aristotelian method (revealed in *Organon*) of the hierarchi-
zation of parts of speech: the most important part possessed the most
modes for being signified (thus, nouns and verbs had more modes than
prepositions and conjunctions). In the framework of these equivalent
segments in Latin and French, Sylvius emphasized the *signs* that constituted and welded the whole: the article, the pronoun, and the preposition. He thus established a *functional* equivalence—which was at the
same time a *logical* one—between a segment in French and the terms
of the same segment in Latin. By doing so, Sylvius *maintained* the
declension in French, as the following passage indicates. "With us, as
with the Hebrews from whom we borrowed it, declension is particularly easy. To form a plural, it suffices to add an *s* to the singular and to
know the articles, whose number is very limited, and which we have
sought among the pronouns and the prepositions." Wanting at any cost
to establish an equivalence with Latin grammar—out of concern for
the logical equivalence between the two languages—Sylvius continued
to use the notion of *declension* to describe French grammar, while
emphasizing the difference between it and Latin grammar. He was led
in this way to valorize the role of the *preposition* and especially that of
the *article* as agents in this French system of declension.

Before discussing the work of the man who, while continuing Sylvius' effort, ended up imposing a serious theoretical and systematical
attitude on the study of language, and thus remedying the defects of
empiricism, let us mention the grammar published in England by Pals-
grave, *L'Esclarcissement de la langue francoyse* (1530). This work followed the tradition of authors like Linacre *(De emendata structura)*,
Erasmus, and Gaza; its aim was to define the organizational laws of a
language that was still far from being stabilized.

But it was especially the work of J. C. Scaliger, *De causis linguae
latinae* (1540), that marked the second half of the sixteenth century.
Although devoted solely to the Latin language, this book went beyond
its era, and figures among the finest examples of linguistic rigor of its
time. As the title indicates, the grammarian intended to discover the
(logical) causes of the linguistic organization that he had set out to

systematize. Like all humanists, he valued usage above all, and relied upon the givens and the facts; but he was no less concerned with the reason underlying these facts. On the contrary, the principal theoretical aim of all his work was to demonstrate the well-foundedness, the *ratio,* that preceded and commanded the linguistic form. "The term is the sign of notions that are in the soul": this definition conveys quite well the conception of language that, according to Scaliger, represented innate concepts, as Cartesians would later say.

While he maintained that "grammar is the science that allows one to speak in conformity with usage," Scaliger nonetheless insisted upon the fact that "even if the grammarian attaches importance to the signified *{significatum},* which is a kind of form *{forma},* he doesn't do it for his own purposes, but in order to transmit the result to the person whose job it is to seek the truth." He was talking, of course, about the logician and the philosopher, and we understand that for Scaliger, as for the entire grammatical tradition, the study of *la langue* was not an end in itself, nor was it autonomous; instead it was part of a theory of knowledge to which it was subordinated. But this gesture of Scaliger's was accompanied by another one that tried to define the field of grammar by first insisting that it was not an art but a *science.* While implicitly immersing it in a logical procedure, he differentiated it from logical science by excluding the science of judgments from grammar. He also differentiated it from rhetoric and the interpretation of authors, in order finally to construct it as a normative grammar, a correction of language with two parts: a study of constituent elements (morphology) and of their organization (syntax).

How exactly was the grammar thus conceived of constructed? "The term," Scaliger wrote, "consists of three modifications: the granting of a form, the composition, and the truth. The truth is the appropriateness of the utterance to the thing of which it is the sign; the composition is the conjunction of elements according to corresponding clauses; the form is given by creation *{creatio}* and by derivation *{figuratio}.*"[2] It was therefore logical that grammar had three types of explanations *{rationes}:* "the first relative to the form, the second to the signification, and the third to the construction."

A constant concern for systematization, inspired by Aristotelian logic, predominated in the book. The analysis had to begin with the *parts* in order to end up with the composition of the *whole.* This method was deemed better "because it follows the order of nature; it is better because it brings out the master's *{tradentis}* superior mind, and because all the elements have to have been put into a well-established order before the mind can be called upon to work on them."

In this order of ideas, Scaliger divided linguistic elements into categories: first, those that made up the word (they could be simple, like letters, or compound, like syllables); next, he obviously must have been thinking about a larger discursive unit than the word, such as the sentence and its subgroups, for within this superior unit he distinguished *nouns* and *verbs.* "But I cannot show you what elements are joined together to form what is called a noun; they are elements that are classified into genres by following so to speak a universal given." We can see that Scaliger refused to analyze parts of speech by their role and position, and instead differentiated them according to their logical import ("universal given").

Now, while the logical given was easily definable—and here was an opening that was later filled by the syntactic reasoning underlying morphology—the same was not true of the linguistic given, which, moreover, did not always cover the logical category (the cause), initially acknowledged as the determining one. The gap created in this way was filled by an analysis of *substitutions, modifications,* and *transitions,* in which a syntax was outlined, this time more clearly than when done by previous grammarians, a syntax that was still, however, mingled with a morphology here called etymology, the science of derivations, declensions, and conjugations. Such analyses testify to Scaliger's interest in studying the functions of terms within the linguistic whole, and his dislike of preliminary, ready-made, morphological definitions. "Since a perfect science is not content with a single definition but requires as well the knowledge of the modalities that an object *{affectus}* assumes, we shall see what ancient authors have said about the modalities of each of the elements and what we, for our part, think about them." Or instead; "No one is less favored by luck than the grammarian, who is a lover of definitions."

The order followed by Scaliger's exposition was the hierarchical order of the Renaissance grammarians:

1. The *sound:* he cut phonemes up into their constituents: $Z = C + D$, and followed the change of letters (vowels and consonants) as they passed from Greek into Latin, and during the course of the evolution of the Latin language.

2. The *noun:* at first defined semantically, in its *logical* cause, it was the "sign of permanent reality," "as if it constituted by itself the cause of knowledge." It was next compared to other parts of speech, such as the pronoun; in the end, it was completely revealed in the light of its modifications: species, gender, number, figure, person, and case. The problem of case led to considerations of an already syntactic order, concerning problems of government *{rection}* and the functional role of the noun—distinguished from its semantic responsibility—in the linguistic whole.

3. The *verb* would be "the sign of a reality envisaged from the point of view of time." The entire group of verbs could be divided into two groups: some designated action, others passion; the two groups could also replace each other in order to express the same signified. Scaliger studied the tense, modes, person and number of verbs. Among other things, he noted the possibility of substituting one verbal category for another, since all of them relied upon the same logical reason (idea). For instance, *Caesar pugnat→Caesar est pugnans→Caesar est in pugna,* was only one of numerous examples which prepared the way for the grammar of Port-Royal, and in which modern transformational grammarians have found their ancestor.

4. The *pronoun* "differed from the noun not in its *signification,* but in its manner of signifying *{modus significandi}.*"

Having constant recourse to the *modi significandi* and constructing his reasoning in this way upon a semantic foundation, Scaliger was therefore looking for the *logique vocis ratio*—or the reason for each term. At the same time, his vision of language was not a parcelled one, but instead operated on vast wholes in which syntax was sketched out, for "the truth resides in the utterance and not in the isolated word." Scaliger's work, written in a style of violent objection to the theories of his predecessors and of constant questioning of his contemporaries, claimed to be, in the words of its author, "a very new book." It was indeed exemplary as a *synthesis* of semantic and formal theories and as a *clarification* of the limited number of constructions (junction and substitution based on an underlying logic) in which *la langue* was organized.

French grammar was then marked by the works of Maigret, Estienne, Pillot, and Garnier and found its culminating point in the books of Ramus, *Dialectique* (1556) and *Gramere* (1562).

Ramus' fundamental methodological preoccupation was to situate his thought process with respect to universal reason (the principles of the logical foundation of linguistic construction), on the one hand, and on the other with respect to experience or "remarkable induction," as he called it, which he defined in this way: "To experiment by usage, to observe by reading poets, orators, philosophers, and, in short, all excellent men." Ramus' reasoning therefore was carried out in a constant coming-and-going from reason to usage, from philosophical principles to observed language. "If a man is knowledgeable in the art but ignorant in the practice, that would be, he [Aristotle] says, [like] Pauson's Mercury, and one wouldn't know if science was inside or outside" *(Dialectique.)*[3]

The *Dialectique* and the *Grammaire* were, so to speak, parallel: the first one tackled the thinking that transcended *la langue,* and the second examined the way in which this thinking was itself transcended. Since logic and grammar were inseparable, grammar was unfolded on the basis of an underlying logic. "There are two parts of Dialectics, Invention and Judgment. The first one states the separate parts of which any aphorism is composed. The second shows the manner and species of arranging them, and so the first part, Grammar, teaches the parts of speech, and Syntax describes the construction." Chevalier has stated it remarkably well: in order to be constructed, syntax had to take advantage of logic, which was supposed to be at the root of *la langue* as the organization of the common core, of universal reason. But this "advantage" didn't go very far, for it prevented syntax from becoming autonomous: syntax constantly had to be referred back to the semanticological definitions of terms, that is, to morphology.

Formal grammar was threatened by its very principles.

Let us mention an important point in the Ramusian conception of the thought/*langue* relation. By assimilating the two, Ramus considered thought according to the image he had of discourse, that is, as a linearity. As a consequence, he "presented three different substitutable kinds of sentences as the fundamental molds for enunciation: a sentence with a full verb, one with the verb to be, and the negative sentence"; he thus established three canonical kinds of sentences with the possibility of substitution. The analysis of *judgments* and *syllogisms* provided the constituent elements of thought and their arrangement, and this guided grammatical reflection and founded the method. But the latter needed a precise observation of enunciation itself in order to be constructed definitively. The following is the Ramusian definition of the dialectic between logic and grammar that founded a method faithful to "nature":

> Let us suppose that all the definitions, distributions, and rules of Grammar have been found, and that each one has been truly judged, and that all the teachings have been written on various tablets, which are all turned over and scrambled together pell-mell in some earthenware jug, as in the game of *blanque*.[4] Now I ask, what part of Dialectics would be able to teach me how to arrange precepts confused in this way and to reduce them to order? In the first place, there will be no need for any scenes of invention, for everything has already been discovered: each particular enunciation has been proved and judged. Neither the first judgment of the enunciation nor the second of the syllogism is necessary. Only the method remains, and a certain path of collocation. The dialectician will therefore choose the definition of Grammar by the light of the natural method in that jug, for this is the most general and he will place it in the highest rank. "Grammar is the doctrine of speaking well." Then, he will search in this same jug for the partitions of Grammar and will allocate them to second rank. "There are two parts of Grammar: Etymology and Syntax." Next, in the same vase he will separate out the definition of the first part, and will adjust it in third place after the previous two. Thus, by defining and distributing, he will descend to the most specialized examples and assign them last place. And he will do the same for the other part, just as we have taken great pains here to arrange the precepts of Dialectics, with the most

general first, the subordinates next, and the most specialized examples last.

The strictly grammatical theories of Ramus were revealed in his *Scholae grammaticae* (1559), a theoretical treatise, as well as in his Latin, Greek, and French grammars. The principle had already been heralded in the *Dialectique:* they would be *formal* grammars, starting from logical bases; to prove their truthfulness, they would come back to these bases. The grammatical constructions interpenetrated each other by substitution or transformation, in conformity with the rules of the context and with the particularities of the forms. Meaning was banished from explicit reflection, and grammar was presented as a *system of marks.* Such a grammar, Chevalier has written,

> was incapable of determining the relations that would allow one to show something other than its own functioning. This system of internal correspondences was extended to the investigation of related languages; the entire model grammar became the framework for other grammars. One cannot speak of universalism here, one would have to speak of imperialism, if one wanted to speak in terms of values or of the impossibility of escaping from one's own system, if one wanted to trace the limits of the formal method. Exactly the same process imposed itself for the description of French. If one adopted the formal system of Latin, it was because a method was necessary. The formal transformations necessary within a language were also necessary in order to pass from one language to another; since the arsenal of procedures for reducing something to the norm was full, this operation was an easy one. Thus, one looked in the prepositions, articles, and ellipses for the *conversion material,* just as when speaking of *monoplata*[5] names or impersonal verbs. . . .

In his analysis of French grammar, Ramus first established the formal principles and the formal distinctions among the parts of speech. "A noun is a word with number and gender." "There are ten nouns that are commonly called pronouns, and seem to have several cases," etc. Besides *morphological* marks, terms were defined by *order.* Thus, one can read in the chapter "On the noun's suitability to the verb" (1572 edition of the *Grammaire française*): "And it seems that where our detractors are the weakest is that, according to Aristotle's advice, transferred words should signify the same thing. We have already shown that French has a certain order in its oration that can in no way be changed." After morphological marks and order, the preposition became an object of study as an important syntactic element. It carried out the change of one construction into another, and was the formal agent of a transformation, which, by the way, far from being part of a dynamic conception of language, fixed it in a representation of *la langue* as a coexistence of parallel and stable structures that responded to one another. Such is the following example of the substitution of a "verbal syntagm" by a "nominal syntagm": "Now the three prepositions *De, Du, Des* ['of,' 'from,' 'by,'], are so efficient that nouns are never governed by a noun or a passive verb unless these three prepositions are used: as in *La vile de Paris, Le Pale' de Roe, La doctrine des Ateniens, Tu es eime de Dieu, du môde, des omes* [the city of Paris, the Palace of the King, the doctrine of the Athenians, you are loved by God, by the world, by men]."

But this formalism was present only to bring logical considerations back to the content; logical methods of classification, judgment, identification of elements, etc., filled the formal framework.

It is obvious that while Ramus' grammar was a considerable step forward in the ordering process and in logical rigor, in systematization and in formalization, it stopped at the threshold of syntactic analysis because it lacked the ability to define the *relations* at work among the formal marks that arranged the utterance in a strict order. Thus one could say with Chevalier that "Ramus' grammar was the first attempt . . . at a formal grammar, but, already, the first failure."

After Ramus, authors such as Henri Estienne in *Hypomneses de Gallica lingua peregrinis eam discentibus necessariae*, 1582, and *Conformité du langage français avec le grec*, 1565, as well as Antoine Cauchie, in *Grammatica gallica*, 1570, continued the task of formalizing the French language, which became more and more detached from the schemas of Latin grammar.

A period of decline in French grammatical theory followed. Great works were elaborated about Latin—a concern for universalism belonging to the apparently nationalistic Renaissance—by Spanish authors such as Sanctius, and German or Dutch ones such as Scioppius or Vossius, etc. The cult of reason became more and more firmly established (usage was bracketed off). This is the case, for example, with the famous work by Sanctius, *Minerve, seu de causis linguae latinae* (Salamanca, 1587), bearing as its title the name of the famous goddess of reason. It is of interest to emphasize that Sanctius chose his title *Minerve* [Athena] to contrast with *Mercurius,* the title of a work by an earlier, rival grammarian. Sanctius therefore consciously replaced the god of commerce and change with the goddess of reason, or, in other words, the conception of languages as fluidity and communication with the conception of language as a logical organization lending itself to rigorous description. *La langue* was therefore thought of in that work as an expression of nature, that is, of reason, and linguistic elements represented logical terms and their relations. Sanctius drew his inspiration from Ramus, but he transferred Ramus' reflection, which was completely attached to the observation of linguistic facts, to a more abstract level. *La langue* for Sanctius had already become a *system:* a concern for logical systematization dominated Ramus' formal, and, in the final analysis, morphological, structuring. "Usus porrosine ratione non movetur" [Custom will not be changed without reason], Sanctius wrote, and he oriented his reflection toward meaning rather than form.

A conclusion arises about the development of linguistic thinking in the sixteenth century. The science of language detached itself from related disciplines and, while continuing to rely upon them—on logic principally—stopped being speculation in order to become observation. Empiricism was joined to metaphysics in order to moderate it, to transfer it to logic and bring about the elaboration of a positivist-scientific process. The old controversy inherited from the Greeks about the conception of *la langue* as natural or conventional was displaced and replaced with another one: the controversy about whether *la langue* was a *ratio* or a *usage.* Physis/thesis became reason or nature/usage. But the two terms of the dichotomy were not mutually exclusive, as was the case during Plato's time. They were superimposed on one another and vertically traversed language which, in this way, split up into two parts: a logical core (rational, necessary, and regulated) and a specifically linguistic enunciation (varied, irreducible to its core, to be grasped in the various manifestations inside a single language or from one language to another). Bacon later said of it (*De dignitate,* 1623): "It is certain that words are the traces or impressions of reason."[6] The concern of grammar became to systematize the diversity-vestige that covered over the rational core: that had been the goal of Ramus and Sanctius.

A procedural modification of grammatical discourse added to the methodical upheaval: it started out being morphological, but gradually worked its way toward a syntax that was both enabled and hindered by logic.

The study of language had not yet become a "pilot science," a model for all thinking that tackled man, as it is today. But in its effort to systematize, clarify, rationalize, and specify itself, grammar became the autonomous and indispensable discipline for anyone who wanted to know the laws of thought. Bacon later formulated it with great precision: "Grammar holds the place of a conductor in respect of the other sciences; and, though the office be not noble, it is extremely necessary" [p. 164].

Henceforth, following the changes in linguistic conception meant following the minute changes of a discourse that was in the process of becoming scientific—logicogrammatical discourse. That is to say, from that point on, the conception of language was clearly linked to the changes undergone by a knowledge uprooted from medieval metaphysics, and to the successive transformations later sketched out there, across the symbolic manifestations of society (philosophy, the various sciences, etc.), including the study of language.

16

THE GRAMMAR OF PORT-ROYAL

After the remarkable works of Scaliger and Ramus, the language studies that appeared at the end of the sixteenth and the beginning of the seventeenth centuries seem to have little scope. These books were meant for pedagogical purposes and brought no theoretical innovation, but instead endeavored to simplify the rules of *la langue* so that students could understand them better. All the same, there was a positive aspect: the number of languages learned grew, and grammars became polylinguistic. English, French, German, and Italian were confronted, and the frameworks imposed by Latin were increasingly weakened.

The concern for regulating *la langue* was felt on the political as well as the rhetorical level. Malherbe (1555–1628) applied himself to introducing discipline into French by purging it of all traces of neologisms, archaisms, or provincialisms. Richelieu was demanding the same thing when he founded the French Academy in 1635: "The principal function of the Academy will be to work with all possible care and diligence in order to give our language sure rules and to make it pure, eloquent, and capable of dealing with arts and sciences," the statutes of the Academy stated.

The tone of that century's debates can be expressed in this way:

regularization, systematization, and discovery of the laws that would enable the French language to attain the perfection of classical speech.

The art of fine speaking became fashionable in France. People at court learned it from Vaugelas' book *Remarques sur la langue française* (1647). Using the ideas of Scaliger and imitating the style of Valla, whose *De elegantia* took up Priscian's teaching from a précieuse perspective, Vaugelas presented in a courtly and agreeable form the "harmonious" French language reduced to a few rules. Oudin, in his *Grammaire française* (1634) devoted himself to developing the grammar of his predecessor Maupas, but basically he only accumulated subtly detailed remarks instead of revealing great theoretical syntheses. The principal aim of these books was to accomodate the properties of a modern language, French, to the old Latin machine, which was based on the noun-verb pair. Articles, prepositions, auxiliaries, etc., had to be inserted. The writers devoted themselves to demonstrating that an expression with a preposition in French was equal to an expression with a genitive or dative in Latin. Vaugelas pointed out that in the example "An infinity of people has taken . . . ." "an infinity" was nominative and "people" was genitive. In other examples he acknowledged the existence of the ablative, and in this way he completed the French declension.

It was absolutely necessary to the dignity of a modern language to prove that it had Latin categories. Great efforts were therefore made to take it back to Latin. Bacon wrote, "It is also worth observing, though it may seem a little ungrateful to modern ears, that the ancient languages are full of declensions, cases, conjugations, tenses, and the like; but the later languages, being almost destitute of them, slothfully express many things by prepositions and auxiliary verbs. For from hence it may easily be conjectured, that the genius of former ages, however we may flatter ourselves, was much more acute than our own." [1]

The impasse of the formal grammar of the Renaissance can be glimpsed here. It had proved that Latin linguistic constructions had *causes,* that is to say, that they were logical and therefore natural. Modern languages had only to follow the same causes; their structures were only formal frameworks that mutually answered each other by relying upon the same logic. Thinking on language thus found itself blocked: grammarians established only the formal correspondences of an already established logical schema, and were unable to discover the new laws governing modern languages.

The way out of this impasse was proposed by *A General and Rational Grammar*[2] by Lancelot and Arnauld, which was founded on the principles clarified by Descartes.

It is known that in an idealistic gesture, Descartes had posited the existence of extralinguistic thought and designated language as "one of the causes of our errors." Since the universe was divided into "things" and "ideas," language was excluded from it and became a hindrance, a useless and superfluous intermediary.

> And finally, because we attach all our conceptions to words for the expression of them by speech, and as we commit to memory our thought in connection with these words; and as we more easily recall to memory words than things, we can scarcely conceive of anything so distinctly as to be able to separate completely that which we conceive from the words chosen to express the same. In this way most men apply their attention to words rather than things, and this is the cause of their frequently giving their assent to terms which they do not understand, either because they believe that they formerly understood them, or because they think that those who informed them correctly understood their signification. (*The Principles of Philosophy*, vol. 1)[3]

While such a formulation objectively clarified the end-state of the theory of Cartesian knowledge, it seemed to pose itself as an obstacle to any serious attempt to study language as a specific material formation. This did not stop the Solitaries of Port-Royal and their successors from being guided by Descartes' conception of human understanding and his principles of reasoning (*A Discourse on Method*), etc., in their search for the laws of language. It is certainly a paradoxical phenomenon that a philosophy, that of Descartes, which bypassed language became—and this is true up until our time—the foundation of the study of language. Seen at its source, Cartesian linguistics is a contradiction in terms (the Cartesian mistrust of language is taken as the guarantee of the absolute reality of a grammatical normality upheld by the subject), which illustrates well the future difficulties of the scientific process in the realm of the human sciences; this process has been caught from its beginnings in the net of metaphysics.

At first glance, the grammar of Port-Royal is not appreciably different from those that preceded it, that is, the formal grammars of the Renaissance, except, no doubt, for its clearness and concision. Indeed, the same correspondences can be found there between Latin cases and the constructions of the French language. However, two fundamental methodological innovations completely renewed the vision of *la langue* proposed by the Solitaries of Port-Royal.

First of all, while taking into account the actual state of the grammar inherited from the Renaissance, they reintroduced the medieval theory of the sign that the humanists-formalists had forgotten, or at least silenced. *La langue* was indeed a system, as Sanctius had demonstrated, but a system of signs. Words and linguistic expressions clothed ideas that referred back to objects. The logical or natural relation, which revealed the truth about things, was at work at the level of ideas: the logical level. Grammar would deal with an object, *la langue,* that was only the *sign* of this logical and/or natural dimension. In this way, *la langue* would depend upon logic, while having its own autonomy. This was the methodological coup de force that allowed a common and necessary *ratio* to be posited as the *core* of *la langue.* On this *ratio,* in relation to it but also at a distance from it, the interplay of specifically linguistic signs—forms—would operate, and the laws of a new linguistic construction could be specified.

Lancelot's and Arnauld's *Grammar* was indissociable from the *Logic*[4] (1662), which was due to this same Arnauld in collaboration this time with Nicole. The projects—grammatical and logical—intersected with and answered each other. Grammar was founded on logic, and logic did nothing but examine linguistic expression. Lancelot acknowledged in his preface to the grammar that the "true foundations of the art of speaking" were dictated to him by Arnauld, the future coauthor of *Logique.* For Arnauld, even if logic refused to deal with linguistic forms and aimed only for a "syntax of the elements of conception," it did not forget about words. He wrote,

Now it is certainly of some use to the end which logic contemplates—*that of thinking well*—to understand the different uses of the sounds devoted to the expression of our ideas, and which the mind is accustomed to connect so closely with them, that it scarcely ever conceives the one without the other; so that the idea of the *thing* excites the idea of the *sound,* and the idea of the *sound,* that of the *thing.*

We may say, in general, on this subject, that WORDS are *sounds distinct and articulate, which men have taken as signs to express what passes in their mind.* And since what passes there may be reduced to *conceiving, judging, reasoning, and disposing* (as we have already said), words serve to indicate all these operations. . . . (*Logic,* 2, 1) [pp. 99–100]

The fact that the publication of the *Grammar* preceded by several years the appearance of *Logic* (even if the two books seem to have been edited in the same way) is without a doubt symptomatic of how the study of language itself became, for the epistemology of the seventeenth century, the initial and determining point of reflection.

What was the theory of the sign that this recasting of logic and grammar placed at the foundation of the *General Grammar?*

The Modists, we recall, distinguished three modes of symbolization: *modi essendi, modi intelligendi,* and *modi significandi.* How did Port-Royal take up this theory again? The *Grammar* opened with the following declaration:

Grammar is the art of speaking.

Speaking is to explain our thoughts by signs, which men have invented for that purpose.

Experience has shown that the most convenient signs are sounds, and the voice. [p. 1]

The *Grammar* did not give any further details about the "model of the sign." These were found instead in the *Logic,* which proposed the geographic map as an example: the idea I form of this map refers back to another object (the real region represented by the map) of which I can formulate an idea through the intermediary of the idea given to me by the sign-map. The sign, a four-term matrix, was defined in the following way in *Logic* (1, 4): "Thus the sign contains two ideas, one of the thing which represents, the other of the thing represented, and its nature consists in exciting the second by means of the first" [p. 42].

This theory of the sign (which was rendered explicit by Michel Foucault in his *Introduction à la grammaire de Port-Royal*) obviously presupposed a critique of the Aristotelian type of reasoning (that is, reasoning by means of predefined objects and categories) and implied a passage to a logical process that examined the ideas and judgments underneath signs. For an entire logic of ideas and judgments lay hidden under linguistic signs, and it had to be grasped in order to "do by means of science what others do only by habit." The fact of seeing a system of signs in *la langue* led to a triple theoretical consequence that was emphasized by Foucault. First, it followed—as the result of a process started more than a century earlier—that the discourse put forth about this *langue* was situated on a different level than it was: one spoke of (linguistic) forms when speaking of the form of the (logical) content. That amounts to saying that *la langue* was delimited as an epistemological realm: "*La langue* as an epistemological realm is not one that can be used or interpreted; it is one whose principles can be uttered in a language of a different level." Moreover, the *General Grammar* "did not define a space common to all languages except to the extent that it opened an interior dimension for each one." And finally, this rationalization of *la langue* was a science of reasoning but not a science of *la langue* as a specific object. "General grammar, as opposed to linguistics, is more a way of viewing one language than an analysis of a specific object, such as *la langue* in general would be."

Nevertheless, with its advantages and its differences, the method of Port-Royal made its contribution to the elaboration of a scientific approach to language.

For the *General Grammar,* the word was not only the form that covered a semantic content. Port-Royal took up again the medieval triad *modi essendi/modi signandi/modi significandi;* it emphasized the difference between *modi signandi* (the idea) and *modi significandi* (the sign), and oriented grammar toward a systematization of the relationship between the two, and by that, with the object. Grammar was no longer an inventory of terms or of the formal correspondences of constructions, but a study of *superior units (judgement, reasoning). La langue* was not a collection or juxtaposition of terms, but an *organism,* a "creation."

This theory of the sign was not explicitly stated in the *Grammar.* It was there in latent form, if you will, but the theory of the various forms of the signification of words clearly revealed it. After having described the phonic aspect of speech ("its material aspect") the *Grammar* (in the chapter entitled "That the knowledge of what passes in the mind is necessary to comprehend the foundation of grammar: and on this depends the diversity of words which compose discourse") continued in this way:

> Hitherto we have treated of words, only with respect to their material part, and as they are common, at least in respect to the sound, to men and parrots.
>
> It remains now that we examine their spiritual part, which constitutes one of the most considerable advantages of man above all other animals, and is one of the most convincing arguments in favor of reason. This is the use we make of them to explain our thoughts, and the marvellous invention of composing out of 25 or 30 sounds that infinite variety of words, which, tho' they have no natural resemblance to the operation of the mind, are yet the means of unfolding all its secrets, and of disclosing unto those who cannot see into our hearts, the variety of our thoughts, and our sentiments upon all manner of subjects.
>
> Words therefore may be defined, distinct and articulate sounds, made use of by men to express their thoughts.
>
> We cannot therefore perfectly understand the different sorts of significations, annexed to words, without considering what passes in our minds, since words were invented only to communicate our thoughts.
>
> 'Tis the general doctrine of philosophers, that there are three operations of the mind: *Perception, Judgment,* and *Reasoning.*
>
> *Perception* is no more than the simple apprehension or view which the understanding forms of the objects acting upon it, whether purely intellectual, as when I think of existence, dura-

tion, cogitation, God; or corporeal and material, as a square, a circle, a dog, a horse.

Judgment is, when we affirm, that the thing which we conceive or apprehend, is so, or not so: as for instance, when I understand what the *earth* is, and what *roundness* is, I affirm, that the *earth* is *round.*

Reasoning is, from two judgments to infer a third. As when having affirmed, that virtue is commendable, and that patience is a virtue, I draw an inference, that patience is commendable.

Hence it is plain, that the third operation of the mind is only an extension of the second. It will therefore suffice, for our present subject, to take only the two first into our consideration, and as much of the first, as is comprised in the second. For men seldom mean to express their bare perceptions of things, but generally to convey their judgments concerning them.

The judgment, which we form of things, as when I say, *the earth is round,* is called a *proposition* [clause]; and, therefore every proposition necessarily includes two terms, one called the *subject,* which is the thing of which the affirmation is; as the *earth;* and the other is called the *attribute,* which is the thing that is affirmed of the subject, as *round:* and moreover the connexion between these two term, namely the substantive verb, *is.*

Now 'tis easy to see, that the two terms belong properly to the first operation of the mind, because that is what we conceive, and is the object of our thoughts; and the connexion belongs to the second, being properly the action of the mind, and the mode or manner of thinking.

Thus the greatest distinction of what passes in our minds, is to say, that we may consider the object of our thoughts, and the form or manner of them, the chief of which is judgment. But we ought likewise to refer thither the conjunctions, disjunctions, and like operations of the mind; as also all the other motions of the soul; as desires, commands, interrogations, &c.

Hence it follows, that men having occasion for signs to express what passes in the mind, the most general distinction of words must be this, that some signify the objects, and others the form or manner of our thoughts; 'tho it frequently happens that they do not signify the manner alone, but in conjunction with the object, as we shall make appear hereafter.

The words of the first sort are those which are called *nouns, articles, pronouns, participles, prepositions,* and *adverbs* Those of the second are *verbs, conjunctions,* and *interjections.* Which are all derived by a necessary consequence from the natural manner of expressing our thoughts, as we shall soon demonstrate. [pp. 21–24]

A careful reading of this chapter shows that, since the language-sign is supported by the core of the idea and the judgment, a major consequence follows for the distribution and organization of grammatical categories. We thus arrive at the second novelty contributed by the *General Grammar.*

Aristotelian logic had proposed a hierarchy of the parts of speech in which the noun and verb held equal rank. By following the generation of judgment and reasoning, the *General Grammar* was able to distinguish, on the one hand, the parts of speech, which were the signs of the "objects of our thoughts" (as will be demonstrated): the *noun,* the *article,* the *pronoun,* the *participle,* the *preposition,* and the *adverb;* and, on the other hand "the form or manner of our thoughts": the *verb,* the *conjunction,* and the *interjection.* The parts of speech were thus seen as participating in an operation, or a process. In this way, from the very first pages, and contrary to what may have been said, the *Grammar* announced its project of elaborating a *construction:* the Solitaries used the lever of the *sign* to propose a syntax, on the logical core, oriented toward a description of the system of meaning, which (for the Renaissance) underlay the arbitrary collection of words. The syntax of the judgment (logical syntax) was working its way toward a linguistic syntax.

For it was the proposition [clause] that became the basic element of grammatical reflection. The key components of the clause were of course the *noun* and the *verb,* but the verb was the determining axis.

Nouns, which included *substantives* and *adjectives,* designated the "objects of our thoughts" which could be either "things as the *earth,* the *sun, water, wood,* that are commonly called *substances";* or "the manner of things, as to be *round, red, hard, learned,* etc., which are called *accidents"* [pp. 24–25]. In the first case the nouns were *substantives,* in the second, *noun adjectives.* Among the modalities of nouns, the case in particular attracted the attention of the *General Grammar.* The reason for this was that the case expressed the *relations* of the terms in the whole of the clause, and that, moreover, these relations were indicated in French by means other than declension—by the preposition, for example.

> If things were always considered separately from one another, nouns would have received only the two abovementioned changes, *viz,* that of number of all sorts of nouns, and that of gender for the adjectives. But since they are frequently considered in the different relations, which they have to one another, some languages have contrived to express these relations, by giving the nouns different terminations or endings which they call *cases;* from the Latin *cadere,* to *fall,* being, as it were, the different falls of a word.
>
> True it is, that the Greek and Latin are perhaps the only languages, in which the nouns have properly cases. Nevertheless as there are very few, which have not some sort of cases in their pronouns, and *as without that it would be difficult to have a right understanding of the connexion of discourse,* commonly called *construction,* it seems almost necessary for the knowledge of any language whatsoever, to know what is meant by these cases. [pp. 36–37; italics added]

However, while nouns and, in general, all parts of speech that designated *conceived* objects were indispensable for the construction of a judgment, and therefore, of a *clause,* its axis, as we have said, was the *verb.* For the grammarians of Port-Royal, the verb was what *affirmed,* and no longer what marked time (as it had for Aristotle) or duration (as it had for Scaliger). In other words, every verb implicitly carried the seme *is,* or every verb was first the verb *to be.*

In the chapter on the verb, the *General Grammar* clearly presented a syntactic conception of *la langue,* with the syntax of the judgment as its basis. In other words, on the basis of the syntax of the judgment, a conception of the syntax of the clause was sketched out. The terms were no longer isolated; they formed a complex centered on the noun/verb relation, which became the *subject/predicate* relation. "This judgment is also called a proposition [clause], and must have, as will be easily seen, *two terms;* the one, that of which we affirm or deny something, called the *subject,* and the other, that [something] which we affirm or deny, called the *attribute* or *praedicate*" [*Logique,* 2, 4) [p. 111].

Since the core of the sentence was thus blocked and closed in upon itself, linguistic syntax, which had been promised by the syntax of the judgment, was stopped. The *General Grammar* offered only four pages of syntax, to which could be added the two pages "Of the figures of constructions." The grammarian, who was above all a philosopher of the judgment, had to introduce *supplements* that could be analyzed by a syntax of governments *{rections}* in order to analyze the specifically linguistic relations that went beyond the matrix of the judgment. However, the *General Grammar* acknowledged only a syntax of *concordance,* not one of government *{régime}:* "On the contrary the syntax of government is almost entirely arbitrary, for which reason it varies greatly in all languages. For one language forms its government by cases; others instead of cases make use only of small particles, which do not even express all those cases, as in French and Spanish they have only *de* and *à,* which mark the genitive and the dative, and the Italians add *da* for the ablative. The other cases have no particles, but only the simple article, nor even that always" [p. 149]. We can see how the impossibility of formulating specifically linguistic government forced the philosopher to take up again the Latin, morphological, conception of the organization of discourse.

However, it would be inaccurate to believe that the syntactic aim of the *General Grammar* did not exceed the limits of the subject/predicate relation.

The chapter "Of the pronoun called relative" testifies to a reflection that embraced fairly extensive linguistic wholes and constructed syntactic schemas that went beyond the simple clause, organizing complex clauses as well. (The second remark below was not added until the

1664 edition, and its importance has perhaps not been sufficiently appreciated):

> What it [the relative pronoun] has particular, may be considered in two different manners.
> The 1. thing, is that it always has a relation to another noun or pronoun called the antecedent; as, *God who is holy: God* is the antecedent of the relative *who*. But this antecedent is sometimes understood and not expressed, especially in Latin, as may be seen in the *New method* of learning the Latin tongue.
> The 2. thing particular to the relative, and which I don't remember to have ever seen observed, is that the proposition into which it enters (and which may be called ancellary) may constitute part of the subject, or of the attribute of another proposition, which may be called principal. [pp. 62–63]

The frameworks of linguistic reasoning first expanded beyond terms to find the clause; then analyzed segments became even bigger than a simple clause, and the analysis took on the relations within the sentence; finally the notion of the *complementarity* of terms seems to have been added to that of *subordination,* so that language was no longer an *oratio,* a formal group of terms, but a system whose principal core was the clause, supported by the affirmation of the judgment. Such are, in summary, the acquisitions enabled by the *logical* conception of the *General Grammar,* which were later developed to become the specifically linguistic science of linguistic relations. It is nonetheless true that the logical thought process of Port-Royal marked the study of language to such an extent, and this is true even to our day, that linguists have had enormous difficulty detaching their analysis from that of logical components, and linguistics has oscillated between an empirical formalism (a description of formal structures) and a transcendental logicism (breakdown of the content into categories borrowed from logic).

While the *General Grammar* dominated the seventeenth century, it nonetheless developed in a context of intense linguistic activity. Several books were devoted to the articulation of sounds and to spelling, such as the study of Petrus Montanus (Holland) *Spreeckonst (The Art of Speaking,* 1635); or of A. Hume, *Of the Ortographie and Congruitie of the Briton Tongue,* 1617. A vast school of phonetics had been at work in England, as the following works testify: Robert Robinson, *The Art of Pronnonciation*, 1617; W. Holder, *Elements of Speech, an Essay of Inquiry into the Natural Production of Letters*, 1669; Dalgrano, *Didoscalocophus, or the Deaf and Dumb Man's Lector*, 1680, etc. The *Traité de physique* of Rohault (1671) and the *De corpore animato* (1673) of Du Hamel are considered the first steps toward scientific phonetics, based on experimentation and anatomical analysis of the phonatory apparatus.

Another particularity of the study of *la langue* in the seventeenth century was the interest in foreign languages and in the constitution of historic theories of language. Let us cite among these polyglot books *Thesaurus polyglottus* by J. Mégiser (1603), as well as several grammars of Russian (by H. G. Ludolf, Oxford, 1696), of Turkish (Mégiser, Leipzig, 1612), the works of the Jesuits on China (see chapter 7), the research by Kircher on Egyptian, etc.

Lexicographic research was intense. After the *Trésor de la langue français* by Nicot in 1606, and the publication of the *Dictionnaire français* by F. Richelet at Geneva, 1679–1680, Furetière published the *Dictionnaire universel contenant généralement tous les mots français, tant vieux que modernes, et les termes de toutes les sciences et les arts* (The Hague, Rotterdam, 1690). The *Dictionnaire de l'Académie* appeared in 1694, with the signatures of Vaugelas and Mézeray; its supplement, the *Dictionnaire des arts et des sciences* by Thomas Corneille, was of considerable importance.

On the basis of linguistic diversity, one endeavored either to establish a common origin of languages (see Guichard, *Harmonie étymologique des langues, où se démontre que toutes les langues descendent de l'hébraïque*, 1606) or to elaborate a universal language (Lodwick, *A Common Writing*, 1647; Dalgrano, *Essay Towards a Real Caracter*, 1668, etc.). The plurality of languages was frightening, so one tried to find a general equivalent for them: hadn't this been the fundamental incentive of the *General Grammar?* The same desire to find a reason for, to make sense of the French language no doubt inspired Ménage in his etymological dictionary *Origine de la langue française* (1650), as well as his observations on the French language (1672). The author "demonstrated," most often while fooling himself, the etymology of French words by deriving them from a Latin or Greek word.

The works of the great rhetoricians, such as the *Rhétorique ou Art de parler* by Father Lamy (1670), *Génie de la langue française* by Aisy (1685), *De oratione discendi et docendi* (on method and linguistic teaching) by Father Jouvency (1692), etc., which came after the *Remarques* by Vaugelas, Bonhours, and Ménage, led, often with subtlety and by following the same aim of finding a common foundation for all languages, to the monumental and eclectic work by François-Séraphin Régnier-Desmarais, permanent secretary of the French Academy, the *Traité de la grammaire française,* 1706. This work was fairly far from the rigor and theoretical orientation of the *General and Rational Grammar of Port-Royal,* for Régnier's reflection was focused on the word and its environment, with no consideration of the clause as a whole or the relations governing its components.

17

THE ENCYCLOPÉDIE:
LA LANGUE AND NATURE

The eighteenth century inherited the rationalist conception of language bequeathed to it by the Solitaries of Port-Royal and their successors. Language was seen as a variety of idioms based on the same logical rules, which constituted a kind of constant: *human nature*. The number of languages studied and taught in school progressively increased; at the same time progress in the natural sciences brought about an epistemological upheaval that oriented studies toward concrete observations: this was the era of empiricism. The result in the realm of language was that philosophers and grammarians sought—more than before— to clarify the particular and specifically linguistic character of each object (language), by completely freeing it from the impact of Latin on the one hand, and on the other, freeing it to a large extent from its dependency on logic, without, however, taking away its universal foundation, which was from then on called *natural* instead of *logical*.

On the philosophical level, this conception of language led to theories on the *origin* of languages. The variety of languages had to be taken back to a common, natural source where linguistic universals were articulated. In order to establish the relation between natural language, real objects, and sensation, a *theory of the sign* was proposed.

On the grammatical level, which was, by the way, inseparable from the philosophical one, since every philosopher in the eighteenth cen-

172

tury tackled languages and every grammarian was a philosopher, the particularity of specifically linguistic relations, differentiated from the (logical) laws of thinking, was brought to light, and led to a *syntactic* description of sentence and inter-sentence relations. The grammar of the *Encyclopédie* was the first to clearly make explicit the effort common to all grammarians for over a century—that of elaborating a syntax.[1]

We will first outline the philosophical theories of language, in order to provide the background necessary to isolate the grammatical conceptions (this order will obviously force us to disregard the chronology of the publication of the works).

The philosophers and grammarians of the eighteenth century who studied the origin and evolution of language had an illustrious precursor who, without sharing the logical vision of the Cartesians and the later Encyclopedists, proposed a general picture of the history of language on the basis of previous research; the principal themes of this picture were seen again later with the Sensationalists, Ideologues, and Materialists. We are referring to G. Vico (1668–1744) and his *Scienza Nuova*. According to Vico, "speech was born in mute times *(tempi mutoli)* as mental language . . . ; the first language in the first mute times of the nations must have begun with signs, whether gestures or physical objects, which had natural relations to the ideas."[2] This first language, which Vico called *divine,* could be glimpsed according to him in the gestures of the dumb, which constitute the principle of the *hieroglyphs* (see below the same themes in Diderot, as well as chapter 3, "The Graphic and the Gestural," and chapter 5) "by which all nations spoke in the time of their barbarism" [p. 226]. This language was followed by *poetic* or *heroic* language: "The first authors among the Orientals, Egyptians, Greeks, and Latins, and, in the recourse of barbarism, the first writers in the modern languages of Europe, were poets" [p. 224]. Vico devoted his research to what he called "poetic logic"—its emblems, its figures, and its tropes: metaphor, metonymy, and synecdoche. The poetic word for him was a "character" or even a "mythographic word"; "every metaphor is a fable in brief" [p. 404]. In last place came "epistolary" language, "born of the lower classes" [p. 439]. Vico examined the different languages known during his time (Greek, Egyptian, Turkish, German, Hungarian, etc.) and their writing systems, in order to divide them into the three categories just mentioned. His research on poetic language influenced the science of poetic language up until our own century, while even his immediate successors took up again the theses of the primitive, nonarticulated, gestural, or deaf-and-dumb language; the influence of natural conditions on the formation of languages; different types of language (such as poetic language), etc. The eighteenth century, however, examined these problems with a positive rigor that broke away from Vico's novelistic style.

Indeed, the study of language did not escape the spirit of classification and systematization that invaded the sciences of that century. *Geometry* seems to be the model upon which the other sciences were tempted to mold themselves. "The order, clarity, precision, and exactness that have reigned in good books for some time now could well have had their first source in the geometric spirit that was becoming more widespread than ever" (R. Mousnier, *Histoire générale des civilisations,* 4:331). Buffier the grammarian wrote that all sciences including grammar "are likely to have demonstrations that are as evident as those of geometry."

The first effect of this geometric process in the realm of language was the tendency toward a systematization of the multiplicity of known languages. The philosophers proposed classifications of languages, all the while trying to bring all these various types back to one original, common, universal, and therefore "natural" language. Leibniz, in his *Brevis designatio meditationem de originibus dictus potissimum ex indicium linguarum* (1710), divided the known languages into two groups: *Semitic* and *Indo-Germanic;* the latter was composed of Italian, Celtic, and Germanic languages on the one hand, and Slavic and Greek languages on the other. The original language, which Leibniz called *lingua adamica,* was supposed to be at the root of this diversity, and that state of human speech could be found again by creating an artificial, purely rational language.

In England, James Harris published *Hermes or a Philosophical Inquiry Concerning Universal Grammar* (1751), a work that tried to establish the universal and rational principles of a general grammar that would apply to all languages. The ideas of Berkeley, Shaftesbury, etc., were at the root of such logical temptations.

Language appeared to be an operational system, a mechanics whose rules could be studied like those of any physical object. President De Brosse published his *Traité de la formation mécanique des langues et des principes de l'étymologie* (1765), in which *la langue* was presented as a system of formal elements, susceptible to change under the influence of geographical conditions. The term "mechanical" became frequent in linguistic description. Abbot Pluche, the author of a scholastic grammar, entitled his book *La Mécanique des langues* (1751), while Nicolas Beauzée (1717–1789) defined the term "structure" in the same way: "Now, I ask you: isn't this word *structure* rigorously related to the mechanism of languages, and doesn't it signify the artificial arrangement of words authorized in each language in order to attain the goal proposed by it, which is the enunciation of thought? Aren't idioms born as well from the mechanism proper to each language?" (Article "Inversion" in *L'Encyclopédie*.)

The study of the mechanisms of languages enabled the elaboration of the comparisons and typologies that prefigured the comparativism of the nineteenth century. Resemblances in the mechanism of various languages were established; this constituted the proof for the thesis of the *common nature* of languages, which, in its *evolution,* had been clothed in multiple expressions. One can see how the principle of a *natural language,* when confronted with the multiplicity of real languages, was able to become the principle of a *common language* from which the others would have developed, and therefore inevitably led to an evolutionist theory of language. The first seeds of this comparativism can be found in the 1767 report by Father Coeurdoux, a missionary at Pondichery, in which he noted the analogies between Sanskrit, Greek, and Latin. Before him, the Dutchman Lambert Ten Kate had published in 1710 a study in which he established the kinship of the Germanic languages. William Jones (1746–1794) inaugurated future comparative linguistics in an undoubtedly decisive fashion when he noticed the correspondences among Sanskrit, Persian, Greek, Latin, Gothic, and Celtic.

However, it was sensationalist and empiricist philosophy that furnished the theoretical foundation on which the grammatical description of the century was built. Locke (1632–1704) and Leibniz, and in

France the "Ideologues" with Condillac (1715–1780) at their head, proposed the *theory of the sign* as the general principle of this common language that had manifested itself in several concrete languages. They revived and transformed in this way theories of the sign from Greece, the Middle Ages, and Cartesian logic. While, for the philosophers of the eighteenth century, thinking was an articulation of signs that were linguistic elements, the problem was to define the *path* that led from *sensation* to the linguistic *sign*.

According to Locke, words were "the marks of the ideas in the minds also of other men, with whom they communicate."[3] They did not for that reason lack a relation to "the reality of things." Locke was categorical about this: the *sign* was not to be obstructed by the relation it might have with reality. "It is perverting the use of words, and brings unavoidable obscurity and confusion into their signification, whenever we make them stand for anything but those ideas we have in our own mind" [p. 11]. The Saussurian definition of the sign (see chapter 1) was being sketched out by Locke when he posited the arbitrary relation between what were later called the "referent" and the "signifier/signified": "Words signify only men's peculiar ideas, and *that by a perfect arbitrary imposition . . ."* [p. 12]. It should be noted that while Locke considered words as signs and studied their diversity (general terms, names of simple ideas, names of mixed modes, etc.), he did not stop with them, but instead considered the *entire* discourse as a *construction,* and envisaged the role of *particles,* for example, as connecting ideas among themselves, in order to show their relation, and to serve as signs of an "action of the mind." It was on the basis of such a "constructivist" conception of the operation of language that grammar was able to elaborate a syntactic approach to *la langue.*

In his *New Essays Concerning Human Understanding*[4] (1765), Leibniz took up Locke's ideas and developed them. Words (book 3), for him "are used to represent and even to explain ideas." While he considered that all languages, no matter how different they were materially, developed on the same *formal* basis, that is, there was one "signification common to different languages," Leibniz did not neglect the *signifying* specificity of every language, or its particular material organization. Thus he wrote:

Philalethes—Men often apply their thoughts more to words than to things, and because they have learned most of the words before becoming acquainted with the ideas they signify, not only children, but grown-up men often speak like parrots. But men ordinarily mean to indicate their own thoughts, and further they attribute to words a secret relation to the ideas of another and to things themselves. For if the sounds were attached to another idea by the one with whom we are conversing, it would be necessary to speak two languages. It is true that one does not stop too much to examine what the ideas of others are, and our idea is supposed to be that which the common people and the scholars of the country attach to the same word. This is particularly the case as regards simple ideas and modes; but as regards substances the belief is more particularly that words signify also the reality of things.

Theophilus—Substances and modes are equally represented by ideas; and things, as well as ideas, in both cases are indicated by words; thus, I see but little difference, save that ideas of substances and of sensible qualities are more fixed. For the rest, it sometimes happens that our ideas and thoughts are the matter of our discourse and constitute the thing itself which we desire to signify, and that reflective notions enter more than we think into those of things. We speak, indeed, sometimes of words in a material way, without in this case being able to substitute with precision in the place of the word its signification or its relation to the ideas or things. This occurs not only in speaking as a grammarian, but also in speaking as a lexicographer, in giving the explanation of the term. [pp. 305–6]

One can see how the notion of metalanguage—language about language—was emerging in these Leibnizian reflections.

Evoking Locke, Condillac supposed that the first humans, using cries that had become signs of passions, first created "naturally the *action* language." "Meanwhile, these men, having acquired the habit of linking some ideas to arbitrary signs, used natural cries as the model for making a new language. They articulated several new sounds; and by repeating them several times, and accompanying them with some gesture that indicated the objects they wanted to point out, they became accustomed to giving names to things. The early progress of this language was slow" (*Essai sur l'origine des connaissances humaines, ouvrage où l'on réduit à un seul principe tout ce qui concerne l'entendement humain,* 1746–1754). A narrative was created in this way, an evolutionist fable that was to be the ideological foundation of the theory of linguistic signs and of their development through various ages and peoples. "There was therefore a time when conversation was maintained by discourse intermingled with words and actions. Usage and custom, just as has happened with most of the other things in life, then changed what had been due to necessity into an ornament: but the practice lasted for a long time after the necessity ceased; this was particularly true for the Orientals, whose character was naturally adapted to a form of conversation that exercised their vivaciousness so well through movement, and satisfied it to such an extent for a perpetual representation of perceptible images" (*Essai sur les hiéroglyphes,* secs. 8 and 9). Condillac considered nonverbal forms of expression and communication as languages, such as *dance,* for example, or gestural language in general, or *song,* thus heralding the modern science of signifying systems, *semiology. Poetry* was also a type of language for Condillac; it imitated action language: "While, in the origin of languages, prosody approached the song, style, in order to copy the perceptible images of action language, adopted all kinds of figures and metaphors, and was a true painting." Condillac insisted nevertheless on the fact that it was the *language of sounds* that had had the most favorable development in order to be able to "perfect itself and finally become the most convenient of all." He studied *composition,* that is, the character of words as different parts of speech, as well as *order,* combination, before concluding in the chapter "Du génie des langues" that every people that had a specific character, determined by climate and government, also had a specific language. "Everything confirms, therefore, that every language expresses the character of the people who speak it." In this way, the principle of the *diversity* of languages and their *evolution* was posited, both relying upon one and the same foundation, signs. Grammar tackled this theoretical model and gave it a minutely detailed description that was also its confirmation. Indeed, we can read in *Principes généraux de Grammaire:* "Just as organization, even though it is the same at the core, is likely to exhibit many varieties depending upon the climate, and even though needs vary in the same way, there is no doubt that men, thrown by nature into different circumstances, embarked upon routes that deviated from one other."

The theory put forward by Condillac on the universal and natural sign, whose variations in different languages were supposedly due to natural and social conditions, had the great merit of offering itself, in a fictional form (that he was aware of), as the ideology of the linguistic description later furnished by grammarians:

> Perhaps this entire story/history will be seen as a novel: but at least one cannot deny it its likelihood. It is hard for me to believe that the method I have used has often caused me to be mistaken: for my object has been to advance nothing except with the supposition that a language has always been imagined on the model of the one immediately preceding it. I saw in action language the seed of Languages and of all the Arts that can be used to express thought; I observed the circumstances suitable to the development of this seed; and not only have I seen the birth of these arts, but I have also followed their progress, and I have explained their different characters. In a word, I have, it seems to me, demonstrated in an appreciable way that the things that seem the oddest to us now were the most natural in their time, and that only what should have happened has happened.

This postulate of the natural necessity of everything, including languages and their development, was orchestrated by Condillac's Ideologue successors. From this point of view, Destutt de Tracy proposed in his *Eléments d'idéologie* (1801–1815) a theory of languages as systems of signs. "All types of knowledge we have are ideas; these ideas only appear to us dressed in signs," he wrote. Using this as his starting point, he considered grammar "the science of signs. . . . But I would prefer people to say, and I wish it had always been said, that it is the continuation of the science of ideas." Not limiting himself to verbal language, Tracy noted that "every system of signs is a language: let us add at this point that every use of a language, every emission of signs is discourse; and let us make of our Grammar an analysis of every type of discourse." Let us point out the universalistic process of such an "ideological" semiotics, which aimed at arranging every discourse in the common rules of ideas: we can see a certain modern tendency of semiotics being heralded here. On the one hand, in the syntactic spirit of eighteenth-century grammar, Tracy noted that "our signs not only have the value proper to each one of them; to this is added a value resulting from the place they occupy." The Ideologues' concern was obvious: the plurality of languages constantly confirmed by grammatical observation had to be historically and logically justified. The postulate of a logical origin necessarily and implicitly found under each of these variables had to be developed. Condillac maintained that the *original* language named what was directly given to the senses: first *things,* then *operations;* first "fruit," then "to want," and lastly "Peter." Latin was the example of this type of language. Next came the analytical languages, which began sentences with the subject and ended them with what one wanted to say about this subject. Evolution and change were likely with both these categories of language for two reasons: climate and government. The idea that social conditions influenced the character of a language seems to be creeping in here, but Condillac exalted the role of the inspired individual much more than that of the social organism. His theory was, nonetheless, materialistic. For, while *la langue* was a rigorous system of signs, which Condillac did not hesitate to compare with mathematical signs (and, in this sense, he considered extreme rigor the condition for the survival and future of a given language), it was not an ideal abstraction given once and for all. It was doubly rooted in the real: first because it was sensations that gave form to the linguistic sign, and next because the development of our sensations and knowledge later influenced the perfection of *la langue* itself. The realism and historicism founded on the perception of the subject-seat of the idea were joined in Condillac's conception. "First, therefore, it is necessary to place oneself in perceptible circumstances in order to make signs that express the first ideas, which one would then acquire by sensation and reflection; and upon reflecting on these, new ones would be acquired, and new names would be made whose meaning would be determined by placing others in the circumstances one would have found oneself in, and by having them make the same reflections one would have made. That way expressions would always succeed ideas: they would be clear and concise, because they would produce only what everyone has experienced with his senses." Therefore, with his *perception* the *subject* produced the *idea,* which he expressed in *language:* the development and perfection of this process was the *history* of knowledge.

One of the major works that came in the wake of Condillac's ideas was the book by Court de Gébelin, *Le Monde primitif analysé et comparé avec le monde moderne* (1774–1782).

This conception of language, which can be defined as a rational and deterministic sensationalism, was opposed by the theories of Jean-Jacques Rousseau (1712–1778) in his *Essai sur l'origine des langues où il est parlé de la mélodie et de l'imitation musicale* (written in 1756, published in 1781). It is true that Rousseau attributed the properties common to all languages to the fact that they played a social role, while their diversity was supposedly due to the difference in the natural conditions in which they were produced: "Speech, since it was the first social institution, owes its form only to natural causes." However, for Rousseau, what was common to languages was not a *principle of reason* but the *personal needs of subjects.* Opposed to the principle that reason molded the core of every language, as well as to Condillac's thesis that needs formed language, Rousseau declared that "the first invention of speech did not come from needs, it came from passions." "The language of the first men was made out to be the languages of geometers, and we (can) see that it was the language of poets. . . ." ". . . The origin of languages was not due to men's first needs; it would be absurd if from the cause that separated them came the means that united them. Where then can this origin have come from? From moral needs, from passions. All the passions bring together men who were forced into fleeing from one another by the need to search for their means of existence. It was neither hunger, nor thirst, but love, hate, pity, and anger that dragged the first cries out of them . . . and this is why the first languages were songlike and passionate, before becoming simple and methodical. . . ."

It was in the work of Denis Diderot (1713–1784), the man who inspired the *Encyclopédie,* that we find a materialistic conception of language; no doubt it influenced the scientific work of the grammarians of the Encyclopedic era. Diderot took up the major themes developed by the Sensationalists and Ideologues: the sign and its relation to the idea and perceptible reality; the types of language in history; the development of language; alphabetism and hieroglyphy; types of signifying systems that were like languages (the arts: poetry, painting, music), etc. He definitively and resolutely placed the rough drafts of the Ideologues and Sensationalists on a rigorously materialist base, by proposing one of the first modern materialistic syntheses dealing with the theory of knowledge, and consequently, of linguistic operation.

Diderot insisted upon the role of "sensible objects" in the formation of language. "Objects that strike the senses are those that are first noticed, and those which unite various qualities which strike the senses are named first, *i.e.* the different objects of which the world is composed. Then the various qualities are distinguished and named, and these form most of our adjectives. Afterwards, these sensible qualities being put aside, some common quality was observed in various objects, such as impenetrability, extension, color, shape, etc., and from these abstract and general names were formed and nearly all substantives. Gradually men became accustomed to think that all these names represented real things; and the sensible qualities were regarded as mere accidents. . . ."[5] Diderot countered the process of ideal abstraction with the thesis that thinking was far from autonomous with respect to *la langue:* "Thoughts, I know not by what contrivance, enter our mind very much in the form in which they appear in speech when they are tricked [dressed] up . . ." [p. 166]. In order to grasp the true mechanism of language while eliminating the grammatical presuppositions bequeathed to him by the study of modern or classical languages, Diderot proposed to examine the gestural discourse of the deaf and dumb with respect to the same message transmitted in verbal language. He ended up establishing the validity of the order of words in the French language—its natural logic—and concluded that it had "an advantage over ancient languages."

Finally, let us point out Diderot's inspired intuition to consider systems of the arts as sign systems, by advocating that it was necessary to study the particularity of each of these sign systems (in music, in painting, in poetry): "The painter shows the thing itself; the expressions of the Musician and the Poet are nothing but hieroglyphs."[6] This theory of certain signifying systems as *hieroglyphic systems,* which has acquired new weight since Freud's work (see chapter 20), was already indicated by Diderot: "Wherever a Western hieroglyph occurs—whether in a line of poetry or on an obelisk, whether in a work of imagination or of mystery—it requires either imagination or an uncommon wisdom to understand it. ... Every imitative art has its own particular hieroglyphs, and one day I would really like to see some informed and delicate mind take on the job of comparing them."

The other Encyclopedists, following Diderot, could not fail to attach great importance to the problems of language. Turgot the economist wrote the "Etymologie" article in volume 6 of the *Encyclopédie* (1756). Voltaire (1694–1775) himself was interested in grammar; in his *Commentaires sur le théâtre de Corneille* (1764), he established or rather defended several grammatical rules, which were eventually accepted because of his authority: I believe + infinitive; I do not believe + subjunctive; do you believe + indicative or subjunctive, according to the meaning, etc. Voltaire worked on the *Dictionnaire de l'Académie* and projected a collective work to be called the *Encyclopédie grammaticale.* His linguistic remarks (collected mainly in his commentaries on the theater of Corneille) reveal a logical mind that considered the just and natural linguistic order to be the analytical order, in accordance with "the natural logic all well-organized men are born with." In fact, no language "could attain an absolutely regular plan, given that none could be formed by a group of logicians"; but "the least imperfect ones are like laws: the best laws are the least arbitrary ones" (*Dictionnaire philosophique,* "Langues" article).

These specifically linguistic theories prolonged and transformed the conceptions of Port-Royal. The radical change consisted of an orientation toward specifically linguistic expression, hereafter clearly distinguished from the logical content. Father Buffier in his *Remarques* (published in *Mémoires de Trévoux,* October 1706) emphasized that "when it comes to language, it is the expression itself one is looking for, much more than the reason for the expression." Languages had a specificity that should not be confused, even if they had a common logical core: "For the arrangement of sentences and the turn of expressions, which constitute the proper characteristics of a language, French is as different from Latin as from any other possible language, and particularly from German" (*Grammaire française sur un plan nouveau,* 1709). Nevertheless, reason had to take hold of all these various linguistic facts and organize them in a system: "What is considered by Philosophy is found in essentially all of them [languages], by seeing them as the natural expression of our thoughts; for just as nature put a necessary order in our thoughts, she put, as an infallible consequence, a necessary order in languages." Buffier's project was therefore what Ramus' had been in the *General Grammar:* logical analysis as a method of systematizing disparate linguistic data.

Buffier's *Théorie de la proposition* was compatible with the theory of the Solitaries, and completed it by first distinguishing types of sentences: "complete, those with a noun and a verb in their proper function," and "incomplete, those in which the noun and the verb are used only to form a kind of noun, composed of several words, without affirming anything, and which can be expressed by a single word" (an example is "that which is true"). Moreover, Buffier's grammar described the construction of the clause in greater detail. Nouns and verbs were given several *modifiers;* the diversity of the modifiers was specified, but they expressed one and the same relation of *complementation:* "We have reserved the term *modifiers* for words that have no other use than to indicate the circumstances of the noun and the verb." The modifying elements related to the verb could be *absolute* (they particularized the action of the verb) or *respective* (with respect to which the verb's action occurs). For example, *Vanity must be sacrificed* (absolute) *to repose* (respective). *Circumstantial modifiers,* which marked the circumstance, were added.

For its part, the work of Du Marsais, *Méthode raisonnée pour apprendre la langue latine* (1722), heralded teaching principles that contributed to the change produced by grammarians like Buffier and thus prepared the way for the *Grammaire* of the *Encyclopédie.* These pedagogical principles consisted of a *dialectic* of the principles *ratio* and *usage,* that is, of logical rules and strictly linguistic observation, as well as of philosophical and formal analyses. This allowed the grammarian to discern, from the grammatical categories inherited from Latin, *relations* between linguistic *terms.* Thus Du Marsais wrote: "One puts into the dative the word that signifies the person or thing to which one gives or attributes something; this is the case of attribution, and that is why it is called the dative case, from the verb *dare*, to give: *date quietem senectuti.* One thus puts in this case words considered to be in relations similar to those of giving, and even taking away: as in the relation of the end, *finis cui.* Usage and examples teach this."

After the grammar of Abbot Fremy, *Essay d'une nouvelle méthode pour l'explication des auteurs* (1722), and under the growing influence of Descartes, on the one hand, but also of Locke and the Sensationalists, on the other, the teaching of French was allowed in university courses, as demonstrated by the *Traité des études*, "De l'étude de la langue française, de la manière dont on peut expliquer les auteurs français" by Charles Rollin (1726–1728). From then on, the need became even more urgent to find a new and specific *metalanguage* that could take into account the particularities in the relations in modern languages, without abandoning the realm of universal relations, or that of *la langue.* The *Principes généraux et raisonnés de la langue françoise* (1730) by Pierre Restaut considered it important to demonstrate the necessity of this junction between the principles of reasoning and the empirical knowledge of linguistic relations (engraved in memory): "Reasoning alone is not enough for the study of a language. Memory must also be loaded and filled with a large number of different words and combinations, whose knowledge can be acquired only by continual exercise, and cannot be part of the spring of any mechanism."

Restaut had the brilliant idea of connecting in the same analysis the terms *subject* and *object,* which had already been used separately before him, in order to design in this way a more complete skeleton of sentence construction. The criteria that presided over the definition of these terms remained semantic: "One still calls *subject,* as we have said, the nominative of a verb, such as it may be. The *object* is the thing at which an intellectual action or an action produced by the soul ends, as when I say: *I love God.*" But Restaut added: "When an action is perceptible, and produces a perceptible effect, the thing at which it ends is also called a subject. Consequently in these sentences: *I tore my book; Cain killed Abel; my book* and *Abel* are the subjects at which the actions of tearing and killing end, and one cannot say that they are the objects of these actions." Situating himself in the schema of formal grammars, Restaut gave semantic correspondences for each form: for instance, the genitive "marks the relation of one thing that belongs to another by production, or by use/possession, or by any other manner." Finally, in place of formalist procedures of substitution, Restaut isolated a *relation* designated by an interrogative pronoun, and possibly preceded by a preposition: "To find the object of an active verb, one asks the question *what* or *who* after the verb or preposition"; for the indirect objects one "asks *from what, from whom, to what,* or *to whom.*" This is exactly the kind of analysis that still goes on in traditional grammar teaching.

Starting from 1750, the activity of formalizing the French language revolved around the *Encyclopédie:* first with Du Marsais, then, after his death in 1756, with Douchet and Beauzée. The dominant idea was, of course, that of a natural language: every language possessed a natural order, *ordo naturalis,* when it approached the models of thinking. Du Marsais wrote: "Everything is in the natural order, an order that conforms to our manner of conceiving [of things] by means of speech, and to the habit we naturally acquired in childhood, when we learned our natural language or some other one; an order finally that must have been utmost in Cicero's mind when he began his letter with *raras tuas {Raras tuas quidem, frotasse enim non perferuntur, sed suaves accipio litteras},* for how could he have given these two words the feminine-gender ending, if he didn't have *litteras* in mind? And why would he have given them the accusative ending if he didn't want to make known that the words were related to *I just this minute got one of your letters: you write to me so rarely, but they always give me an appreciable pleasure?*" To find this natural order, covered over by the later concern for elegance and rhetoric, the grammarian had to "perform the anatomy of sentences," Du Marsais said.

With a similar aim, the observation of the diversity of languages and their reduction to the natural order, Abbot Girard (*Les Vrais principes de la langue française ou la parole réduite en méthode conformément aux lois de l'usage,* 1747) established a typology of languages according to the type of *clause construction.* Even if every language had its proper genius, the abbot said, "languages can nevertheless be reduced to three types." In first place were *analytical* languages (which obeyed the natural order): French, Italian, and Spanish. "In these languages, the acting subject comes first, followed by the action accompanied by its modifications, and then what makes up the object and the term." In second place came *transpositive* languages (which did not follow the natural order) such as Latin, Old Church Slavonic, or Old Russian; these "put at the beginning sometimes the object, sometimes the action, sometimes the modification and the circumstance." In third place were *mixed* or *amphibiological* languages, such as Greek and Old German. As can be seen, this typology was founded on a syntactic analysis that became the outstanding phenomenon of the linguistic thinking of the second half of the century.

The components of the clause were still defined in a semantic manner, and by the relations of the elements. The clause was with the help of the preposition a *system of complementation,* and no longer a function defined in logical terms. The preposition "consisted of an indication of determinative relation, by means of which one thing affected another. The preposition always announced the thing that affects, called the complement of the relation, and it is for this reason that the preposition has this thing as its object." Clauses were "incomplete, limiting themselves to Subjective and Attributive, the essential members," or "complete, those which, besides Subjective and Attributive, also had the three following, Objective, Terminative, and Circumstantial. . . ." Here then is the complete table of the syntax of the clause with its seven parts "which can be accepted into the structure of the sentence, to make of it the picture of thought. I find that first a subject is needed and an attribution for this subject; without these one says nothing. I see then that the attribution can have, besides its subject, an object, a term, a modifying circumstance, a connection with another one; merely to be a means of support for one of these things, or express a movement of sensitivity that occurred in the soul of the one speaking."

Du Marsais went on to use this admirable synthesis of Abbot Girard, who had known to join Port-Royal and formalistic grammars, in order to isolate an analysis of the functions and forms that are expressed. Chevalier has remarked that Girard's innovation consisted of introducing more logical rigor in order to clarify the content of the term *complement* and establish the difference between *agreement* and *government {régime}.* Du Marsais developed his theories on the origin of language, its character as a *sign,* and its dependence on climate, theories he had inherited from the Ideologues, in his *Fragments sur les causes de la parole,* as well as in his *Logique* (the posthumous edition). He revealed his ideas about the organization of the clause for the most part in the chapter "De la construction grammaticale" of his *Principes de grammaire* and in the article "Construction" in the *Encyclopédie.* He distinguished two levels of analysis, a grammatical and a logical one: "When one considers a grammatical clause, one pays attention only to the reciprocal relations that exist among the words; whereas in the logical clause, one pays attention only to the total meaning that results from the collection of words." Grammar was to deal with the "arrangement of words in discourse" and syntax the constant laws of these arrangements, not by closing itself up in the narrow frameworks of logical affirmation but by considering every affirmative or negative utterance as well as the enunciation of "certain views of the mind."

The true pivot of syntax became the nature of the *complement,* which was isolated through and with the help of the identity/determination distinction. The relation of identity dealt with the name and the adjective. The relation of determination "regulated the construction of words." "A word must be followed by one or more determiner-words every time that it, by itself, composes only one part of the analysis of a particular meaning; the mind then finds itself forced to wait and ask for the determiner-word in order to know the particular meaning, which the first word announced only in part." Here is a precise example of this notion of determiner-object: "Someone tells me that the king *gave.* The word *gave* is only part of the particular meaning; the mind is not satisfied, it isn't moved. One expects or one asks (1) What did the king give? (2) To whom did he give? One answers the first question, for example, with *The king gave a regiment;* now the mind is satisfied with respect to the thing given: *regiment* is in this respect the determiner of *gave.* Next one asks, *To whom did the king give the regiment?* One answers, *To Mister N.* . . . Thus the preposition *to,* followed by the name that determines it, forms a partial meaning that is the determiner of *gave* with respect to the person *to whom."*

Once this analysis of the relations of the parts of speech had been done, declension, which had long been carried on using the Latin model, definitively disappeared. *Prepositions* were given the task of articulating relations in the sentence, and there was no need for formal marks corresponding to the six cases. "For example, the proposition *for/in order to* indicates a motive, an end, a reason; but then the object that is the term of this motive must be uttered, and that is what is called the *complement of the preposition*. For example, in *He works for the country, country* is the complement of *for. . . ."*

While we have been able to follow here the elaboration of the syntactic concept of the *complement* in Du Marsais, one would search in vain for a grammatical theory in the article "Complément" in the *Encyclopédie*. Beauzée noted later, in the article "Régime," that in the article "Gouverner" it was only insinuated that "the name complement should be given to what is called government *{régime}*" and that "these two words should not be confused as synonyms; I am going to determine the precise notion of each of these in two separate articles; and by doing that I will replace the article 'Complément,' which M. Du Marsais omitted, even though he frequently used the term." The history of linguistics nevertheless considers Du Marsais the inventor of this analysis; Thurot clearly stated it in his Introduction to Harris' *Hermes:* "Du Marsais is, I believe, the first to have considered these words from this point of view."

De Wailly's *Grammaire françoise* (1754) was followed by Beauzée's *Grammaire générale* (1767), which developed and detailed the analysis of complements. The descriptions wandered from logicism to semanticism or went back to Aristotelian categories, but the framework of the syntactic study was fixed and has remained so for scholastic grammarians up to the present. The bourgeoisie had succeeded in forging a sure ideological weapon for itself: it surrounded language with the logical framework classicism had bequeathed it, while granting it suppleness and relative autonomy when it turned the analysis slightly toward linguistic "facts." Universalism and empiricism, interpenetrating one another, modeled this conception of sentence construction that the grammar of the eighteenth century had been able to elaborate on the foundation of a "natural" conception of language. In closing, let us quote from the article "Langage" in the *Encyclopédie*, which condensed in its ideological form what grammarians had done on the level of "scientific" description:

> Article III. *Analysis & comparison* of languages. All *languages* have the same aim, which is the enunciation of thoughts. To arrive at this, they all use the same instrument, which is the

voice: it is like the body and soul of language; now there are, up to a certain point, *languages* considered in this way, just as there are men who speak them.

All human souls, if one believes the Cartesian school, are of the same type and nature; they have the same faculties to the same degree, the seed of the same talents, the same mind, the same genius, and between them there are only numerical and individual differences. The differences between souls that one can note in what follows are due to external causes: to the intimate organization of the bodies they animate; to the various temperaments established there by circumstances; to occasions that are more or less frequent, more or less favorable for exciting ideas in them, for bringing them together, for combining and developing them; to more or less fortunate prejudices received from education, customs, religion, political government, domestic, civil, and national contracts, etc.

About the same is still true of human bodies. They were formed in the same way, and when one considers the principal traits of the face, it appears so to speak to have been cast in the same mold: nevertheless, it has perhaps not yet happened that one man has had a very exact bodily resemblance to another. No matter what physical connection exists from one man to another, as soon as there is a diversity of individuals, there are more or less perceptible facial differences, besides those that are inside the machine—these differences are more marked as the causes converging on the same effects diminish. In this way all the subjects of the same nation have among themselves individual differences from the traits of the national resemblance. The national resemblance of one people is not the same as that of a neighboring people, even if there are characteristics of approximation between the two: these characteristics grow weaker and the differential features increase as the terms of comparison draw apart, until the very great diversity of climates and the other causes that more or less depend on that only allow to persist features of specific resemblance in the differences between Blacks and Whites, Laplanders and southern Europeans.

Let us likewise distinguish the mind & body in *languages:* the common object languages propose to themselves, & the universal instrument they use to express it, in a word, the thoughts & the articulated sounds of the voice. We will sort out what in all this they necessarily have in common, & what is specifically theirs under each of these two points of view, & we will put ourselves in a position to establish reasonable principles about the generation of *languages,* about their mixture, their affinity, & their respective merit.

The human mind ... manages to distinguish parts in its thought, even though this thought is indivisible, by separating, with the help of abstraction, the different ideas that constitute the object & the various relations they have among themselves, because of the relation they all have to the indivisible thought in which they are envisaged. This analysis, whose principles are due to the nature of the human mind, which is the same everywhere, must show the same results everywhere, or at least similar results; it must cause ideas to be envisaged in the same way & establish in words the same classification.

Here therefore is what is found universally in the mind of all *languages:* the analytical succession of partial ideas that constitute the same thought, & the same types of words to represent the partial ideas envisaged with the same aspects. But they allow all the differences, on these two general objects, that come from the genius of the peoples who speak them & and which themselves make up both the principal characteristic of the genius of these *languages,* and the principal sources of the difficulties that arise when translating exactly from one to another.

1. With respect to analytical order, there are two means by which it can be rendered perceptible in the vocal enunciation of the thought. The first is to arrange the words in the articulation according to the same order that results from the analytical succession of partial ideas; the second is to give to words that can be declined the inflections or endings relative to the analytical order, & then to regulate the arrangement in the

articulation by other principles capable of adding some perfection to the art of speech. From this comes the most universal division of *languages* into two general types, which Abbot Girard (*Princ. disc.* 1:23) has called *analogues* and *transpositives,* and for which I'll keep the same names because they seem to me to characterize very well the distinctive genius.

Analogous languages are those whose syntax is submitted to analytical order, because the succession of words in discourse in these languages follows the analytical gradation of ideas; the functioning of these *languages* is actually analogous and in a way parallel to that of the mind itself, whose operations it follows step by step.

Transpositive languages are those in which the articulation gives words endings related to the analytical order & which acquire in this way the right to make them follow in discourse a functioning that is free and completely independent of the natural succession of ideas. French, Italian, Spanish, etc., are *analogous* languages; Greek, Latin, German, etc., are *transpositive* languages.

A fairly natural question presents itself here. The analytical order and the transpositive order of words presuppose completely different views in *languages* that have adopted them in order to regulate their syntax: each one of these orders characterizes a completely different genius. But since there was at first only one language on earth, is it possible to determine what type it was, and whether it was analogous or transpositive?

Since the analytical order is the invariable prototype of the two general types of languages, & the unique foundation of their respective communicability, it seems fairly natural for the first *language* to have scrupulously attached itself to analytical order & that this *language* subjected the succession of words to that order. . . .

— 18 —

LANGUAGE AS HISTORY

The end of the eighteenth century marked a change that manifested itself in ideology as well as in philosophy and the sciences that developed in the nineteenth century. The description of *mechanisms* (including that of *la langue*) and the *systematization* of types (including those of various languages) were succeeded by an evolutionist, *historical* conception. One was no longer content with formulating the operational rules or correspondences between the wholes being studied: they were taken in in a single glance that arranged them in an ascending line. *Historicism* became the fundamental mark of thinking in the nineteenth century, and the science of language did not escape from it. Where did it come from?

It is generally admitted that Herder's book *Outlines of a Philosophy of the History of Man* (1784–1791) was the first global formulation of historicism. In it Herder proposed constructing "a philosophy and science of what concerns us most nearly, the history of mankind at large."[1] Among the motives that made him designate the realm of the "human" as an object of science, Herder cited the progress of physics, the formation of natural history (to make an anthropological map of the world, on the level of the one with which Zimmerman had enriched zoology), but first "metaphysics and morals," "and lastly religion above all the rest" [p. vii]. The fact that this admission by Herder was not a coincidence but the true ideological foundation of his historicism was demonstrated by his commentators. In Edgar Quinet's introduction to the French edition of *Outlines of a Philosophy of the History of Man* (1827), the reader can clearly grasp that Herder's course was a transcendental reaction to the radical social changes experienced by the eighteenth century: the collapse of empires, and the transformation of states under the influence of the revolution. "Thinking no longer relied upon each of them in isolation. To fill the void, they were added on to each other; one took them in in a single glance. Individuals no longer succeeded one another, but instead one squeezed collective beings into tight spheres. Then seeing that that also served only to indicate nothingness one applied oneself to looking to see if there wasn't, at the heart of this instability, a permanent idea, a fixed principle around which the accidents of civilizations succeeded each other in an eternal order. . . ." The near-collapse of social structures placed thinking in front of the vertigo of nothingness, of the void that it strove to fill: "For the rest, if this philosophy of history should ever become a resource in either public or private distress . . ." *(ibid.).* The historicism of the permanent idea, of the fixed principle of evolution, became the coup de force with which idealism reacted to the materialism of the French revolution. Its task was to efface the void in which idealistic thought found itself, uprooted from its refuges by the gap that the revolution had created in the static universe of "natural logic." Historicism gave its *reason* for the *rupture* in order to find continuity after division. Herder (1744–1803) formulated its principles, the precursors of the Hegelian dialectic: "The general composition [series] of Powers and Forms is neither retrograde nor stationary, but progressive" [p. 114]. *Organization* is only "their [the forms'] conductor to a higher state" [p. 114]. "Every demolition is but a passage to a higher sphere of life" [p. 115].

But where could one find the *reason* or the *logic* that would explain the revolutionary and materialist rupture by using it in the fixed, reassuring principle of evolution? It could be found where logic is produced, where one finds it when one wants to prove it: *in language.*

While the grammarians of Port-Royal had demonstrated that language obeyed the principles of the logic of judgment, and while the Encyclopedists wanted to see in it the logic of perceptible nature and the confirmation of the influence of material circumstances (climate, government), the nineteenth century wanted to demonstrate that language itself also had an evolution, so that on this evolution they could base the principle of the evolution of the idea and of society.

Evolutionist ideology found in the discovery of Sanskrit and in the kinship of the Indo-European languages the linguistic corollary indispensable to its own establishment. Society was then conceived of using the model of language, which was seen as an evolving line; or, even better, the model used was that of *phonetic evolution,* that is, the change in the signifying form, detached from its signified content. This admirable juncture of the Idea and the Voice in evolution, which had been disjoined by Plato, was found again in Friedrich Hegel (1770–1831), where they confirmed each other. Evolutionism went so far as to borrow *linguistic terms* to "clarify" the operations suspended in the nonachievement of a failed act, interrupted in "eternal time." Quinet thus spoke of a "harmony of the Ages": "Every people that falls into the abyss is an accent of its voice; every city is itself only an interrupted word, a broken image, an unfinished verse of the eternal poem that time is charged with unfolding. Can you hear the immense discourse that runs on and grows with the centuries, and which, always taken up again and always left hanging, leaves each generation unsure about the way of speech that is to follow? It has, like human discourse, its circumlocutions, its angry exclamations, its movements, and its repose. . . ."

Comparative linguistics and *historical linguistics* were born and developed on this ideological core. These types of linguistics drew upon the general principles of Romanticism and German evolutionism, but also acquired autonomy from them; they were able to develop as an objective science, independent of the ideological exploitation of objective science that would later occur. They used Romantic thinking to react against what Bréal later called "the somewhat naked simplicity, the somewhat dry abstraction of our Encyclopedists of the eighteenth century." The linguistics of the nineteenth century replaced the syntactic ordering of the eighteenth-century grammarians with a *genealogical* vision of languages. Languages were grouped into families by deriving each member from an initial source.

In this work, the linguistics of the nineteenth century used above all the discovery, made by the linguists of the previous century, of Sanskrit and its kinships with certain European languages. For the knowledge of Persia and India attracted the attention of scholars. An "Asiatic Society" was formed at Calcutta that published works on the Indian language. Remember that in 1767 Father Coeurdoux had sent a paper entitled "Question proposed to Abbot Barthélémy and the other members of the Academy of Belles-Lettres and Inscriptions: how is it that in the Sanskrit language there are a large number of words that this language has in common with Latin and Greek, but especially with Latin?" The Academy left this essential question about linguistic kinship unanswered.

In the meantime, the translation of Indian literary texts was progressing. William Jones translated *Shakuntala,* and noticed in 1786 a kinship between Sanskrit, Greek, and Latin "that cannot be attributed to coincidence."

In the atmosphere of this growing interest in India, its language, and the relations between it and other European languages, a circle of Sanskritists was organized in Paris at the beginning of the nineteenth century, with the participation of A. Hamilton, a member of the Calcutta Society, of Father Pons, of F. Schlegel, of the Indianist Chézy, of Langlès, of Fauriel, of the Arabist Sacy, and later of August Wilhelm von Schlegel. Adelung published *Mithridate* (1808), the first global compendium of the knowledge about numerous languages.

Moreover, the teaching of Leibniz and Mercier, which had proclaimed the necessity and possibility of making a science out of grammar, joined with the historical interest to give birth to *historical, linguistic science.*

It was India, however, that excited the enthusiasm of philologists and linguists. It was seen as the "lost origin," and its language as the abandoned "mother tongue"; it had to be taken up again in order to animate knowledge, which was in a state of wild confusion. F. Schlegel wrote (*On the Language and Philosophy of the Indians,* 1808), "I only wish that Indian studies may find some of the disciples and protectors that Italy and Germany saw rise up suddenly in the fifteenth and sixteenth centuries in Greek studies and accomplish so many things in so little time! The renaissance of knowledge about antiquity is transforming and promptly rejuvenating all the sciences: one can add that it is rejuvenating and transforming the world. We dare to affirm that the effects of Indian studies would not be any less great today, nor of a less general scope, if they were undertaken with the same energy, and introduced into the circle of European knowledge."[2]

The birthday of comparative linguistics, and from that, of historical and general linguistics, is considered to be the publication in 1826 by the German Franz Bopp (1791–1867) of his paper, *On the Conjugation System of Sanskrit, Compared to That of Greek, Latin, Persian, and German.* To this work, to which we will return, can be added the research of the Danish scholar Rasmus Rask (1787–1832) on the kinship of European languages; the discovery by Jacob Grimm in 1822 in his *Deutsche Grammatik* of the phonetic laws of *Ablaut* (alternation of vowels) and *Umlaut* (change in the timbre of a vowel under the influence of a neighboring, closed vowel), as well as the rules of consonantal shift, *Lautverschiebung* (the Greek consonants π, τ, χ, and the Latin p, t, k, corresponded to the Germanic consonants f, p, h, etc.)

Let us not for the moment follow the chronological order of these discoveries. Instead, let us examine first Rask's contribution. For the Danish linguist, despite being along with Bopp and Grimm one of the founders of the historical method in linguistics, was nonetheless, because of his conceptions and the nature of his research not part of the great evolutionist current that carried the linguistics of the nineteenth century. He was not a historicist, he was a *comparativist.*

Rask's empirical discoveries, of which the main work was entitled *Investigation of the Origin of Old Norse or of Icelandic* (1814) consisted first of all in his demonstration that the Lithuanian and Lettish languages formed a separate family of Indo-European languages, and that the Iraqi or Avestan language was an independent Indo-European language. He described with much rigor the *phonetic changes* corresponding to a *common structure.* For instance, when he compared the "Thracian" (Lithuanian, Slavic) class of languages with Greek and Latin, Rask noticed that "not only do several words resemble one another to a certain extent, according to their form and meaning, but these resemblances are of such a number as to enable the rules of letter changes to be deduced, whereas the entire structure of the languages is the same in both classes."

Rask's in-depth studies of Nordic languages made him without a doubt the founder of Nordic philology. The discovery of the first phonetic law, the *Germanic shift* (as, for example, the regular correlation at the beginning of a word of Latin *p*'s and *t*'s with the Germanic *F*'s and *P*'s: *pater, tres > Fathir, Priz*) belonged to him.

Rask's theoretical aim was not at all historical. With his logical, systematizing mind, he belonged more to the era of the Encyclopedists than to that of the Romantics, an era he hated. He was not interested in the hypothesis of a historical line of languages whose roots came from Sanskrit. He did everything he could to avoid the trip to India imposed upon him by the authorities; when he found himself forced to go anyway, to the great disappointment of his contemporaries, he didn't bring a single document back from the countries he visited (Russia, the Caucasus, Iran, and India). While he was inspired by discoveries in the natural sciences and did consider, as was common later in the nineteenth century, that *la langue* was an *organism,* Rask was more concerned with classifying languages, as eighteenth-century linguists had done, or as Linnaeus had done in botany, than with discovering their historical development, as Darwin had done in zoology. As L. Hjelmslev has remarked (*Commentary on the Life and Work of R. Rask,* 1950–1951)—and his opinion is not just due to his structuralist bias—Rask's science was *typological* and not *genetic.* "He discovered the method to follow in classifying languages by families, but, for him, this classification was only a typological one." This is true because for Rask there was no change in *la langue:* it could only disappear, as was the case with Latin; it could not evolve and transform itself into other languages. When he did note the phonetic or grammatical correspondences among various languages, he allied them and made a family out of them, and no more. For him, "a family of languages was a system of languages, and, therefore, a system of systems"; it was not a family tree. Moreover, Rask's philosophical creed (which he described in his course, circa 1830) confirms Hjelmslev's conclusions. After declaring that *"La langue* is an object of nature" and that "the knowledge of *la langue* resembles natural history," Rask continued, *"La langue* presents us with two objects for philosophical consideration: (1) the relation between objects, that is, the system; and (2) the structure of these objects, that is, physiology. It isn't mechanical; on the contrary, it is the supreme triumph of the application of philosophy to nature, if it enables one to find the true system of nature and to demonstrate its truth." Hjelmslev distinctly emphasized that for Rask language study presupposed two levels that intersected each other: the *explanation,* which produced dictionaries and grammar and which was a theory of the *linguistic form;* and the *investigation* or the theory of the *content,* "the scientific examination of thought hidden in the structure of *la langue,* that is, the ideas expressed by the forms of derivation and inflection, etc." Thus, while Rask was interested in *phonetic* correspondences, it was the correspondences in the *structures* of the content that were decisive for him. He was never able to cut himself off from them in order to listen only to phonetic correlations and to isolate in this change of the signifier the evolving line of the *history of language,* as Grimm and Bopp were doing. If he succeeded anyway in classifying Indo-European languages in the same family, that was because in most cases the phonetic correspondences went hand in hand with structural correspondences (signified, logical correspondence, correspondence of content). So we will say with Hjelmslev that "the history of *la langue* did not interest Rask; the linguistic system and its structure did," and that his comparative linguistics was not genetic, but general, and was related to the Encyclopedists' concern for logical systematization. That didn't stop him from being the author of the first attempt at a comparative Indo-European grammar.

Bopp was the one who formulated the principle of the change in languages which, originally identical, underwent modifications prescribed by certain laws, and resulted in idioms as varied as Sanskrit, Greek, Latin, Gothic, and Persian. After a sojourn in Paris from 1812 to 1816, where he became acquainted with the work of the Parisian Sankritists and Orientalists, Bopp published his paper *On the Conjugation System. . . .* "We must above all," he wrote, "be acquainted with the conjugation system of Old Indian, and we must run through while comparing them the conjugations of Greek, Latin, Germanic, and Persian. In this way, we will perceive their identity. At the same time, we will recognize the progressive and gradual destruction of the simple, linguistic organism and we will observe the tendency to replace it with mechanical groupings, which resulted in the appearance of a new organism when the elements of these groups were no longer recognized."

To prove this principle without leaving the territory of grammar, Bopp demonstrated, contrary to Schlegel, that inflections (a notion used by Schlegel) were old *roots*. "If *la langue,*" he said, "used, with the genius of foresight proper to it, simple signs to represent the simple ideas of people, and if we see that the same notions are represented in the same way in verbs and in pronouns, then it follows that the letter had a signification in the beginning, and that it has remained faithful to it. If there was in the past a reason for *mām* to signify 'me' and for *tam* to signify 'him,' then it is no doubt the same reason that makes *bhavā-mi* signify 'I am' and *bhava-ti* 'he is.' "

Bopp went on to publish in succession *Vergleichende Zergliederung des Sanscrits und der mit ihm verwandten Sprachen* (1824–1831) and *Vergleichende Grammatik* (1833–1852).

Compared to the work of Rask, that of Bopp covered a less vast field in the beginning. Bopp dealt with Sanskrit, which Rask had neglected, but he did not take Lithuanian into account until 1833, Slavic until 1835, or Armenian until 1857. The kinship with Celtic was only barely noticed in 1838, and Albanian was not included until 1854. Moreover, his work dealt only with inflections, and there was hardly any phonetics. He did, however, contribute to the search for phonetic laws by demonstrating, contrary to Grimm, that the *Ablaut* (for example, sing-sang-sung) was not significant; it was due to the laws of phonetic equilibrium and to the influence of tonic stress. Bopp enlarged his investigative field when, in the English edition of *Konjugations System,* he took declension into consideration.

While Bopp's evolutionist intention was well within the line of the ideology of the era, his research nevertheless distanced itself from the mystical and metaphysical idealism of the German Romantics (such as Bopp's teacher, Windischmann, as well as Herder and Schlegel), and came close to a positive attitude as far as *la langue* was concerned. This was because he still believed that he would succeed in finding the "common origin" of languages by means of Sanskrit; later he did modify his initial conception to consider Sanskrit not the original language but part, like other idioms, of the "gradual modifications of one and the same primitive language." Bopp confessed to having this conception, which even led him to try to establish kinship ties between the Caucasian, Indonesian, Melanesian, and Polynesian languages and the Indo-European ones, starting with the preface to the first edition of his *Comparative Grammar of Indo-European Languages* in 1933. It was, however, moderated by furtive warnings about the search for the mystery of the sign (that is, of the signification of the first sounds, or of the roots), such as the following:

> I am proposing to give in this book a description of the organism of the various languages named in its title; to compare among them facts of the same nature; to study the physical and mechanical laws that govern these idioms; and to research the origin of the forms that express grammatical relations. The only thing we will refrain from penetrating is the mystery of roots or, in other words, the reason for which such and such a primitive conception is marked by such and such a sound and not by another. We will not, for instance, examine why the root *I* signifies "to go" and not "to stop," and why the phonic group *STHA* or *STA* means "to stop" and not "to go." Except for this point, we shall try to observe language in, if you will, its blooming and development. . . . Primitive signification and consequently the origin of grammatical forms reveal themselves for the most part of their own accord, as soon as one opens the circle of one's research and brings together languages issued from the same family, which, despite a separation dating several thousand years, still bear the indisputable mark of their common descent.

This tendency to extricate oneself from the mysticism of the era in order to look for a positive basis in the very substance of *la langue,* studied for itself and in itself, was confirmed by Bopp in a famous sentence from his preface to his *Comparative Grammar,* in which some people see already foreshadowed Saussure's theories: "The languages treated by this work are studied for themselves, that is, as an object, and not as a means of knowledge." That amounts to saying that *historical linguistics will be the true linguistics,* and not a study of ways of reasoning (as was the *General Grammar*): an analysis of the specific fabric of linguistic construction, throughout its specific evolution.

Bopp's great contribution remains, therefore, in having incorporated Sanskrit into the positive study of *la langue.* As Pederson has written,

A mere acquaintance with this language had revolutionary effects, not only because it was something new, something which lay well outside the old circle of knowledge, something to which scholars came unhampered by the old misconceptions, which were not easy to shake off when Greek and Latin were discussed, but also because Sanskrit is so extraordinarily perspicuous in structure. Just as its clear structure had brought the admirable clarity of Indian grammar, so it produced comparative grammar when it acted upon the minds of European scholars. Although Rask's work was in many respects more mature and more thorough, Bopp's book, in spite of its many shortcomings, could not fail to provide a much stronger stimulus to future research, stronger even than the stimulus which Rask's could have provided if it had been written in a world language. Bopp's little essay, therefore, may be regarded as the *real beginning* of what we call comparative linguistics.[3]

Through his idealism and despite his errors, Bopp marked a true epistemological break. Bréal (*Introduction à la Grammaire de Bopp*, 1875) provided the following formulation of this: "The chain must be relinked in order to understand facts encountered at a given moment in their history. The error of the former grammatical method was in believing that an idiom formed by itself a completed whole that was self-explanatory."

The importance of the writings of W. von Humboldt (1767–1835), who was a friend of Bopp's and was initiated by him into Sanskrit, needs to be emphasized, since they were at the origin of the comparativist and historicist view of language. More of a philosopher than a linguist, but possessing a vast knowledge of numerous languages, Humboldt has remained famous for his works: *Ueber das Entstehen des grammatischen Formen und ihren Einfluss auf die Ideenentwicklung* (1822), *Ueber die Kawi-sprache auf der Insel-Java* (1836–1840), *Letter to M. Abel Rémusat on the Nature of Grammatical Forms in General and the Genius of the Chinese Language in Particular,* etc. His influence and authority were such that he was considered the "true founder of comparative philology." Humboldt's philosophical position (see V. A. Zvegentzev, in *Texts of Nineteenth-Century Linguistic History,* Moscow, 1956) was that of Kant. For him, consciousness was an entity, independent of objectively existing matter, and obeying its own laws. "Language is the soul in its totality. It develops according to the laws of the mind." But, at the same time, Humboldt defined language as the instrument of thought, while emphasizing that *la langue* was not a sum of traits, but the group of means that realized the uninterrupted process of linguistic development. Hence the distinction he established between *la langue* and discourse: "*La langue* as the sum of its products is different from discursive activity."

One of the major themes of Humboldt's texts was the establishment of a *typology* of the structures of languages and a classification based upon it. Each structure corresponded to a way of understanding the world, for "nature consists of pouring the material of the perceptible world into the mold of thoughts," or "the diversity of languages is a diversity of world views." While such a theory can lead to a "racist" thesis (a racial superiority corresponds to a superiority of the language), it has the considerable advantage of insisting upon the inseparable union of thinking and *la langue,* and seems to herald Karl Marx's materialist thesis, namely, that language is thinking's only reality. Humboldt's typological vision was, of course, dominated by the evolutionist principle; languages had a perfect origin, followed by a period of development, and then one of decadence. Modern thinking, on the other hand, is discovering in Humboldt certain principles that current science and philosophy seem to be taking up again: such as the principle that *la langue* is not an oeuvre, ἔργον, but an activity, ἐνέργεια; this principle has seduced transformationalists like Chomsky. Humboldt is also credited with the discovery of the concept *Innere Sprachform,* an interior linguistic form that precedes articulation; L. Tesnière has relied upon this concept, which is also echoed in structural semantics and in all semiotics.

One can see how, with the help of the Romantic reaction, the science of language was constituted by comparing itself to two epistemological facts: the logical system of the previous century and the development of the natural sciences of its time. The study of language "stopped taking logical categories for explanations," Meillet later said, thinking of the encyclopedist grammarians (*Introduction à l'étude com-*

parée des langues indo-européennes, 1954, 7th edition). It wanted to mimic the study of "living beings," *organisms,* and it used these organisms as the example with which to consider societies. Language "does not, for the most part, allow itself to be reduced to abstract formulas like a fact of physics" *(ibid.).* The logic of systems was followed by the *vitalism of the logos.* This change was experienced as a reaction to the logical, a priori method, which (in reference to Archimedes, Galileo, and Newton) had marked the previous era:

> Method had arrived at its perfection, and the only thing left to do was to apply it with ever-growing precision to all the objects it enabled one to study. In contrast, the method of historical explanation was an invention of the nineteenth century (and already to a certain extent of the end of the eighteenth century). The earth's crust, organized beings, and societies and their institutions appeared to be products of a historical development whose detail could not be guessed at a priori, and could not be accounted for except by observing and determining, as exactly as the data allowed, the succession and conjunctions of the particular events by which they were realized . . . ; inorganic bodies themselves have a history.

This reasoning of Meillet's sketched out the trajectory by which evolutionism moved away from a metaphysical search for "origins" and became an *exact description of a history*—a historical positivism. The *comparative* linguistics of the beginning of the century became *historical,* via Bopp, to the extent that it demonstrated the genetic kinship of languages that descended from one another and could be traced back to the same origin; this was especially true with Grimm (*Deutsche Grammatik,* 1819, vol. 1; following vols., 1826, 1831, 1837). Grimm abandoned the thesis of kinship and devoted himself to a chronological study of a single language. This chronology, minutely followed, step by step, had been lacking in the comparatists; it definitively founded linguistics on exact bases.

Pederson has pointed out that this decisive turn took place circa 1876; it was therefore prefigured by Grimm, as well as by Franz Diez (*Grammatik der romanischen Sprachen,* 1836–1844). But Diez, a German Romanist, had predecessors who followed Bopp's and Grimm's example and elaborated the comparative and historical grammars of various languages. E. Birmpoif (1801–1852) dealt with Iranian, and Dobrovsky (1753–1829) devoted himself to the Slavic languages, which enabled F. Miklosisch (1813–1875) to publish his *Comparative Grammar of Slavic Languages.* Later E. Curtius (1814–1896) applied the comparative method to Greek (1852), and Theodor Benfey (1809–1881) dealt with Egyptian. An unknown professor, J. K. Zeuss (1806–1856) elucidated the place of Celtic in the Indo-European family, in his *Grammatica celtica* (1853). But the work of Dicz, the founder of Romance studies (see L. Wagner, *Contribution to the Prehistory of Romanticism,* 1950–1955), was stimulated in the beginning by the book of the Frenchman François Raynouard (1761–1836), *Choix de poésies originales des troubadours contenant la grammaire comparée de la langue des troubadours* (1816–1821). The author developed Dante's erroneous theory that stated that Provençal was the mother tongue of the Romance languages. However, he displayed an enormous amount of linguistic material (French, Spanish, Italian, Portuguese, Ferrarese, Bolonese, Milanese, Bergamese, Piedmontese, Mantouan, Frioulan, etc.), whose elements were compared on lexical, morphological, and syntactic levels. Prompted by the studies of scholars who had looked into Provençal (Achard, Féraud, etc.), Raynouard's work broke off from the whole of the French linguistics of the era, which, faithful to Port-Royal and the *Encyclopédie,* hesitated to adopt the Romantic views of the Germans, and because of that, remained reserved about comparative grammar. As Meillet has said, Condillac blocked Bopp's way. A. W. von Schlegel responded to the work of Raynouard, whose conception he criticized in his book *Observations on the Language and Literature of the Troubadours* (1818).

The young Diez therefore inherited these studies, and having made his début with his literary studies of the poetry of the troubadours, devoted himself definitively to a historical analysis of the French language, which he compared to other Romance languages. It was Diez who, in contrast to Raynouard, noticed that Romance languages had come from Latin Vulgate. While he did not include Catalan, Rhaeto-Romanic, and Sardinian in this line, he did distinguish Romanian as a Romance language.

With Romance linguistics thus founded, several works were devoted to a historical study of French, such as: the first *Descriptive Grammar of Old French* by Conrad von Orelli (1830); *Recherche sur les formes grammaticales de la langue française et de ses dialectes au XIIIe siècle*, by Gustave Fallot (1839); *Histoire de la formation de la langue française* by J. J. Ampère (1841); *Variation de la langue française depuis le XIIe siècle* by F. Génin (1845); *Histoire des révolutions du langage en France* by F. Wey (1848), etc., and ending with the *Histoire de la langue française*, in two volumes, by E. Littré (1863).

This evolutionist period of historical linguistics, even though it started to turn toward positivism with the constitution of Germanic and Romance, etc., studies, found its *genetic* apogee in the work of August Schleicher (1821–1868), which was in harmony with the outstanding phenomena of the era's epistemology: the science of Darwin and the philosophy of Hegel. Here is how Schleicher impregnated his linguistic reflection with biological terms and concepts: "To use a comparison, I am thinking about calling roots the simple cells of language in which special organs do not yet exist for grammatical functions such as the noun, the verb, etc., and in which these same functions (grammatical relations) are still as little differentiated as, for example, respiration or nutrition in monocellular organisms or the fetus of superior animals." Referring to Darwin's thesis of the natural selection of organisms in the struggle for survival, Schleicher considered that languages as well as living organisms were concerned by it. "In the current period of the life of humanity," he wrote, "the victors in the struggle for survival are especially the languages of the Indo-Germanic family; their distribution constantly continues by ousting other languages." Moreover, and still echoing Darwin, Schleicher's linguistic theses seem to transpose the Hegelian conception according to which a language was richer when it was not developed, therefore at the primitive stage of peoples, and, on the contrary, grew poorer in the course of civilization and the formation of grammar.

For Hegel, *la langue* was like a "depot" for thought. He proposed a hierarchical arrangement of languages according to their aptitude for expressing logical operations, by means of their grammatical categories. One will note in the following passage just how much these logical operations, given as omnivalent, were exact copies of the model of the modern Indo-European languages, even of German, and how, consequently, Hegel's logicism led him not only to ignore the particularity of other languages (Chinese, for example), but also to propose a discriminatory conception of language:[4]

It is in human Language that the Forms of Thought are manifested and laid down in the first instance. In our day it cannot be too often recalled, that what distinguishes man from the beasts is *the faculty of Thought.* Language has penetrated into whatever becomes for man *something inner*—becomes, that is, an idea, something which he makes his very own;— and what man transforms to Language contains—concealed, or mixed up with other things, or worded out to clearness—a Category; so natural to man is Logic—indeed, Logic itself is just man's peculiar nature. But if Nature in general is opposed, as *physical,* to what is *mental,* then it must be said that Logic is rather that something Super-natural which enters into all the natural *behaviour* of man—Feeling, Intuition, Desire, Need, Impulse—and thereby alone transforms it all to something human—to ideas and purposes—though, perhaps, only formally human. It is a great advantage to a language when it has a wealth of logical expressions—that is, expressions characteristic and set apart—for the determinations of thought; of prepositions and articles many belong to those relationships which depend upon thinking; the Chinese language is said not to have developed so far, or only in a very small degree; these particles in fact perform an entirely subordinate office, the same as prefixes and suffixes, and in an only slightly more independent form. It is much more important that in a language the determinations of thought should be manifested in Substantives and Verbs and thus receive the stamp of objective form; the German language has here many advantages over other modern languages; indeed, many of its words have the further peculiarity that they have not only various, but even opposed, meanings, so that we must recognize here a speculative spirit in the language; it is a joy to thought to stumble upon such words, and to meet with the union of opposites (a result of Speculative Thought which to Human

Understanding seems senseless) in the naïve shape of one word with opposite meanings registered in a dictionary.

Schleicher, a convinced Hegelian, botanist, and admirer of Darwin, published in 1863 *Die darwinische Theorie und die Sprachwissenschaft,* and in 1865, *Ueber die Bedeutung der Sprache für die Natürgeschichte des Menschen.* He remains famous in the history of linguistics for his effort in presenting a reconstructive schema of the evolution of languages by trying to go all the way back to the most archaic forms witnessed. Schleicher proposed a hypothetical form of an Indo-European language that would thus have been the origin of all the others. Languages would thus have proceeded from one other according to a family tree. It was a seductive theory, and was generally accepted until it was refuted and replaced by that of Johann Schmidt, who proposed another schema called the "linguistic waves" theory. Indo-European *dialectology* was later founded on this last schema.

Schleicher himself, however, truly believed in the existence of this hypothetical primitive Indo-European language (whose hypothetical forms are indicated by an asterisk in current linguistic science). In order to arrive at this conception, Schleicher took up the evolutionist thesis, and proposed in this way the first great synthesis of linguistic knowledge. He did this by demonstrating that the evolution of language took place in two stages, a (prehistoric) *ascending* stage which led to inflected languages, and a (decadent or historical) *descending* stage, which was marked by the disintegration of the inflection system. In fact, this conception did no more than arrange the typology of languages into three classes (inherited from Schlegel, Bopp, and Humboldt) according to an "ascending–descending" schema. There were isolating languages (Chinese, for example), agglutinating languages (Hungarian, for example), and inflected languages (Sanskrit, for example). Schleicher only added to these a fourth stage that constituted a "historical" decline of the first three.

Sanskrit was therefore no longer the first language for Schleicher, as it had been considered at the beginning of the "comparativist" period. The "original form" had to be reconstructed; this was for Schleicher "the shortest method of indicating later changes in the individual languages," Pederson noted [p. 267]. Pederson went on to say, "The necessity of reconstruction compels the student to give his individual attention to every detail in the development of sounds. Therefore the method has maintained itself to this day, and must be regarded as indispensable. Reconstructed forms are usually indicated nowadays by an asterisk placed before them (for example, Indo-European *ekwo-s, or, more exactly, *äkwä-s, ('horse'), so that they may not be confused with historically authentic forms like Latin equ-us, Greek hippo-s, Sanskrit ásva-s, Avesta aspa-, Old English eoh, Old Irish ech, West Tokharian yakwe, East Tokharian yuk, etc. This practice, too, goes back to Schleicher" [p. 267]. Today, of course, "we have a lot less confidence than Schleicher did in the possibility of linguistics reconstructing a language which, if it did exist, disappeared thousands of years ago" [p. 268]. But we must emphasize that Schleicher, for his part, didn't have the slightest doubt about it—he even "translated" into Indo-European a fable entitled "The Ewe and the Horses"!

This linguistic objectivism, which led Schleicher to consider *la langue* an organism subject to *necessary laws,* made of this German linguist one of the pioneers of *general linguistics,* which succeeded historical linguistics. He wanted to call this discipline *Glottik,* and to found it on the basis of laws analogous to biological laws. But this positivism, mechanically transferred from the natural sciences to the science of signification, could only be idealistic, since it did not take into account the specificity of the object being studied: *la langue* as a system of signification and as a social product. It immediately found, by the way, its complement, which appeared to be its opposite but was profoundly necessary, and its ideological correlate for the realm of the study of society in Hegelianism, which posited itself as the *historical* consciousness of the expansion of the mode of bourgeois production. Hegel's influence on Schleicher was, moreover, visible in the theory of the ascendancy of languages during the stage of their formation and of their decline during the stage of their free development. The Hegelian influence exerted itself even on Schleicher's phonetic classifications, such as, for example, the triadic classification of sounds in Indo-European. Pederson has noted that this threefold scheme revealed the philosophical admiration Schleicher felt for Hegel, but did not correspond to the reality of languages. Here is this triad of sounds, which linguistics later greatly corrected and refined, and which even the

Indian grammarians had presented in a more precise and less symmetrical fashion:

Original vowels (*grundovokal*)	a	i	u
1st "increment" (*erste Steigerung*)	aa(à)	ai	au
2nd "increment" (*zweite Steigerung*)	àa(à)	ài	au
Consonants	r	n	m
	j	v	s
	k	g	gh
	t	d	gh
	p	b	dh
			bh

This effort of constructing a genetic table of languages was pursued by the etymologist August Fick, as well as by Friedrich Max Müller in *Lectures on the Science of Language,* 1861 and 1864.

The development of sciences toward the end of the nineteenth century, crowned by the creation of a positivist ideology that found its expression in the *Cours de philosophie positive* (1830–1842) by Auguste Comte (1798–1857), had two effects on the scholarship of its day. Not only did it encourage rigor in linguistic research by separating it more and more from general philosophical considerations, but it also witnessed the appearance of the forerunner signs of a true, autonomous linguistic science, isolated from grammar and philology.

The role of Comte in the development of positivist processes in the so-called "human" sciences cannot be overemphasized. From the perspective of the progress of sciences themselves, which we have just mentioned and which also concerns the science of language, it was indeed Comte who made himself the ardent defender of the transfer of exact methods to the study of social phenomena, thus propagating the positivist philosophy of "the serene order." "The only thing left, as I have explained, is to complete positivist philosophy by including in it the *study of social phenomena,* and then to summarize all this in a single body of homogeneous doctrine. When this double work has been sufficiently advanced, the definitive triumph of positivist philosophy will take place spontaneously, and will reestablish order in society" (*Cours de philosophie positive,* vol. 1, 1830).

The outstanding moment of this change of historicism toward positivism was, as Meillet has pointed out, the work of the *neogrammarians* Brugmann (1849–1919) and Osthoff (1847–1907). The important point of their research is that it put an end to the doubts about the phonetic changes comparative linguistics had been establishing since Rask, Bopp, and Grimm; they affirmed that these transformations were *necessary laws* like those of physics and biology. "Every phonetic change, since it proceeds mechanically, takes place without exception according to laws, that is, the direction of the change is always the same in all members of a linguistic community—except in the case of dialect separation—and all the words with the sound that is subject to change are affected, without exception."

Bréal since 1867, Verner in 1875, Scherer in 1875, G. I. Ascoli since 1870, Leskien, etc., all these men had already had inklings of this thesis of the regularity of phonetic changes, but it was definitely Brugmann and Osthoff who defined it most clearly. Hermann Paul (1846–1921), in his *Prinzipien der Sprachgeschichte* (Principles of Language) in 1880, magisterially revealed the theories the neogrammarians had promoted in opposition to traditional scholars.

Nonetheless, the neogrammarians have been the subject of vigorous criticism in the twentieth century. Among their critics was Hugo Schuchardt (1842–1928), who criticized the phonetic laws as well as the genealogical perspective; he recommended etymological and dialectological studies, while supporting the theory of the transformation of languages according to the geographic situation. Another critic was K. Vosseler (1872–1947), who published in 1940 his book *Positivism and Idealism in Linguistics,* in which he examined in particular the relations between French language and culture, exalted the role of the individual in linguistic and aesthetic creation, and profoundly stimulated linguistic and stylistic studies.

While imposing a regulated vision of *la langue* (phonetic laws), the neogrammarians nevertheless defended a certain historical position: they were opposed to Schleicher's thesis of a prehistory of language, and wanted to establish phonetic laws for the Indo-European language itself. Brugmann wrote, "We should formulate for ourselves a general representation of the development of linguistic forms, not through a hypothetical original linguistic symbol, nor even through the most ancient forms of Sanskrit, Greek, etc. ever transmitted, but instead on the basis of linguistic events whose antecedents, thanks to documents, can be followed over a longer period of time, and whose point of departure is directly known to us."

This positive historicism found its apotheosis in the work of Paul mentioned above:

> Conditions of development cannot possibly be studied with as much precision in any other realm as in that of language. That is why no other human science exists whose method can be taken to such a degree of perfection as the method of linguistics. No other science has been able up until now to penetrate so far beyond monuments; no other one has been as constructive as it has been speculative. It is exactly because of these particularities that linguistics seems so close to the natural and historical sciences; this could have led to the absurd tendency to exclude it from the field of historical sciences.

Paul distinguished two groups of historical sciences, the natural sciences and the cultural sciences: "The characteristic trait of culture is the existence of the psychical factor." And, as a matter of fact, linguistics was beginning to become more and more the terrain of *psychology*.

Brugmann saw in it a means of combatting logical schemas, and recommended that "historical linguistics and psychology keep in closer contact." It was in G. Steinthal's (1823–1899) *Grammar, Logic, and Psychology: Their Principles and Relations* (1855), and *Introduction to the Psychology of Linguistics* (1881, 2d ed.) that psycholinguistic principles were systematized. Steinthal refused to confuse logical thinking and language: "The categories of language and of logic are incompatible and can no more be related to one another than the concepts of circle and red." He tried to get to the "laws of the spiritual life" of the individual in various societies and collectivities (nations, and political, social, or religious groups) by establishing a relation between the language and the psychology of a people (ethnopsychology). The Russian linguist A. A. Potebnia (1835–1891), while inspired by Steinthal's work, developed an original theory of psychical activity and language, by drawing attention above all to the fact that language is an *activity*, a process in which *la langue* is constantly renewed: "The reality of the word . . . comes into being in discourse. . . . The word in discourse corresponds to one act of thinking, and not to several. . . ." "In fact . . . there is only discourse. The word removed from its relations is dead. . . ." We can see being sketched out here a theory of discourse that was later attentively developed by modern linguistics, on the basis of psychoanalytic research.

The development of psychology, accompanied by the growing interest paid to it by linguists, did not fail to bring into the field of linguistics the question (somewhat forgotten after so many studies of phonetic, morphological, and syntactic evolution) of *signification*. G. Grote in his *Glossology* (1871) opposed the *phone*, or word as phonetic form, to the *noeme*, or word as thought; however, his complex terminology (dianocmantism, semantism, nomato-semantism, etc.), did not succeed in becoming accepted. Wilhelm Wundt (1832–1920) dealt with the process of signification and spoke of two types of association, by similitude and by contiguity, by distinguishing between the phonic form and meaning, and consequently, between transfer of sounds and transfer of meaning (metaphor). For his part, Schuchardt contrasted *onomastics* (the study of names) and *semantics* (the study of meaning). The paternity of this last term seems to belong, however, to Bréal (1832–1915), who, in an article in 1883, "Les Lois intellectuelles du langage, fragments de sémantique," defined semantics as needing to deal with the "laws that preside over the transformation of meanings." His *Semantics: Studies in the Science of Meaning* appeared in 1896 [English edition, 1900]. Historical linguistics was by then no longer a description of the evolution of forms; it looked for the rules—the logic—of the evolution of meaning. Such was the subject of *The Life of Words Studied in Their Situation* (1886) by Darmsteter (1846–1888), who turned to rhetoric to explain changes in meaning.

Thus, having gone through the history of *la langue* and its relation to the laws of thought, the evolutionism of the beginning of this century was ripe for becoming a general science of language—a *general linguistics*. As Meillet has written, "it has been noted that linguistic development obeys general laws. The very history of languages is enough to show this from the regularities that can be observed there." That amounts to saying that once grasped in its past and present, *la langue* appeared as a system that extended to the present as well as to the past, to phoneticism and grammar as well as to signification. For it was a system of signs, as the Solitaries and Encyclopedists had thought, but this notion, which reappeared in the context of the concrete knowledge of *la langue* furnished by comparative and historical linguistics, had from then on a new meaning: it was no longer logical or sensationalistic, but was instead rooted in a specifically linguistic fabric.

Ferdinand de Saussure, the Swiss linguist (1857–1913), is considered the founder of this vision of *la langue* as a system. From his first *Mémoire sur le système primitif des voyelles dans les langues indo-européennes* (1878), Saussure rigorously and systematically fixed the Indo-European vowel system in a coherent classification that embraced all the data. He no longer considered the closed vowels *i and *u essential vowels: they became the vowel forms for *y and *w, just as *r, *l, *n and *m were the vowel forms for *r, *l, *n, and *m. Indo-European, as Meillet has summed up, really had only one vowel, which appeared with the *e and *o timbres, or which was lacking. Every morphological element had a vowel pattern of the *e degree, the *o degree, or a no-vowel degree.

While scholars such as Meillet, Vendryes, or Bréal had tried to reconcile historical linguistics with general linguistics, Saussure was the first to produce a *Course in General Linguistics* (1906–1912). He became the indisputable father of general linguistics, which Meillet, who was more historical than Saussure, later defined this way:

> A discipline which only determines possibilities, and, which, since it cannot ever exhaust the events of all languages at all moments, must proceed by induction, by relying on the one hand on certain clear and characteristic facts, and on the other hand, on the general conditions where these facts were produced. *General linguistics is to a large extent an a priori science. . . .* It is based on descriptive and historical grammar, to which it owes the facts it uses. Only anatomy, physiology, and psychology can explain its laws. . . . Finally, it is only under conditions specific to a given social state, and in virtue of these conditions, that such-and-such possibilities determined by general linguistics are realized. Thus one can see the place general linguistics has, between descriptive and historical grammars on the one hand, which are sciences of particular

facts, and anatomy, physiology, psychology, and sociology, on the other hand, which are vaster sciences, dominating and explaining among other things the phenomena of articulated language.

The tranformation of historical linguistics into general linguistics was also no doubt influenced and accelerated by the introduction of exact methods into language studies and, more specifically, into the realm of *phonetics*. The invention of the laryngoscope in 1855 by Manuel V. Garcia, and its use in the study of vocal cords and how they work by the Czech doctor Czemak (1860); the transcription of sounds (a graphic marking that noted their breakdown into articulatory elements) by A. L. Bell, and, finally, the publication of *Grundziige der Lautphysiologie* (Foundations of Phonetic Physiology) by Edward Sievers in 1876 were the various stages enabling the constitution of a phonetic science in itself. The names Vitor, Paul Passy, Rousselot, Sweet, Jones, and Jespersen are connected with this work. Phonetics thus began to describe the current state of the phoneticism of a language, by furnishing detailed and complex physiological descriptions of various sounds, without being able, however, to explain the fact that the different ways of pronouncing a phoneme, for example, did not take away its permanent value in the voiced chain (for example, the different ways of pronouncing the French *r* do not interfere with the comprehension of the message). Phonology later made this explanation its work (see chapter 19). However, with experimental phonetics, linguistics became definitively oriented toward studying the current system of a language, and looking for concepts to organize it.

For instance, the Polish linguist Jan Baudouin de Courtenay (1845–1929), who taught linguistics at Kazan, Krakow, and St. Petersburg, borrowed the term *phoneme* from Saussure and gave it its current meaning, for he distinguished the physiological study of the sounds of language from the psychological study that analyzes acoustic images. For Baudouin de Courtenay, the phoneme was "the sum of phonetic particularities which constitute an indivisible unit in comparisons, whether in the framework of a single language, or several related languages." This definition of Baudouin de Courtenay's was refined by his student Kruscewski, and was taken up again by twentieth-century phonologists; they purged it of its psychologism and used it to build *phonology,* and with that, structural linguistics.

Let us add to the list of works that founded general linguistics by clearing the way for the structural renewal brought about by the contemporary era, the work of the American linguist W. D. Whitney (1827–1894) and in particular his book *The Life and Growth of Language* (1875). Saussure admired this text and had been working on an article about it. Indeed, in it can be found the notion of the *sign,* a typological outline of communication systems, a study of linguistic structures, etc.

Born of history, linguistics is now focusing on the current state of *la langue* and proposes to systematize it in two directions.

In the first direction, the linguistic process is keeping in mind the discoveries of the historical period and is interested in shedding some historical or social light on its reflections and general classifications, while keeping close to the specific linguistic material of the concrete language. Such was the case of Meillet, and of Benveniste in France, or to a certain extent of the Linguistic Circle of Prague and Jakobson. In 1906, Meillet translated the concerns of sociological linguistics in this way: "Which social structure a given linguistic structure answers to must be determined, as well as how, in a general way, changes in the social structure are translated by changes in the linguistic structure."

In the second direction, linguistics is censoring what the historical study of concrete languages has brought to the knowledge of symbolic operation, and is striving to elaborate a logical-positivist theory of linguistic structures, more or less abstracted from their signifying materiality.

━━━ 19 ━━━
STRUCTURAL LINGUISTICS

It is obviously difficult to have, as of now, a clear and definitive view of the exact place currently occupied by language in the entire set of areas in which it has become an object of study or a model of investigation. Indeed, while linguistics is relentlessly proposing new approaches to the system of language, it is not the only field dealing with it. Philosophy, psychoanalysis, literary theory, sociology, the study of the various arts, as well as literature and the arts themselves, all these are exploring in their own way the laws of language. This exploration, together with specifically linguistic description, constitutes an immense spectrum that reveals both *modern conceptions* of language and the *mechanism* of the various discourses that propose these conceptions.

Discussing this complexity poses several problems. First, we don't have enough distance from it yet to appreciate it. Nor do we have enough space to study it in this brief summary. However, while linguistic science proper does take on aspects that vary greatly, it nevertheless obeys several constant principles that differentiate it from the preceding "historical" period.

First of all, modern linguistics is dedicated to the description of the system of *la langue* as seen through the concrete national language or languages in which this system manifests itself. In this way it hopes to find the general principles and elements, which one can call the linguistic *universals. La langue* therefore appears to be not an evolution, a family tree, or a history, but a *structure,* with laws and operational rules that must be described. The separation *langue*/speech *{parole},* paradigm/syntagm, synchrony/diachrony (see part 1) indicates very well this orientation of linguistics toward *la langue, paradigm,* and *synchrony* rather than toward speech, syntagm, and diachrony.

This does not mean that structural study cannot shed some historical light on the subject and show, for example, the historical difference between the structures of the same or two different languages.

Then, however, it would be a completely different history, and not a linear, evolving history that would apply itself to explaining the progressive change of one structure into another according to the laws of evolution. Instead it would be an *analysis of blocks,* of structures of signification, whose typological differences present a terracing, a layering, a *monumental history,* or it would be an analysis of the internal changes of a structure that *transforms* itself (as generative grammar sees it) without looking for an origin or following an evolution. "It is not so much the historical point of view that is thus condemned as a certain way of 'atomizing' language *{la langue}* and of making history mechanical. Time is not the agent of evolution; it is only its framework. The reason for the change that affects a certain element of a language *{la langue}* lies, on the one hand, in the nature of the elements of which it is made up at a given moment, and, on the other hand, in the structural relationship among these elements," Benveniste wrote.[1] Thus, since *history* is back in the right place, *logic* is too: logical categories, extracted from a single language unbeknownst to the linguist, were no longer omnivalent. And, to a certain extent, each language had its logic: "It can be seen that 'mental categories' and 'laws of thought' in large measure do nothing but reflect the organization and the distribution of linguistic categories" [p. 6]. One could even say that although the study of *la langue* as a structure or transformation does echo the tendencies of current sciences (physics or biology), which examine the internal structure of matter by breaking it down into constituent parts (as in nuclear or bionic theories), it is also clearly the best-placed discipline for transferring this state of science to ideology, while contributing in this way to a reevaluation of the concept of *history.* Indeed, using as its bases scientific data (including that of linguistics), the modern representation of history is no longer a linear one, as it was in the nineteenth century. Without falling into the excesses of certain idealist philosophies, which would lead to a total ahistoricism, materialist theory envisages (economical or symbolic) systems in change, and guided by linguistics teaches us to analyze the laws and transformations inherent to each system.

Even though such a transformation of the concept of history is manifest in the structuralist current, one cannot say that it is always consciously practiced in contemporary studies. On the contrary, structuralist thought has a tendency to flee history and use the study of language as its alibi for this flight. It is true, however, that the study of language in primitive societies (prehistoric ones, such as the tribes of North America) probably lends itself to such a flight.

Be that as it may, by abandoning the historical and psychological presuppositions of previous periods, and by devoting itself to an object it wanted to describe in an exact and precise fashion, linguistics found an example of rigor in the *mathematical* sciences, whose models and concepts it borrowed. For a time this mathematical rigor was believed to be absolute; no one considered that a mathematical model (like any formalist model, by the way), once applied to a signifying object, requires some justification and is only applicable because of the implicit justification the researcher gives it. The ideology one wanted to escape from thus turned up again in latent form in the *semantic root* of the model applied to the description of language.

In this way, by moving away from empiricism, the study of language should enable science to understand that its "discoveries" depend upon the conceptual system that is applied to the object being studied, and that these discoveries are more or less given ahead of time. In other words, linguistics believes that its discoveries of the properties of language are dependent upon the *model* used in the description, even upon the *theory* the model belongs to. This has resulted in considerable interest in the innovation of theories and models, rather than a sustained investigation enabled by the use of a single model. Linguistics doesn't describe language as much as make its own language. This turnabout, which seems paradoxical, has a double consequence. On the one hand, theoretical research in no way implies that language remains unknown, buried under the mass of forever-new models of linguistic operation. But, on the other hand, the attention of scientific discourse is drawn to the very process of knowledge as a process of the construction of a model, which is overdetermined by a theoretical, or even ideological agency. In other words, the science of language is not oriented solely toward its object, *la langue;* it is also oriented toward its own discourse, its own foundations. Every discourse about language is thus *required* to think about *its* object, *its* language, through the model it has chosen for itself, that is, through its own matrices. Without ending up in a relativism and an agnosticism that would deny the objectivity of all knowledge, such a means of proceeding forces linguistics (and every science that follows its path) to question itself about its own foundations, to become a science of its *process,* while remaining the science of an *object.*

It should be carefully noted that this analytical perspective, implicitly open to linguistic science and modern epistemology in this way, is far from being admitted to and consciously practiced in structuralist works. On the contrary, the greater part of linguistic research does not in any way question itself about the procedures, presuppositions, and models it uses, and, while it is becoming more and more formal and formalized, linguistic research seems to believe that these formulas are neutral facts and not logical constructions applied, for a semantical reason whose ideological foundations must be questioned, to an irreducible object, language.

Moreover, studying language as a system of *signs,* linguistics has forged the conceptual means for the study of *every system of signification* as a "language." Thus, the different types of social relations invested in language, culture, codes, and rules of social behavior, religions, arts, etc., can be studied as systems of signs with particular structures, or as so many types of language. Linguistics has become a part of *semiotics,* the general science of signifying systems, which it made possible by thinking of language as the first system of signs.

Finally, and as a consequence of what we have just said, the study of language is extending far beyond the framework of linguistics alone, and its analysis has been undertaken from angles that if not unexpected are at least radically new.

For instance, certain *philosophical theories,* postulating that the world exists for thought only to the extent that it is organized through language, are studying philosophical categories as linguistic or logical categories. In this way, language is also becoming the mold for every philosophical construction.

Psychoanalysis has found in language the real objects of its investigation. For it is indeed in linguistic structures and in the relation between the subject and his discourse that psychoanalysis analyzes the structures known as psychical.

Finally, the *literature* and *art* being developed in this climate of the detailed analysis of their own material—language and systems of signification in general—are, in what is called the "avant-garde," constructing fictions that enable them to look into the laws of that construction. Literature is becoming a self-analysis, an implicit research into the rules of literary language, just as modern art is pulverizing the descriptive opacity of the previous type of painting and exposing its components and laws. Here, language is no longer an object of study, but a practice and knowledge, or an analytical practice, an *element* and *work* in which and through which the subject knows and organizes reality.

We are first going to follow the principal moments in the visions of languages such as they have been elaborated by modern linguistics, and then we will tackle the expansion of the analysis of language beyond the strictly linguistic field.

LOGICAL RESEARCH

It is true that it was Saussure who, in a period dominated by the neogrammarians, first set forth the principles of *la langue* as a *system of signs*. He thus founded modern general linguistics, which later became structural and highly formalized. Nevertheless, it is in the work of a philosopher that we find established the conception of language that underlies current linguistics. By here designating Husserlian phenomenology and, more particularly, the conception of the sign and meaning in Husserl (1859–1938), we would like to insist upon structuralism's unacknowledged debt to phenomenology.

In 1900–1901, Edmund Husserl's *Logical Investigations* appeared; its fundamental points were clarified without being radically modified in his later works, *Formal and Transcendental Logic,* etc. By taking on the concept of the *sign,* which he wanted to elaborate without presuppositions, Husserl remained riveted to the metaphysical project of the sign itself, a metaphysics Derrida described as "restored to the original purity in its historical achievement."[2] Husserlian reflection on the sign was submitted to a logic: without questioning this logic, Husserl presented language through the system of this logic, which was clearly seen as providing linguistic order with normality. Thus, when he was studying grammatical order, the morphology of signs, the rules enabling the construction of a discourse that had meaning, one realizes that this grammar was *general,* purely *logical,* and that it did not take into account that real variety of language. Husserl talked about "the entire *a priori* of general grammar—there is, e.g., a peculiar *a priori* governing relations of mutual understanding among minded persons, relations very important for grammar—talk of pure *logical* grammar is to be preferred."[3]

This logical apriorism, which we will find again in the first structuralists, goes hand in hand with the privilege accorded to the *phōnē,* which Husserl understood not as a physical vocalism but as a spiritual substance, "the voice in its transcendental flesh." The concept of *signified* was later attached to the *signifying* phonic complex through the intermediary of the *word,* and linguistic reflection took up residence in the logical transcendence that phonetics (later called phonematics) not only manifests but *is.*

Without developing a general theory of the sign, Husserl distinguished between signs that express something, or that *mean* something —he grouped these under the concept *expression*—and signs that are deprived of "meaning"—which he designated by the concept of *indicative sign.* The two systems, moreover, could become confused: the discursive sign that *means* is always indicative. Indication on the contrary establishes a much larger concept and can consequently also present itself outside this confusion. That amounts to saying that discourse is caught in the indicative gesture, or in *indication* in general, and consequently could cover all of language by making reductions (factuality, worldly essence, etc.). In this way it made its way toward a more and more marked reduction of the conceptual pairs fact/essence, transcendentalism/worldliness, even meaning/form. This doctrine of the *expressive sign* as different from the *indicative sign,* far from being included in and assimilated by the metaphysical system of the sign, shows itself furtively in certain descriptive theories, where the reduction of the transcendental meaning of language operates under the cover of indicative signification, of the signifier that has no "meaning."

One last point on Husserlian doctrine that we would like to make here is the limitation of Husserl's *pure logical grammar.* Even though it was much more formal than rational grammar, its formality was limited. For the *pure form* was held by the concept of *meaning,* which depended upon a relation to the *real object.* And so one can understand why no matter how formal a grammar is, it is always delimited by a *semantics* it doesn't acknowledge. Here is an example. Among the three formulas "the circle is a square," "green is or" and "abracadabra," only "the circle is a square" makes any sense, even though that clause doesn't correspond to any object. This is because the grammatical form (noun-verb-attribute) is the only one of the forms given capable of having an object. The other cases, as well as several examples of poetic language or music, without lacking signification, don't have any (Husserlian) *meaning,* for they don't have a logical relation to an object. One can see that in the final analysis the formal-grammatical criteria ("the discourse makes sense if it obeys a grammatical rule") is limited by the semantic rule of a relation with the object. This thinking should be related to Chomsky's example on grammaticality (see chapter 19, "Generative Grammar"), whose fundamental weakness it demonstrates.

Husserlian phenomenology, of which we have only indicated some essential points, became the basis for this century's theory of signification, to which, consciously or not, explicitly or not, linguistic theories refer.

We are going to mention several of the most important ones.

THE PRAGUE LINGUISTIC CIRCLE

The Prague linguistic circle was without a doubt the linguistic "school" that most profoundly marked the linguistic science of the first third of this century. Created in 1926 by the Czech linguists V. Mathesius, B.

Havránck, J. Mukarovsky, B. Trnka, J. Vachek, and M. Weingart, the circle also brought together foreign linguists, among whom were the Frenchmen L. Bruo, L. Tesnière, J. Vendryes, E. Benveniste, and A. Martinet and the Russians R. Jakobson and N. S. Trubetskoi. The circle's theories were revealed in the *The Works of the Prague Linguistic Circle* [WPLC] (published 1929–1938), a collective work containing the principal theses of the group. Inspired by Saussure's principles, the circle set out to study *la langue* as a system, "a functional system," without ignoring either concrete linguistic facts or the comparative methods of the study of the evolution of language—for synchronic analysis of language does not suppress an interest in history.

For this reason the Circle's program was entitled "METHODOLOGI-CAL PROBLEMS STEMMING FROM THE CONCEPTION OF LANGUAGE {*la langue*} AS A SYSTEM AND THE SIGNIFICANCE OF THIS CONCEPTION FOR SLAVIC LANGUAGES (the synchronic method and its relation to the diachronic method, structural comparison versus genetic comparison, the accidentality or the developmental regularity of linguistic phenomena)."[4]

The circle defined *la langue* as a "goal-oriented means of expression" [p. 5], and affirmed that "the essence and nature of a system of language can best be discovered through a synchronic analysis of today's languages which alone provide complete material and which can be directly experienced" [pp. 5–6]. The changes undergone by *la langue* cannot possibly be envisaged "without regard for the system to which it belongs" [p. 5]. "On the other hand, neither can a synchronic description absolutely exclude the notion of evolution, for such a synchronic moment reflects the disappearing, present, and coming stages. Stylistic elements perceived as archaisms as well as the distinction between productive and nonproductive forms are evidence of diachronic phenomena, which cannot be eliminated from synchronic linguistics" [p. 6].

The first task to be taken on in the study of a linguistic system defined in this way was research related to the *phonic* aspect of the language. The sound was distinguished "as an objective physical fact, as a representation, and as an element of a functional system" [p. 8], that is, as a *phoneme*. From the phonological level one passed to the *morphological* one—to the morphological utilization of phonological differences (morpho-phonology). "Morphonemes, the complex representations of two or more phonemes capable of replacing one other within the same morpheme according to the conditions of the morphological structure of a word, play an essential role in Slavic languages (e.g., in Russian there is the morphoneme *k/č* in *ruk/c—ruka, ručnoj*)" [p. 9].

Next, one considered the *designating activity* of language. By means of the act of designation, language "analyzes reality—whether external or internal, material or abstract—into linguistically graspable elements" [p. 10]. A theory of syntagmatic procedures was put on the circle's program: *"Predication is the fundamental correlating {syntagmatic} act, and at the same time it is the intrinsic sentence-creating act"* [p. 10].

Finally, the circle studied these sytematizations not in abstract theoretical frameworks but in the material language, which was itself considered through its material manifestations in *communication.* From that ensued the circle's interest in literary language, art, and culture in general. Research was undertaken on the different functional and stylistic levels of language.

In this collection of quite vast and varied research, a major place was occupied by *phonological* theories, which were due primarily to the work of Trubetskoi and Jakobson.

Starting from Saussure, for whom phonemes were "the first units obtained by cutting up the spoken chain" [p. 40] and which he had defined as "above all, oppositional, relative, and negative units," Jakobson wrote, "We shall call the *phonological system* of a language the repertory, proper to this language, of 'significant differences' that exist among the ideas of the acoustico-motor units, that is, the repertory of oppositions to which can be attached, in a given language, a differentiation of significations (repertory of *phonological oppositions*). All terms of phonological opposition that cannot be dissociated into smaller phonological sub-oppositions are called *phonemes"* ("Remarks on the Phonetic Evolution of Russian Compared to that of Other Slavic Languages," WPLC, 1929, vol. 2).

Trubetskoi revealed his theses in his *Grundzge der Phonologie* (WPLC, 1939, vol. 7; French translation, *Principes de phonologie,* Paris, 1949). He took up and clarified certain definitions of the phoneme—differential, representative element; *sound-image,* and not physical *sound;*

atoms of the spoken chain—owing to Russian linguists such as L. V. Scerba or N. E. Jakobov, and especially to Jakobson (WPLC, 1929, vol. 2). Indeed, Scerba had written in 1912, "[The phoneme is] the briefest general phonic representation that, in the language being studied, has the power to be associated with other given representations or meanings, and to differentiate words." For Plyvanov, the phoneme was "the briefest generic phonetic representation, proper to a given language and capable of being associated with semantic representations and of being used to differentiate words," while Jakobson wrote that the phoneme was "each phonic particularity that can be removed from the spoken chain as the briefest element capable of being used to differentiate signified units."

From the first pages of his *Principles,* Trubetskoi clarified the difference between *phonetics*—the science of the sounds of speech—and *phonology*—the science of the sounds of *la langue.* While phonetics was "the science of the material side of the sounds of human language," phonology studied "how elements of differentiation (or marks, according to K. Bühler) behave among themselves and what rules determine how they combine with one another to form words and sentences." "Phonology should only consider as a sound that which performs a determined function in *la langue.*" Now, since *la langue* was a system of differences, the function of an element was not fulfilled unless this element, which was connected to the others, was distinguished from (opposed to) another element. For instance in French the phoneme {p} is opposed to the phoneme {b}, for the substitution of one for the other can produce changes in signification (*pas/bas,* not/low). *In contrast, any individual pronunciation change* of {p} or {b} that did not lead to a change in meaning was not *pertinent;* it did not produce a change of phonemes; it only introduced variations of the same phoneme. "We shall call the phonic oppositions which, in the language in question, can differentiate the intellectual meanings of two words, *phonological oppositions* (or distinctive phonological oppositions or perhaps *distinctive* oppositions)."

The terms of such an opposition were called "phonological units." Phonological units could sometimes be broken down into even smaller phonological units called "acoustic atoms." Now phonological units that, from the point of view of the language in question, were not able to be analyzed as even smaller, successive phonological units were called "phonemes." "The *phoneme* is thus the smallest phonological unit of the language being studied. The signifying side of every word that exists in the language can be analyzed as phonemes and represented as a determinative series of phonemes." All the while insisting upon the difference between the phoneme and the concrete sound ("Concrete sounds that figure in the language are rather the simple material symbols of phonemes"), Trubetskoi was opposed to the tendency to "psychologize" the phoneme and to see in it a "psychological equivalent of the sounds of language" (Baudouin de Courtenay), as well as the tendency to confuse it with the phonic image. "The phoneme is the sum of the phonologically pertinent particularities comprising a phonic image." For what constituted a phoneme was its *distinctive* function in the whole of the spoken chain. It was isolated by a *functional* (structural and systematic) analysis of each concrete language, and in no way depended on a psychological support; instead it depended on the system proper to that language. Indeed, functional oppositions were not the same in all languages. Palatal vowels (oral) in French for example are divided into two series, rounded (*u, oe,* and *o*) and nonrounded (*iè, é,* and *è*). However, Italian and Spanish do not have the rounded series (*peu, deux* are hard to pronounce for Spaniards and Italians). Nor does Spanish differentiate between half-*closed* vowels and half-*open* ones (*élè, ólò*).

This descriptive procedure of phonology, which analyzes the spoken chain in distinctive units, was taken up by other branches of language study, and is today the basis of structuralism. M. Leroy (*Les Grands courants de la linguistique du XXe siècle,* 1963) has pointed out that phonology has renewed as well the view of traditional historical and comparative grammar. For instance, it was realized that the phonological principle of *alternation* plays an important role in the morphology of various languages. For example, the formation of the feminine in French is done either by a voicing alternation (*neuf, neuve*) or by a zero degree/full degree alternation (that is, by adding a consonant [sound], as in *vert, verte, grand, grande*). Moreover, the method of phonology was applied to comparative linguistics; this led to the compilation of an inventory of phonetic changes by placing them in a system. In this vein, Jakobson published in 1931 *Principles of Historical Phonetics,* and

Proposition 22 of the circle proclaimed that "The problem of the purpose for which changes have taken place must be posed. Historical phonetics is transformed in this way into a history of the evolution of a phonological system."

Diachronic phonology thus became necessary. It was elaborated by A. Martinet (*Economie des changements phonétiques, Traité de phonologie diachronique,* Berne, 1955).

However, the radical development of the phonological theses of the Prague school, which constituted the foundation of the structural method that was already in an embryonic stage in Trubetskoi, was due to the work of Jakobson. He put into place the theory of *distinctive features:* every distinctive unit of language was composed of *features* in binary opposition. The pertinent oppositions number a dozen in all the languages of the world. *La langue* was therefore a system whose distinctive elements were in *binary opposition;* the other oppositions, which did not have a distinctive value, were called *redundant.*

The binarist hypothesis was unveiled with much rigor in *Observations on the Phonological Classing of Consonants* (1938). What are these binary oppositions? They function on the basis of terms that are *contradictory* (presence/absence: for example, long vowels/short vowels) and *contrary* (maximum/minimum: for example, low vowels/high vowels). Consonants can also be grouped along the axis of these oppositions. The difference in the place of articulation can be systemized into two phonological oppositions, front/back and low/high (figure 19.1).

p	t	front
k	c	back
high	low	

Figure 19.1

By using modern techniques of recording and sound reproduction, Jakobson and his team were able to establish a general phonological theory based on the principle of binarism. The complete exposition can be found in the book by Jakobson and M. Halle, *Fundamentals of Language,* 1955. The twelve binary oppositions established by the binarists were neither provisional nor arbitrary; they answered an empirical necessity. They do nevertheless have a universal character. Thus for Jakobson the triangle shown in figure 19.2 represents the optimal differentiation of phonemes.

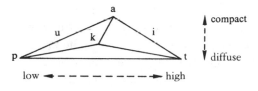

Figure 19.2

Jakobson also proposed an interesting theory about synchrony and diachrony, which remedied the usual static state of structural theories. Synchrony, for him, was dynamic. The synchrony of film was not a juxtaposition of images, it was a synchronic totality in motion. As for phonetic changes, they were not due to a cause, but a *purpose,* which reestablished the principle of phonological differentiation; they operated by *leaps.*

True to the program of the Prague Linguistic Circle, a major part of Jakobson's research analyzed the *linguistic act* and the *functions* of language.

It was probably Jakobson's interest in the poetic functioning of language, as well as in linguistic functioning in aphasics and children, that allowed him to revise the Saussurian theory of the *linearity of the signifier.* In his *Course,* Saussure had maintained the thesis of the *linking* of linguistic elements, and had presented discourse as a spoken *chain.* Other works by Saussure, the *Anagrammes* (published in part initially by J. Starobinski in 1964) showed another conception of the signifying combination, one that corresponded to a *tabular* rather than to a *chain* model. Before the publication of these works, Jakobson had been the first to question the linearity of the signifier by studying not only the combination but also the *selection* of linguistic signs, not only their linking but their *competition.* He isolated two axes in poetic language:

metonymic (the linking of units by contiguity; characteristic of prose, the epic, and realism), and metaphoric (by resemblance; characteristic of lyric poetry, etc.) Aphasic problems could be classified on these two axes.

THE COPENHAGEN CIRCLE

Structuralist principles were espoused with much rigor, bias, and exigency, and on bases that were more logical than phonological, by the Copenhagen Linguistic Circle. In 1939 the first issue of the review *Acta Linguistica* appeared, in which was published Viggo Bröndal's "structuralist manifesto," "Structural Linguistics." Bröndal first established an indictment of comparative grammar: it had been "inspired by an interest in tiny true facts," and was qualified by him as "positivist," "purely physiological and psychological," and "legal" to the extent that it was able to become more and more rigorous and methodical by formulating "more and more of its results (for the most part historical and phonetic at the same time) in the forms of laws." Having done this, he went on to recall that all the sciences of his time had changed their view. Quantum physics with Planck, biology with de Vries, etc., all had given in to "the necessity of isolating, of carving out in the flux of time the proper object for a science, that is, of positing on the one hand states that would be considered stationary and, on the other hand, sudden leaps from one state to another." The same thing had happened in linguistics with the Saussurian distinction synchrony/diachrony. Still emphasizing the same epistomological break, Bröndal recalled that sciences had understood "the necessity of the general concept, the only unit possible in particular cases, in all the individual manifestations of the same object. Such is the concept of a genotype in biology, of a social fact (Durkheim) in sociology, or of *la langue*—at once species and institution—in linguistics. As a consequence, science therefore had taken "a closer look at the rational connections inside the object being studied." The term *structure* used in physics, biology, and psychology translated the belief that "reality must have in its totality an internal cohesiveness, a particular structure." Bröndal saw the premises of such an approach to linguistics in Saussure, who had spoken of the "system of *la langue*," in Sapir (see below) and in Trubetskoi, who, "to his great credit, founded and elaborated structuralistic doctrine for phonetic systems."

Structural linguistics relied upon three concepts: *synchrony* (or the identity of a given language), *la langue* (or the unity of the language identified by synchronic study), and *structure* (or the totality of a language whose identity and unity had already been recognized). The structure was penetrated by establishing among these identified elements all the constant, necessary, and, therefore, constitutive connections. "For it is not until successive states of language have been established—two worlds, varied and closed like *monads* with respect to one other, despite their conformity in time—that one will be able to study the modalities of the reorganization rendered necessary by the transition of one into the other, and the historical factors responsible for this transition." While he admitted that "time is emphasized inside synchrony," Bröndal was already heralding the shape of ahistorical, universalist structuralism by envisaging a "panchrony or achrony, that is, universally human factors that persist throughout history and inside the state of any language."

Bröndal's manifesto formulated two warnings that *glossematics,* professed by the Copenhagen school, had noticeably neglected. The first concerned the relation between abstract *theory,* which posited the object of study, and the material *experience* of language: "It in no way follows that we have underestimated the value of the *empiric.* Increasingly detailed observations and an increasingly complete verification will, on the contrary, be required in order to fill in and give life to the frameworks posited by theoretical construction." The second has to do with the philosophical study of the categories making up the system, or its foundations: "The elements that make up a system cannot possibly be considered simple derivatives of structural correlations or oppositions. . . . The study of real categories, whether as the content or basis of systems, will not be any less important than that of the formal structure. *Husserl's penetrating meditations on phenomenology will in this case be a source of inspiration for every logician of language"* (italics added). Unfortunately, this *substantialism* was neglected by Bröndal's successors and by Bröndal himself in his later work.

Applying his theses in a more precise fashion in his book *Essays in*

General Linguistics (Copenhagen 1943), Bröndal proposed describing every morphological system by a combination of four terms, of which A was neutral (thus the indicative in verb modes, or the third person, the "impersonal" form of persons) and was contrasted with B, which was positive or negative. The C term was complex, and could be complex-negative, or complex-positive (among the modes, this was the optative one; among tenses, the preterite-present, etc.) With the help of these four terms, and by applying Leibnizian logical rules to them (Leibniz was frequently Bröndal's referent), the author was able to calculate the number of possible morphological systems that had occurred during the course of the changes in languages. He felt that neutral forms had become more and more widespread in modern languages (English had eliminated [certain] modes, aspects, and tenses, while impersonal forms predominate in it, etc.) or that they were frequent in the languages of ancient civilizations (Chinese), but were much more rare in ancient Indo-European languages. One can see the *logical* orientation of linguistics in Bröndal who, while emphasizing the "mutual autonomy, equal importance, and complementary nature of the system of syntax, of *la langue,* and discourse," insisted upon the fact that structural linguistics had much to learn from logic.

It was the work of Hjelmslev, however, which made famous the linguistic conception of the Copenhagen school. In 1928 he published his *Principles of General Grammar;* he later continued his research with P. Lier and H. Uldall by elaborating a linguistic conception designated by the name *glossematics.* This theory, perfected over a period of some years, was revealed in its definitive form in *Prolegomena to a Theory of Language* (1943, English edition 1953).[5]

Taking Saussure and Weisgerber (*Muttersprache und Geistesbildung,* Göttingen, 1928) as his starting point, the author in this book considered *la langue* not as a conglomerate of nonlinguistic phenomena (for example, physical, physiological, logical, or social) but as a self-sufficient totality, as a sui generis structure [p. 2]. Hjelmslev criticized as humanistic the conception of language that contrasted the character of language with that of natural phenomena, and which believed that language could not be grasped by "mere description" [p. 4]. He himself was convinced that "for every *process* there is a corresponding *system* by which the process can be analyzed and described by means of a limited number of premises" [p. 5].

What should this linguisitic discourse that would isolate the rigorous systematicity of language be like? Hjelmslev devoted a large part of his work to the description of the methodological procedures of linguistics, which above all had to *elaborate* its object: *la langue* as a system. *"The description shall be free of contradiction (self-consistent), exhaustive, and as simple as possible. The requirement of freedom from contradiction takes precedence over the requirement for exhaustive description and the need for exhaustive description takes precedence over that of simplicity"* [p. 6; italics in the original]. This linguistic method was designated as "necessarily empirical and necessarily deductive" [p. 7]. That amounts to saying that to a certain extent theory is independent of experience, and that it contains premises whose validity need not be demonstrated by the theoretician, because previous experience has convinced him of them. Theory was therefore first *arbitrary,* and next *appropriate* to the empirical data [p. 8]. What would the criteria be for the acceptance of such-and-such basic postulate of this theory? While advocating that linguistic theory should consist of the least possible number of implicit or intuitive premises (wasn't that Husserl's initial requirement?), Hjelmslev believed that the linguist must "invade the domain of epistemology," for "we leave it to epistemology to decide whether our linguistic theory has need of such premises [axioms and postulates] beyond those explicitly introduced by linguistic theory" [p. 8]. Our procedure here is based upon the conviction that *"it is impossible to elaborate the theory of a particular science without an active collaboration with epistemology"* [p. 9; italics added].

Linguistics defined in this way took as its object of study *texts* considered as *processes,* which it had to understand by elaborating self-consistent and exhaustive descriptions, or in other words, descriptions through which it could find the *system* of *la langue.* However, since the process consisted of elements in various combinations or *dependent* relations, linguistics' only aim was to describe these relations. "A dependence that fulfills the conditions for an analysis we shall call a *function.* The terminals of the function we shall call *functives,* understanding by a *functive* an object that has function to other objects. . . .

By a *constant* we shall understand a functive whose presence is a necessary condition for the presence of the functive to which it has function; by a *variable* we shall understand a functive whose presence is not a necessary condition for the presence of the functive to which it has function" [pp. 20–21]. Starting from there, there were three types of functions: *interdependence* (a function between two constants), *determination* (a function between a constant and a variable), and *constellation* (a function between two variables) [p. 21]. Another distinction between functions concerned the *both-and* function (conjunction) and the *either/or* function (disjunction). In the process or text, the function was conjunctive; in the system or *la langue,* the function was disjunctive [p. 22]. For instance, Hjelmslev gave the example of two English words, *pet* and *man,* to illustrate these two functions. "By interchanging *p* and *m, e* and *a, t* and *n,* respectively, we obtain different words, namely, *pet, pen, pat, pan, met, men, mat, man.* These entities are *chains* that enter into the linguistic process (*text*); on the other hand, *p* and *m* together, *e* and *a* together, *t* and *n* together produce paradigms which enter into the linguistic system. In *pet,* there is conjunction, or coexistence, between *p* and *e* and *t* . . . , in the same way there is conjunction or coexistence between *m* and *a* and *n.* But between *p* and *m* there is disjunction or *alternation* . . . , in the same way there is disjunction or alternation between *t* and *n*" [p. 22].

Global analysis of the text presupposes that the linguist coordinate the system, by considering the text as a *class* of segments. *Induction* and *synthesis* provide the object as a segment of a class, and not as a divided class. Once the entities have been inventoried, they must be *reduced,* that is, they must be *identified* in order to find the *variants* and the *invariants.* It is in this way that a rigorous system of *la langue* can be built.

Such a logicoformal conception of *la langue,* which had been reduced to an abstract structure of correlates of a formal if not mathematical nature, clearly needed a theory of the *sign.* The sign was first defined as a *sign function* between two entities: a *content* and an *expression.* "The sign is an *expression* that points to a *content* outside the sign itself" [p. 29]. Moreover, and in itself, this function is the *sign* of something else, *meaning* or *purport,* "an entity defined only by its having a function to the structural principle of language [*la langue*] and to all the factors that make languages different from one another" [p. 31]. Its structure could first be analyzed by a nonlinguistic science (physics, or anthropology), whereas, by a series of deductive operations, linguistic science could produce the *linguistic schema,* which was manifested by *linguistic usage.*

In this way Hjelmslev distinguished on the one hand the material of the expression and the content, and, on the other hand, the form. For him, each language *formed* in a different way the amorphous "mass of thought" that only existed as a substance for a form.

For instance, the phrases

jeg véd det ikke (Danish)
I do not know (English)
je ne sais pas (French)
en tiedä (Finnish)
naluvara (Eskimo)

despite their differences, have a common factor, which is precisely the "purport" or the thought itself, the meaning [p. 31].

"We thus recognize in linguistic *content,* in its process, a form, the content-form, which is independent of and stands in arbitrary relation to, the *purport* and forms it into a *content-substance*" [p. 32]. In the same way, the *expression-form* transforms the *expression-purport* into the *expression-substance.* The four terms can be combined according to a schema, and these combinations partition different planes in the analysis of *la langue* (figure 19.3).

	form	substance
content		
expression		

Figure 19.3

"Expression-plane and content-plane . . . are structured in quite analogous fashions . . ." [p. 37].

While *la langue* was an unlimited process in which the number of signs was also unlimited, it was constructed into a system with the help of a small number of *nonsigns* or *figures.* Thus, *la langue* could be considered a *system of signs* from the perspective of its relations with nonlinguistic factors and—within itself—as a *system of figures* that construct *signs.*

The object language of this glossematics had to find its place in the whole of semiotic structures. Hjelmslev envisaged the semiotic domain as an *absolute totality* that included all scientific objects likely to have a structure analogous to that of language: semiology "is a hierarchy, any of whose elements admits of a further division into classes defined by mutual relation, so that any of these classes admits of a division into derivates, defined by mutual mutation" [p. 65].

In order to introduce into semiology objects other than natural languages, Hjelmslev first defined in an even more precise way his concept of *language,* which could be extended beyond natural languages. According to him, language was any signifying structure that could be interpreted on the two planes of content and expression. Games, for example, are not languages because they cannot be interpreted on these two planes: "if two planes are tentatively posited, the functional net[work] will be entirely the same in both" [p. 72] Systems like those of mathematical or logical symbols, or music, are probably not languages according to Hjelmslev's meaning: he proposed calling them *symbolic systems.*

Inside *languages* themselves, another clarification was made with the help of the concepts *denotation* and *connotation.* For indeed every text is composed of derivatives based upon different systems (style, type of style, national or regional language, etc.). "The individual members of each of these classes and the units resulting from their combination we shall call *connotators*" [p. 74]. In other words, connotators are the parts that enter into functives in such a way that the functives are never without ambiguity, and are found in both planes of language. The language of connotation is built upon or rests upon the language of denotation. "Its expression plane is provided by the content plane and expression plane of a denotative language" [p. 76]. Thus, the schema or schemas and linguistic usages that we call the French language are the *expression* of the connotator "French." It is therefore a language in which one of the planes, that of expression, is a language.

In contrast, if a language furnishes the plane for the content of another language, then the latter is the metalanguage of the former. Linguistics, for example, is a metalanguage because it is built on the content plane of language. Starting from this definition, Hjelmslev was able to redefine semiology: "A metalanguage whose object language is a non-scientific language" [p. 77]. But this construction of overlapping languages contained a final level—*metasemiology*—which is a scientific metalanguage whose object languages are semiologies.

This totalizing and ambitious project of Hjelmslev's is far from being completed, and its abstract character is no doubt the major obstacle to its fulfillment. Moreover, the logical orientation that the theory of language took with Hjelmslev is far from being strictly rigorous, and in practice often proves to be intuitive. Finally, the concrete descriptions attempted on the basis of this theory are extremely complex. Since the theory is still in the process of being elaborated today, it is difficult to judge its qualities. Nevertheless, one can note as of now its apriorism and ahistoricism, which betray the well-known metaphysics of the "systematized totality." Lacking any interrogation of the presuppositions of such a constructivism, glossematics is symptomatic of the "belle époque" of systematizing Reason, convinced of the omnivalence of its transcendental operation. Nonetheless, the fact still remains that the glossematicians were the first, if not the only ones, in modern structural linguistics to have suggested epistemological problems. In this way they have managed to avoid the naïveté of "objective" descriptivism, and to call attention to the role of scientific *discourse* in the construction of its object.

AMERICAN STRUCTURALISM

Since the beginning of this century, American linguistics has been oriented toward the current of structural linguistics by the work of scholars such as Boas, who was trained in the neogrammarian school, and who in 1917 founded *The International Journal of American Lin-*

guistics, but especially by scholars like Sapir (1884–1939) and Bloom-field (1887–1949).

While European linguists understand a structure to be "the arrangement of a whole into parts and the demonstrable coherence of these reciprocally conditioned parts in the whole," American linguists have in mind primarily "the distribution of the elements as it is observed, and the capacity of these elements for association and substitution."[6] American structuralism is thus notably different from the structuralism we have seen in Europe. It divides the whole into its constitutive elements and "defines each of these elements by its position in the whole and by the variations and substitutions possible in this same position" (Benveniste, "Recent Trends . . ." [p. 8]).

Sapir's work as a whole (his book *Language,* 1921, as well as his collected works—see *Selected Writings on Language, Culture, and Personality,* ed. D. G. Mandelbaum, 1949) are distinguished by a vast conception of language that is in strong contrast to both the overly theoretical tendencies of glossematics and the technical nature of the American structuralism that came later. For Sapir, language was a communicative, social activity. He did not neglect its different functions and aspects; he took into account scientific and poetic language, the psychological aspect of the utterance, its relations to thought, reality, and language, etc. While his position was generally structuralist, it was moderated: for him, language was a historical *product,* "the product of long-continued social usage" [p. 2]. "Speech . . . varies as all creative effort varies—not as consciously, perhaps, but none the less as truly as do the religions, the beliefs, the customs, and the art of different peoples. . . . Speech is a non-instinctive, acquired, 'cultural' function" [p. 4]. Language was a representation of real experience: "the essence of language consists in the assigning of conventional and voluntarily articulated sounds, or of their equivalents, to the diverse elements of experience" [p. 11]. Elements of language (Sapir had words in mind) did not symbolize an object, they symbolized the "concept," that is, "a convenient capsule of thought that embraces thousands of distinct experiences and that is ready to take in thousands more. . . . The actual flow of speech may be interpreted as a record of the setting of these concepts into their mutual relations" [p. 13]. Nevertheless, for Sapir, "language and thought are not strictly coterminous. At best, language can but be the outward facet of thought on the highest, most generalized level of symbolic expression" [p. 15]. "The most rarefied thought may be but the conscious counterpart of an unconscious linguistic symbolism" [p. 21]. Sapir even went so far as to consider the existence of communication systems "outside of speech," although they would *necessarily* exist through "the intermediary of a truly linguistic symbolism." [p. 21]. The possibility this "speech symbolism" has of being transferred to systems of communication other than speech itself implied for Sapir that "the mere sounds of speech are not the essential fact of language, which lies rather in the classification, in the formal patterning, and in the relating of concepts" [p. 22].

Sapir formulated his structural conception of language in this way: "Language, as a structure, is on its inner face the mold of thought" [p. 22]. This structure is universal: "There is no more striking general fact about language than its universality. . . . The lowliest of the South African Bushmen speaks in the forms of a rich symbolic system that is in essence perfectly comparable to the speech of the cultivated Frenchman" [p. 22].

Sapir studied the elements of speech, and first of all, *sounds.* While he did describe their articulation and their value, he did not develop a phonological theory. In his later works, however, he had already begun to distinguish between a "sound" and a "phonic element."

In *Language,* Sapir studied *forms in language;* he analyzed "grammatical processes," that is, the formal methods (the composition of words, the order of words, etc.), and the "grammatical concepts." Sapir first examined the "world of concepts in so far as the world is reflected and systematized in linguistic structure" [p. 82]. He used an English sentence as his example for analyzing the *concrete concepts:* the object, the subject, the action, etc., expressed by a radical element or by a derivational element, and the *relational concepts:* reference, modality, personal relations, number, and time [p. 88]. Having done this, he then noted that the same concepts may "not only be expressed in different form, but may be differently grouped among themselves" in other languages [p. 90]. Having established this commonality of the conceptual structures of languages, Sapir sketched out a *typology* of linguistic structures. This enabled him to give his interpretation of language in history: how language was shaped by history; how phonetic laws show that *la langue* is a product of history; and how languages reciprocally influence one another (borrowing of words, phonetic modification of borrowed words, morphological borrowings, etc.) Sapir refused to consider language through mechanistic methods and was opposed to the behaviorism that resulted from them. He insisted above all on the *symbolic* character of language, on its complexity, which was due to the intersection of the *configuration system,* the *symbolic system,* and the *expressive system,* and finally on its primary function, which for Sapir was *communication.*

Sapir's tendency, often characterized as "mentalistic," was opposed by Bloomfield's behaviorist conception of language, which he revealed in his main work, *Language* (1933).[7] This materialistic and mechanistic conception (see G. C. Lepschy, *Structural Linguistics,* Turin, 1966, French edition, 1968) is based upon the famous *stimulus-response* schema:

$$S \rightarrow r \cdot \cdot \cdot \cdot \cdot \cdot s \rightarrow R$$

A stimulus (S), which is a real event, can be mediated by discourse: it is therefore replaced by a *vocal movement,* speech (r). This produces a *vibration* in the listener's *tympanic membrane;* for the listener, the vibration is a *linguistic stimulus* (s), which is translated into a practical response (R). The r . . . s connection is called a *speech event* or a *speech-utterance.* In agreement with the doctrines of J. B. Watson (*Behaviorism,* 1924) and A. P. Weiss (*A Theoretical Basis of Human Behavior,* 1925), Bloomfield refused to accept any psychological interpretation of the linguistic fact, and demanded a strictly mechanistic approach. According to him, the linguist should deal only with events that in both time and place were accessible to any observer; that is, events had to be located in the coordinates of time and space. Theoreticism was replaced by *physicalism:* the linguist had to use rigidly defined terms that could be derived from a collection of daily terms dealing with physical events.

This scientific extremism was no doubt in reaction to mentalism, which was considered imprecise. It responded to the need for language study constructed on rigorous bases. One cannot, however, avoid emphasizing the theoretical blindness of behaviorism and its genetic inability to think about mechanistic ideology pertaining to its technicist presuppositions. It is obviously impossible to explain the complexity of the discursive act by the S-r . . . s-R schema alone. Language is not a sensory mechanics, and to refuse the relative autonomy of the sign and the field of signification it governs is in fact to explain nothing about the functioning of language.

Bloomfield also rebelled against the linguistic theories of the *signi-fied.*[8] Since he considered the signified the whole of the practical events linked to the utterance, he affirmed that linguistic science would never be able to tackle it without taking into account the "state of the speaker's body" and the "predisposition of the nervous sound system, which results from all of his experience, linguistic and other, up to this very moment—not to speak of hereditary and pre-natal factors" [p. 141]. The accuracy of this remark, which unveils the weakness of mentalism, no doubt designates that more work—which has yet to be done—is needed to get out of logicism and to elaborate, without falling into mechanistic behaviorism, a theory of language linked to the corporal and physical materiality of the speaking subject and his environment.

Bloomfield proposed precise formalist descriptions of grammatical phenomena. We shall present here some of these descriptions, which can be summed up by the schema in figure 19.4 [p. 264].

		lexical	grammatical
minimal unit deprived of signified	phememe	phoneme	taxeme
minimal unit with signified	glosseme	morpheme	tagmeme
signified of such units	noeme	sememe	episememe
unit with signified (minimal or complex)	linguistic form	lexical form	grammatical form

Figure 19.4

The morpheme is a simple form that cannot be analyzed any further: it is an *ultimate constituent,* but at every stage of the analysis one must look for the *immediate constituents.* The sememe is the morpheme's signified. The lexical forms formed by the phonemes and the grammatical forms formed by the taxemes result in two parallel series that constitute the "meaningful features of linguistic signaling" [p. 264].

As for the phonemes themselves, they are composed of *distinctive features* accompanied by other features; they play a specific role in "the structural grouping of linguistic forms." They therefore depend upon "structural facts" and not only upon mechanistic description. Consequently, they are the object of a *phonology* that is distinct from phonetic description and "practical phonetics."

Taking Bloomfield's work as its inspiration, American structuralism devoted itself exclusively to a description of the syntagmatic structure. This way of proceeding accentuates the rigorous application of basic concepts in descriptive as well as historical research. These concepts encompass the phoneme, morpheme, and other units of linguistic analysis that Bloomfield had used, and are used to build a general theory of linguistic structure. Linguistic analysis was considered a logical calculus leading to the discovery of the basic units of language and their formal arrangement. John B. Carroll (*The Study of Language: A Survey of Linguistics and Related Disciplines in America,* 1953) has written that this procedure can in principle be followed without any reference to the external signification of linguistic forms. This author has noted that the method of American linguists "often seems to be a compulsion to carry such a procedure to its logical conclusion, even when the results may seem somewhat absurd from a common-sense point of view."[9] Further, he stated, "A general characteristic of the methodology of descriptive linguistics as practiced by many American linguists today, is the effort to analyze linguistic structure without reference to meaning. It is thought possible in theory that one could identify the phonemes and morphemes of language purely on the basis of their *distribution,* that is, by noting the linguistic environments in which they occur. Such a type of analysis would be desirable, it is thought, because unconscious biases might lead one to prejudge the analysis if one makes references to meanings" [pp. 31–32; italics added].

Such a conception was therefore inspired by Bloomfield's principle of *immediate constituent analysis*. One takes an utterance, divides it into two parts, which are in turn divided into two parts, etc., until one arrives at the minimal elements that can no longer be divided using the same criteria. In this way one finds the immediate constituents but one doesn't name them; they are "without labels," and are indicated instead by parentheses (by unlabeled bracketing). Thus the sentence "La vieille mère de Jean écrit une longue lettre [John's old mother is writing a long letter]" can be divided as in figure 19.5 where the two segments immediately to the right or left of a vertical bar are the immediate constituents of the segment they form.

	vieille	mère					longue	lettre
La	vieille	mère	de	Jean		une	longue	lettre
La	vieille	mère	de	Jean		une	longue	lettre
La	vieille	mère	de	Jean	écrit	une	longue	lettre
La	vieille	mère	de	Jean	écrit	une	longue	lettre

or instead:

La vieille mère de Jean écrit une longue lettre

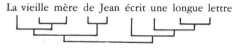

Figure 19.5

It can be seen that this is a matter of purely formal description that doesn't seem to take classical grammatical categories into account, much less the philosophical categories that established the classical analysis of the sentence (subject, predicate, etc.). This formal analysis proposed by American structuralism has one important advantage: it frees up the logical categories explicitly used in the analysis of language, and offers the possibility of studying languages that do not need these logical categories to construct a signifying system. The Chinese language, for example, does not need to clarify tense in the verb form, or determination by an article. The Indian language Yana for its part

introduces a grammatical category unknown in Indo-European languages: it indicates whether the utterance is assumed by the speaker,
or whether he is referring to an authority, etc. Certain linguists also
believe that formalization can free linguistic analysis from the presuppositions formed on the basis of Indo-European languages, and therefore free it from Eurocentrism.

But in fact these grammatical categories are implicitly admitted,
without being directly questioned. For, limiting ourselves to the example given above, the cuts that isolate the immediate constituents
obey the "intuitive feelings' of the analyst. He puts together "long"
and "letter," "old" and "mother," by relying upon his knowledge of
determination and government *{rection}*. He brings "writes" and "letter" together by relying upon his knowledge of objects, etc. We therefore note that in fact a whole implicit traditional knowledge underlies
a description that is presented as being purely formal. Nevertheless,
an epistemological break is manifest in this abandonment of the traditional principles of linguistic description and in the use of a method
that claims to be neutral.

Benveniste suggested that this change was due to the fact that American linguists have had to describe numerous unknown languages, and
have thus been *forced* to opt for a neutral description, which wasn't
supposed to refer to how the researcher conceived of the language.
The reason for this was that since he did not know how the informant
conceived of the language (one of Bloomfield's rules was to not ask the
informant what he thought of his language), the researcher ran the risk
of transferring his own language's way of thought [to the language
being studied]. One can point out in this respect that while the discovery of Sanskrit forced European linguists to situate their national languages with respect to it and to promote a comparative method, the
discovery of American languages that were very different from English
forced American linguistics into a theoretical abstraction that clung to
technical cut-outs in order to avoid having to deal with *philosophy*
(ideology). This was so because the philosophy of the informant could
not be known, and that of the researcher had to be effaced. Let us add
to this situation the fact that most American linguists don't know
foreign languages and base their reflections solely on their own language. These objective "constraints" no doubt do not diminish the

importance of the *theoretical choice* of American linguistics, which censors psychosociological investigations from its own processes and applies a formalization founded on presuppositions laden with signification, presuppositions that European philosophy has been discussing for years. A technical description of language results from this, one that is no doubt mathematically manageable and can be used for automatic translation when it is not inspired by it, but which does not provide an explanatory hypothesis of linguistic functioning. One could even say that the epistemological break introduced by structuralism, of which American structuralism is the extreme formalizing tendency, consists not in *explaining,* but in offering—in accordance with logical positivism—a flat *description,* one blind to its own foundations and technical in its procedure, of what language has become: a static object, without subject or history.

But what aspect, starting from such theoretical bases, do semantics, morphology, and phonetics take on?

American linguistics has a habit of presenting itself in one of the six following forms, which Carroll has described in this way:

Phonetics is the name of the discipline that examines the sounds of language from an articulatory and acoustical point of view.

Phonemics also classifies the sounds of language; it groups them into units called phonemes, which play a differential role in the utterance.

Morphology studies the construction of words by identifying *morphemes* (the smallest structural units that have a grammatical or lexical signification), their combination and change in words and various grammatical constructions.

Morphophonemics, a branch of morphology, is the study of the phonetic construction of morphemes, as well as of the phonemic variation of morphemes in different grammatical constructions.

Syntax studies the construction of the clause, but is directly dependent upon morphology. Syntax has even been supplanted by a morphology that cuts the sentence order up into segments and units, and which is presented as an analysis that takes the place of syntax.

Lexicography, finally, compiles a list and an analysis of all the meaningful elements in the system of language [see p. 24].

Let us first emphasize the fact that by renouncing the classical categories of linguistic description and by adopting a formal description,

American structuralism was forced not to treat *syntax*. By breaking the utterance up into segments that one then tried to arrange into paradigms according to their distribution, American linguistics was not able to elaborate propositions about the *relations* of the terms of the sentence. It became mechanically analytical, without being able to grasp the laws of the synthesis of the constituents in the whole of the utterances. To remedy this lack, Chomsky could not do without a theory of the subject of the signification, or in other words, a philosophy. By going back two centuries, he found it in the *Grammar* of Port-Royal.

In the realm of *phonemics,* let us mention the work of M. Swadesh, W. F. Twadell, B. Bloch, and finally C. F. Hockett's book *A Manual of Phonology* (1955). The fundamental principle of phonemics is the definition of a formal criterion for identifying phonemes. This criterion, called *complementary distribution* or *patterned congruence* states that two sounds that are phonetically similar cannot contrast with each other to the point of producing differences in meaning (for instance, *t* and *t* in *tone* and *stone* in English, while being phonetically different, one aspirated and the other not, do not produce a difference in meaning). The two sounds are called *allophones* of the same phoneme. Patterned congruence consists more precisely in grouping the sounds of a language with respect to the kinds of phonetic environments; this reveals certain changes in the behavior of partially similar sounds (see Carroll) [pp. 33–34].

These identification procedures for phonemes can be applied to the morphological units of language, as well as to complex signifying systems, such as literature, dance, etc.; this is the starting point for the structural method in the so-called human sciences (see, at the end of this book, the chapter on semiotics).

Morphemics has an important place in American linguistics. Let us mention, among the books devoted to this problem, Z. Harris' *Structural Linguistics* (1951). The analysis of languages other than Indo-European ones showed that traditional morphological categories such as the noun (designating the thing), the verb (designating the action), etc., which correspond to a logical analysis (see Port-Royal) could not be applied. The word cannot be identified with the concept it expresses, and psychological and psychoanalytic experience prove that a word is not made up of only one concept or meaning. The formal method of phonemics has also been transferred to morphemics: the *morpheme* in morphology corresponds to the phoneme in phonemics. "Any form, whether free or bound, which cannot be divided into smaller parts is a *morpheme*. Thus, *man, play, person* are words consisting of a single morpheme each; *manly, played, personal* are complex words since each of them contains a bound morpheme (*-ly, -ed, -al*)."[10] Such are the definitions given by Bloch and Trager in *Outline of Linguistic Analysis* (1942). Just as phonemes have positional variants called allophones, morphemes have positional variants called *allomorphs* that can be quite different phonemically—for instance, among the allomorphs of the morpheme *be,* one finds *am, are,* and *is.* As we have said, once the morphemes have been identified, morphology establishes the *classes* of morphemes according to their "differential positioning in the utterance,"[11] as, for example, the class of morphemes that can be substituted for "courage" in "courageous" and for "courage" in "encourage." Finally, and starting from the two preceding stages, an immediate constituent analysis can be carried out; this analysis takes the place of classical syntactic analysis.

As we can see, the morpheme is the minimal element of this analysis. It takes up the *semanteme* and the *lexeme* of the current vocabulary, and is then located on the level of vocabulary and semantics rather than on that of grammar, while grouping certain problems of syntax to the extent that each morpheme undergoes immediate constituent analysis. By dividing the utterance into segments, morphemes can be identified without taking entities such as the "word" into account.

After the very complex theory Bloomfield established for the morpheme, and after a long period of silence in this realm, his research has been taken up again by contemporary linguists. Hockett uses the terms "entities and process" to mark in a dynamic fashion the distinction between two similar forms as being due to a *change:* for instance, *finissons* [first person plural of the French verb, "to finish"] becomes *finissez* [second person plural]. From a static point of view and using the terms "entities and dispositions," one can say that *finissons* and *finissez* are two dispositions of three morphemes, taken two at a time: finiss ô e.

For Harris, morphematic analysis is comprised of three stages: (1)

the transcription and isolation of minimal parts that in other utterances have the same signification—these are called morpheme alternates; (2) the constitution of a single morpheme, starting from the morpheme alternates that have the same signified, are in complementary distribution, and do not have a greater distribution than the other particular alternates; (3) the establishment of general definitions for morphemes that have the same differences between alternates.[12]

In 1964 Harris published his book *String Analysis of Sentence Structure,*[13] in which he proposed a conception of the sentence that differed from immediate constituent analysis as well as from transformational analysis. "Each sentence," Harris wrote, "consists of one elementary sentence (its center), plus zero or more elementary adjuncts, i.e., word sequences of particular structure which are not themselves sentences, and which are adjoined immediately to the right or to the left of an elementary sentence or adjunct, or of a stated segment of an elementary sentence" [p. 9]. The difference with respect to constituent analysis is that the latter cuts the sentence up into lower descriptive levels that include one other. Harris noted that most constituents either consisted of a single word, or instead a word that characterized the constituent, plus another word; he defined such a constituent in clause A as *endocentric* [p. 12]. In other words, he expanded the constituents' characterizing category by adding adjuncts, so that each constituent could be replaced by its characterizing category, and a sentence B could be obtained that was related to A as a constituent-expansion of A. This differs from transformational analysis, which reduces every sentence to elementary sentences, whereas *string* analysis isolates only one elementary sentence out of each sentence.

In the realm of syntagmatic analysis, let us also mention E. A. Nida's study (*Morphology,* 1944), which gives striking examples of the positive results as well as the inadequacies of morphematics.

The theories of K. L. Pile, *Language in Relation to a Unified Theory of Human Behavior* (1954 and following years) are situated in Sapir's perspective and try to utilize exact analyses without, however, forgetting semantic problems and cultural criteria. The author distinguished two types of linguistic elements: *-etics* (based on the example of phonetics) and *-emics* (on the example of phon-emics); the first were physical or objective, the second significant. He analyzed utterances in three layers: lexical (where one finds morphemes), phonological (phonemes), and grammatical (composed of units called grammemes or tagmemes). He called his theory "grammemics" or "tagmemics," and offered graphs representing the intersections of complex grammatical relations.

In the realm of *semantics,* American structuralists have maintained a Bloomfieldian mistrust of the signified, and look for the *formal features* capable of revealing it: "The signified is a contextual element." They have proposed the notion of *distribution* for classifying different signifieds. To find out if two words have the same signified, one has to show that they have the same distribution, that is, that they participate in the same context. It is less a question of a syntactic framework than of a lexical site, for a syntactic context can easily tolerate the replacement of one of its terms by another, without using the global meaning to differentiate the signifieds of the two terms. But, even if it is a question of distribution at the lexical site, it is practically impossible to give a list of all the contexts in which the two terms participate. There is no way of proving that if one chooses a finite list from this infinity of contexts, it will contain the "critical" contexts. Synonymy is another obtacle for this theory. If context *a* signifies *b* (*a* and *b* are synonyms), this is not necessarily the same as *b* signifies *a*. It would be better to refer to extralinguistic criteria (the referent) or to a theretico-philosphical interpretation. But then one would find oneself in contradiction with Bloomfieldian principles (see Lepschy, *Structural Linguistics*).

MATHEMATICAL LINGUISTICS

Mathematical linguistics came into being for technical reasons: the construction of electrical computer circuits designed to read or write, and machines designed for automatic translation. To be programmable into a computer, linguistic matter must obviously be treated in the most rigorous and precise fashion. American structuralism, of which we have isolated a few characteristics, blazed just such a rigorous trail; for the rest, it was strongly influenced by the needs of this applied linguistics known as the mathematical.

But mathematical linguistics strictly speaking constitutes an autonomous realm in which two branches must be distinguished: *quantitative* or *statistical* linguistics, and *algebraic* or *algorithmic* linguistics. The first branch operates by using numerical considerations of linguistic facts. The second uses symbols on which it effects operations.

Statistical linguistics counts the linguistic elements and by putting them in relationship with each other formulates quantitative laws; intuition itself might have been able to suggest these, but they would not have taken on the form of laws without a quantitative demonstration. While such research has been accepted in traditional linguistics (counting the terms of a given writer's vocabulary), it did not gain autonomy until the 1930s. It requires of the researcher a patient study of large corpora[14] as well as mathematical experience. Let us mention here one of the first to work in this realm, G. K. Zipf (a synthesis of his research can be found in his book *Human Behavior and the Principle of the Least Effort: An Introduction to Human Ecology,* 1949), as well as Guiraud in France (*Problèmes et méthodes de la statistique linguistique,* 1960), G. Herdan in England (*Quantitative Linguistics,* 1960), and C. F. Hockett (*Language, Mathematics and Linguistics,* 1967), etc.

Information theory gave rise to another mathematical conception of language. It is known that the founders of this theory, Hartly and Shannon, postulate that it is possible to accurately measure a *given aspect* of the transmission of a message, that it, the *relative frequency* of a symbol *i* (or of the quantity that depends upon it). Before going further, let us clarify that "quantity of information" here means a function relative to the rarity of certain symbols, and that a semantic or psychological meaning is not given to the term "information." Bar-Hillel insists upon the fact that it is a question of the *transmission* of symbols that have been deprived of signifieds. The quantity of information was found to be the logarithmic function of the inverse of such a relative frequency:

$$\log \frac{I}{f^r(i)}.$$

The term used, *binary digit (bit),* is a unit of measure whose logarithm is in base 2. The number of bits must correspond to the number of binary cuts that need to be made in order to identify an element in an inventory. For instance, a message composed of a symbol chosen between two equipotent symbols *a* and *b* would have one bit of information. But if the symbol is chosen from among 26 other symbols (let's say the letters of the alphabet) the message would have 5 bits of information. This binarism evokes that of Jakobson's phonological theory. If one admits that a computer can produce infinite information, then the value of the frequency is called the "probability" $p(i)$, and the quantity of information associated with the symbol is

$$\log \frac{1}{p(i)}.$$

Another branch of mathematical linguistics deals with so-called mathematical or automatic translation. Starting from an original language, from which one translates and which is called the *source language*, automatic translation produces a text in the language into which one is translating, or the *target language*. In order to do this, it is necessary, of course, to program into the computer not only lexical correspondences from the source language to the target language but also the formal relations between the utterances of the source language and those of the target language, and between their parts.

One of the tendencies of automatic translation consists of analyzing the periods of the source language, and of synthesizing those of the target language, without directly dealing with translation. The passage from the source to the target language can take place in either a direct, or bilateral, fashion or through the intermediary of a third language, the machine's language, which would be composed of linguistic universals, and, in this way, could serve as passage from every source to every target language. This solution, practiced in the Soviet Union, is situated in the direction, common to several linguists, of a search for the universals of *la langue*.

Let us now clarify the terms *analysis* of the source language's structure, and *synthesis* of the periods of the target language.

The central principle is the determination of *syntactic function:* there is no longer any recourse to the context or to semantics, but only to the formal, syntactic relations of the constituents. The previous analysis presupposes a distribution of words into different syntactic classes which, subsequently, and in order to synthesize satisfactory utterances, must satisfy the machine's rules, as for example in the sentence: NP + VP; NP = V + NP; NP = A + N; A = the; N = ball, man, etc.; V = hit. The machine would thus produce: *The man hit the ball.* But it could also produce: *The man hit the hypoteneuses,* which would not be acceptable. To avoid such cases, the grammar must be composed of complex, prohibitive rules.

From the invention of the first translation machine by the Russian Piotr Petrovic Smirnov-Trojansky in 1933, to the work of Booth and Weaver (1946), and including Bar-Hillel's research, automatic translation has been advancing and is providing more and more satisfactory results. The mutual emulation of the United States and the Soviet Union has, in this realm, produced work of obvious interest. But once the early enthusiasm, which led one to believe that every translation could be done by a machine, had died down, it clearly appeared that the semantic factor, and therefore the role of the speaking subject, was essential for the translation of many texts (literary, poetic, even the discourse of daily life which is laden with polysemy) and that the machine was not able to decide all this. The affirmation of the machine's all-powerful translating ability is considered today by Bar-Hillel, for example, a simple expression "of the will to work toward a certain goal, even if its practical content is almost nothing." Moreover, the positive results obtained by computers in automatic translation have not furthered our theoretical knowledge of the functioning of *la langue.* Automatic translation puts into a rigorous form, for automatic treatment, a preformed conception of language; and in the search for more perfect rigor it can indeed advance syntactic theory (as in Chomsky's case) without, however, drastically changing the generally accepted meaning of linguistic functioning specific to a certain formal conception of language. On the contrary, it indicates perhaps that the path taken by formal analysis—which loses interest in the fact that language is a system of signs and that its layers must be thoroughly gone into—despite its undeniable contributions, is not the one to lead us to a knowledge of the laws of linguistic functioning.

GENERATIVE GRAMMAR

The decade of the 1960s was marked by a theory of language that gained currency not only in America but everywhere in the world, by proposing an original conception of the *generation* of syntactic structures. We are referring to the work of the American linguist Noam Chomsky, whose book *Syntactic Structures* appeared in 1957. Chomsky continued his research, clarifying and often notably modifying his initial postulates. The continued changes in Chomskian theory on the one hand, and the advanced technical nature of its descriptions on the other, make it impossible to present here the totality of his research, and to draw all the implications for the theory of language. We will therefore limit ourselves to a few aspects of generative grammar.

Let us first emphasize the "climate" in which it developed and against which it reacted. This is, of course, "post-Bloomfieldian" linguistics, that is, above all an analytical, structural description that breaks the utterance down into watertight layers. This is the so-called "separation of levels" principle (phonemic, morphemic, etc.); each level functions for itself, and one cannot refer to morphology if one is conducting a phonemic study, although the opposite is possible. Moreover, this linguistics does not under any circumstances want to take the speaker and his role in the constitution of the utterance into account; instead it proposes an empirical description, which claims to be "neutral" and "objective," of the spoken chain in itself (see above, "American Structuralism").

Chomsky remained faithful to the demands of the "post-Bloomfieldians" for rigor, and neutral and formal descriptions, as well as to their mistrust of the signified. Taking a close interest in the problems posed by automatic translation, and concerned with solving certain problems that syntagmatic analysis proved incapable of addressing, Chomsky tried to create a new grammatical theory, a sign of the technical and scientific nature of a mathematical formulation, without having recourse to semantics. He had Harris as his teacher and inspired precursor; he took up certain of Harris' concepts (including that of *transformation*), analyzed them, and gave them a new interpretation. But the resemblances to his predecessors should not mask the profound novelty of Chomskian theory.

In place of an *analytical* approach to structure, Chomsky proposed a *synthetic* description. The sentence should no longer be broken down into immediate constituents; instead one should follow the *synthetic process* that leads these constituents to a syntagmatic structure, or transforms this structure into another one.

This operation is based above all and principally on the speaker's implicit linguistic intuition, which is the only criterion for the *grammaticality* or *agrammaticality* of a sentence. "The fundamental aim in the linguistic analysis of a language L is to separate the *grammatical* sequences which are the sentences of L from the *ungrammatical* sequences which are not the sentences of L and to study the structure of the grammatical sequences." [15] "In this respect, a grammar mirrors the behavior of the speaker who, on the basis of a finite and accidental experience with language, can produce or understand an indefinite number of new sentences. Indeed any explication of the notion 'grammatical in L' (i.e., any characterization of 'grammatical in L' in terms of 'observed utterance of L') can be thought of as offering an explanation for this fundamental aspect of linguistic behavior" [p. 15]. Chomsky noticed that the notion of grammaticality could not be identified with that of "meaningful" from a semantic point of view, since, of the two sentences (1) *Colorless green ideas sleep furiously* and (2) *Furiously sleep ideas green colorless,* while both are nonsensical, the first is grammatical and the second is not for an English speaker. However, Husserl's observations, which we have quoted above (see "Logical Research" in this chapter), should be recalled; according to him, grammaticality always covers over if not expresses a certain meaning. According to these remarks, sentence 1 is grammatical to the extent that it is the syntactic form enabling a connection to a real object. It can be seen that the theory of the sign cannot be eluded once one goes deeper into a principle as apparently formal as that of grammaticality.

By means of this grammaticality, founded on the "speaker's intuition," Chomsky's rigorously formalized theory is infiltrated by an ideological foundation, namely, the *speaking subject* the "Bloomfieldians" had wanted to chase out of their analysis. In 1966, Chomsky published his book *Cartesian Linguistics,* in which he looked for the ancestors of his theory of the speaking subject. He found them in the Cartesian conceptions that had been known in Europe two centuries earlier, and, more precisely, in Descarte's *cogito,* which implied the universality of the subject's innate ideas, the guarantee of the normality—Chomsky would say the "grammaticality"—of the thoughts and/or utterances.

In agreement with these theories, to which he added Humboldt's conceptions, Chomsky distinguished *competence,* that is, the speaking subject's capacity to form and recognize grammatical sentences from among the infinity of possible constructions in a language, from *performance,* that is, the concrete realization of this capacity. Far from accepting the behaviorist postulate that *la langue* is a "system of habits," therefore, Chomsky opted for the idealist Cartesian position of "innate ideas." The universal character of these ideas demands of the linguist a highly abstract theory capable, starting from each concrete language, of finding a universal formalism valid for all languages, of which each language realizes a specific variation. "More generally, linguists have been concerned with the problem of determining the fundamental underlying properties of successful grammars. The ultimate outcome of these investigations should be a theory of linguistic structure in which the descriptive devices utilized in particular grammars are presented and studied abstractly, with no specific reference to particular languages" [p. 11].

It can therefore be seen that for Chomsky, grammar is less an empirical description than a *theory of la langue,* and that it consequently and at the same time leads to a "condition of generality." The grammar of a given language must be considered in accordance with the specific theory of linguistic structure in which terms like "phoneme" and "syntagm" are defined independently of any particular language.

How did Chomsky establish the rules of his theory?

First, he examined two types of grammatical description. One, suggested by the terms of one of Markov's processes *(model of finite states of an infinite language),* he dismissed because it could not explain the speaker's ability to produce and understand new utterances, whereas this same speaker rejects other new sequences as not belonging to his language. The other was the *syntagmatic linguistic* description [phrase structure], formulated in terms of constituent analysis, which analyzed terminal languages that were not necessarily finite.[16] It too was rejected by Chomsky, since it was inadequate for describing the structure of English sentences. Here are the elements of Chomsky's critique.

Let us take the English sentence *The man hit the ball,* and apply to it the rules of constituent analysis. There are three steps: (1) grammatical analysis; (2) derivation of analysis 1 applied to the particular sentence *The man hit the ball;* and (3) a summary diagram [pp. 26–27].

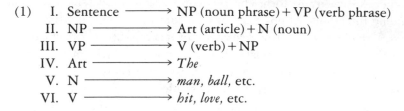

(1) I. Sentence ⟶ NP (noun phrase) + VP (verb phrase)
    II. NP ⟶ Art (article) + N (noun)
    III. VP ⟶ V (verb) + NP
    IV. Art ⟶ *The*
    V. N ⟶ *man, ball,* etc.
    VI. V ⟶ *hit, love,* etc.

(2) Sentence

NP + VP	I
Art + N + VP	II
Art + N + V + NP	III
The + N + V + NP	IV
The + *man* + V + NP	V
The + *man* + *hit* + NP	VI
The + *man* + *hit* + Art + N	VII
The + *man* + *hit* + *the* + N	VIII
The + *man* + *hit* + *the* + *ball*	IX

(3)

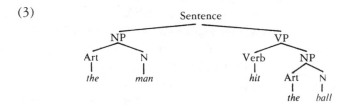

One can see that in diagram 1, each rule merely signifies that one can "rewrite" Y in place of X, and that diagram 2 is only the application of these rules, since each line of diagram 2 refers back to a rule of grammar (diagram 1). To clarify the signification of these rules, one can add supplementary indications (which indicate, for example, that the article can be either *a* or *the,* that NP and VP can be singular or plural, etc.) Diagram 3 only presents the derivation more clearly.

The syntagmatic model thus seems very convincing. By means of several examples, however, Chomsky showed its limitations. From what has been stated, it follows that if one had two sentences, Z + X + W and Z + Y + W, and if X and Y are the "constituents" of these sentences, one could in principle form a new sentence, such as Z-X + *and* + Y-W. Here is an example of this:

(4)   I. A. *The scene of the movie was in Chicago.*
          B. *The scene of the play was in Chicago.*
      II. C. *The scene of the movie and of the play was in Chicago.*
          [p. 35]

If, however, X and Y *are not* the constituents, then the formula cannot be applied, for it would produce, for example:

(5) III. A. *The money left the country.*
          B. *The police controlled the country.*
          C. *The money left and the police controlled the country.* [Kristeva's example.]

These examples prove that in order to apply syntagmatic rules to a language like English, one needs to know not only the final shape of sentences but also the structure of their constituents, or their "history of derivation" [p. 37]. But Chomsky has demonstrated that the "effective content" of a given sequence is what determines whether or not each rule "X → Y" of syntagmatic grammar applies to that sequence. The question of the *progressive formation* of the sequence is therefore not a pertinent one in syntagmatic grammar. This led Chomsky to devise new rules that had not necessarily been part of that grammar. Here is one of the rules, which can be applied to the previous case:

(6) If S_1 and S_2 are grammatical sentences, and S_1 differs from S_2 only in that X appears in S_1 where Y appears in S_2 (i.e., $S_1 = \ldots X \ldots$ and $S_2 = \ldots Y \ldots$), and X and Y are constituents of the same type in S_1 and S_2, respectively, then S_3 is a sentence, where S_3 is the result of replacing X by X + *and* + Y in S_1 (i.e. $S_3 = \ldots X + and + Y \ldots$). [p. 36]

We can see that for Chomsky syntagmatic grammar is inadequate for a language like English, unless new rules are incorporated into it. But doing that completely changes the conception of the linguistic structure. Chomsky therefore proposed the concept of a "grammatical transformation," which he formulated in this way: *"a grammatical trans-*

formation T operates on a given string (or . . . on a set of strings) with a given constituent structure and converts it into a new string with a new derived constituent structure" [p. 44; italics added].

The principle of transformational grammar was formulated in this way. Its essential properties were then clarified, for example, the order in which these transformations are applied. Moreover, some transformations are obligatory while others are optional. The transformation that governs the addition of affixes to a verb root is necessary in order to produce a grammatical sentence; it is therefore obligatory. Since passive transformation may not apply to every particular case, it is optional. In the vocabulary of transformational grammar, the *kernel* of the language is the set of sentences that are produced by applying obligatory transformations to the terminal strings of syntagmatic grammar. The sentences obtained by applying optional transformations are called *derived* [p. 45].

Grammar therefore had a succession of rules of the $X \rightarrow Y$ form (as in diagram 1 above); in addition, corresponding to the syntagmatic level, it had a succession of morpho-phonological rules that have the same basic form, as well as a succession of transformational rules linking the first two levels. Here is how Chomsky described this process:

> To produce a sentence from such a grammar we construct an extended derivation beginning with *Sentence*. Running through the rules of F we construct a terminal string that will be a sequence of morphemes, though not necessarily in the correct order. We then run through the sequence of transformations $T_1, \ldots T_j$, applying each obligatory and perhaps some optional ones. These transformations may rearrange strings or may add or delete morphemes. As a result they yield a string of words. We then run through the morphophonemic rules, thereby converting this string of words into a string of phonemes. The phrase structure segment of the grammar will include such rules as those of (1). The transformational part will include such rules as (6), formulated properly in the terms that must be developed in a full-scale theory of transformations. [p. 46]

For Chomsky, transformational analysis has a power he calls explicative. For instance, the sentence *The war was begun by the aggressor* is, from a transformational point of view, the result of a series of transformations effected on the kernel sentence *The aggressor began the war.* That amounts to saying that the structure $NP_1V_tNP_2$ (where V_t is a transitive verb) became the structure NP_2V_p by NP_1 (where V_p is the passive verb to be + past participle of the verb), which lexically corresponds to the initial sentence we wanted to explain.

Moreover, transformational description can resolve a sentence's ambiguity without having to resort to semantic criteria by merely reestablishing the transformational rules that produced it.

The Chomskian approach obviously offers a dynamic vision of syntagmatic structure that was lacking in structural grammar, and also eliminates the atomization of *la langue* that accompanied "post-Bloomfieldian" methods. It proposes instead a conception of *la langue* as a process of production in which each sequence or rule stems from a coherent whole centered on the consciousness of the subject-locutor whose freedom consists of submitting to the norms of grammaticality.

On that subject let us recall the tremendous amount of work that was done by the *General and Rational Grammar of Port-Royal,* and especially by the grammarians of the *Encyclopédie,* in order to elaborate a syntactic conception of *la langue.* Chomsky has obviously adopted this way of thinking; among other things, he took from them his conception of the subject as the free possessor of ideas whose transformation he controls. The search for *syntactic structures,* as opposed to the morpho-semantic splitting *la langue* had been subject to in former studies, reveals a conception of *la langue* as a collection of coordinated terms. One could say that it is no longer a question of *linguistics* in the sense this word had when it was coined in the nineteenth century, that is, as a science of the specificities of the body of *la langue.* For *la langue* fades from view underneath the formal network that engenders the linguistic cover of reasoning, and transformational analysis presents the syntactic schema of a psychological process envisaged according to a rationalistic conception of the subject. The *General and Rational Grammar of Port-Royal* was not a linguistics, for it was a science of reasoning. Generative grammar, though, is both more and less than a linguistics, for it is the syntactic description of a psychological doctrine. Syntax, which used to be a science of reasoning, has become the science of normative psychological behavior.

The novelty of the Chomskian approach thus appears to be a variation on a former concept of language, which had been formulated by the Rationalists and had been centered upon the logical categories forged from Indo-European languages and from communicative-denotative discourse. It is striking that the *universalism* of this linguistic conception has not (yet) shown an interest in languages other than Indo-European ones, nor in the functions of language that are different from purely informative ones (such as, for example, poetic language, dream language, etc.). The acuteness of Chomskian description, and the pleasure its rigorous and dynamic method elicits in the reader searching for rational certitude, do not mask the underlying foundation of this approach. It studies neither *la langue* in its diversity nor discourse in its multiple functions. It demonstrates instead the coherence of the logical subject-predicate system made obvious by Port-Royal, which has been transformed into various final sequences all of which obey one reason, the one which founds the subject, his "linguistic intuition," and his logical analysis. Chomsky himself claims to be more of an analyst of psychological structures than a linguist. He is no doubt a describer-in-detail of a given structure, the one the rationalists of the seventeenth century gave birth to. But is that the only structure? Should the enormous variability of linguistic functioning be subordinated to this one structure? What do concepts like "subject," "intuition," or "innate ideas" mean today after Marx and Freud? Isn't Chomskian-Cartesian analysis too blocked theoretically by its own presuppositions, and because of that unable to see the plurality of signifying systems recorded in other languages and discourses? This is only one of a series of general problems posed by Chomsky's work; the rigor of his analyses (which are nothing but the apogee of positivism, since he has acknowledged Descartes as his father) should not allow these problems to be passed over without comment.

Transformational grammar is carrying out in a more marked and revealing fashion the same reduction that structural linguistics, and especially American linguistics, effects in its study of language. Pure signifier without a signified, grammar without semantics, *indices* instead of *signs:* the orientation is clear-cut, and is even more marked in Chomsky's later unpublished works. One could say that the formalism of Husserl's project is being achieved by abandoning what there was in Husserl of semanticism and the object theory of truth. Indeed, in order to neutralize *empirical subjectivity* in the study of language, linguistics has reduced the constitutive elements of the spoken chain, the signs, to indices or marks that show but do not demonstrate elements that mean nothing more than their grammatical purity. Next, coming back to constitutive subjectivity and finding once more the Cartesian subject as generator of *la langue,* transformational grammar opted for an eclecticism that can momentarily reconcile the theory of a psychological subject and an indexing of less and less expressive linguistic components. This reconciliation (which is difficult, for one can hardly see how a reasoning subject could be in keeping with a nonexpressive grammar) finds itself confronted by the following alternative: either the formal indices that make up the generative-transformational operation will become laden with meaning, and will be the bearers of significations that will need to be integrated into a theory of truth and its subject, or instead the very concepts of "subject," "truth," and "meaning" will be dismissed as incapable of resolving the order of indicative language. In that case, linguistics will no longer claim to be a *Cartesian grammar,* but will instead become oriented toward other theories offering a different view of the subject: a subject who destroys and reconstructs himself in and through the signifier. This second possibility has working for it the pressure from psychoanalysis and the extensive reshaping of the very conception of *signification* heralded by semiotics. That this path seems to open up the Cartesian enclosure in which transformational grammar wants to confine linguistics; that such a way of thinking makes it possible to take back mastery of the signifier and to break out of the metaphysical isolation linguistics is being kept in, in order to formulate the theory, in the plural, of the signs and modes of signification in history—this is what we shall try to show in the following chapters.

PART THREE

LANGUAGE AND LANGUAGES

20

PSYCHOANALYSIS AND LANGUAGE

We have just seen that contemporary linguistics has taken paths that have led it to a rigorous, even mathematical description of the formal structure of *la langue*'s system. But that is not the only way in which current sciences have been tackling the study of language. As a signifying system in which the speaking subject *makes* and *unmakes* himself, language is at the center of psychological and more particularly psychoanalytic studies.

Since the beginning of the century, one may recall, the psychological problems posed by language have preoccupied certain linguists.[1] These problems have since been abandoned by linguistics, but philosophers and psychologists continue to explore language in order to study the speaking subject. Among the recent psychological schools that often refer to linguistic usage in order to analyze psychical structures, we must above all mention Piaget's school and all of genetic psychology. Research dealing with language learning by children, and with the logical categories they elaborate as they grow up in order to understand the world, is constantly oriented toward language and casts light on its functioning in a way formal linguistics never could.

The fundamental period of the study of the relationship between the subject and his language, however, was no doubt marked well before the beginning of the twentieth century by the magnificent oeuvre of

Freud (1856–1939), who opened up a new perspective in the representation of linguistic functioning, and who overturned the Cartesian conceptions modern linguistic science had been relying upon. The repercussions of Freud's work—which we cannot yet completely measure—are among the most important to mark the thinking of our era.[2]

The problem of the close relations between psychoanalysis and language is complex, and we will deal here only with a few of its aspects. Let us first emphasize that psychoanalysis sees the patient's speech as its object. The psychoanalyst has no other means within his reach, no other reality with which to explore the conscious or unconscious functioning of the subject, than speech and its laws and structures. That is where the analyst discovers the subject's position.

At the same time, psychoanalysis considers every *symptom* as language: it makes of the symptom a type of signifying system whose laws, similar to those of a language, must be discovered.

The dream, which Freud studied, is also considered above all a linguistic system to be deciphered, or better, as *writing,* with rules similar to those of hieroglyphs.

These opening remarks render psychoanalysis inseparable from the linguistic universe. Conversely, psychoanalytic principles, such as the discovery of the unconscious, the laws of "dream work," etc., have profoundly modified the classical notion of language.

While the psychiatrist may look for a physical lesion as the cause of a disturbance, the psychoanalyst refers only to what the subject says, but not in order to find there an objective "truth" that would be the "cause" of the problems. He listens with as much interest to the real as to the fictitious part of what the subject tells him, for both have an equal *discursive reality.* He discovers in this discourse first the unconscious, then the more or less conscious *motivation* producing the symptoms. Once he has uncovered this motivation, all the neurotic behavior denotes an obvious logic, and the symptom appears as the symbol of this finally rediscovered motivation.

"It is essential to abandon the overevaluation of the property of being conscious before it becomes possible to form any correct view of the origin of what is mental. In Lipp's words, the unconscious must be assumed to be the general basis of psychical life. The unconscious is the larger sphere, which includes within it the smaller sphere of the conscious. Everything conscious has an unconscious preliminary stage; whereas what is unconscious may remain at that stage and nevertheless claim to be regarded as having the full value of a psychical process. The unconscious is the true psychical reality," Freud wrote in *The Interpretation of Dreams.*[3]

While it presents itself as a vertical or historical ascent into the subject's past (memories, dreams, etc.), this quest for unconscious motivation in and through discourse takes place, in fact, in and through a discursive, horizontal position: the rapport between the subject and the analyst. In the psychoanalytic act, we find the subject-addressee chain, and the fundamental fact that every discourse is destined for an other. ". . . There is no speech without a reply, even if it is met only with silence, provided that it has an auditor . . ." (Jacques Lacan, *Ecrits,* 1966).[4] Further on, Lacan wrote:

> Is it not rather a matter of a frustration inherent in the very discourse of the subject? Does the subject not become engaged in an ever-growing dispossession of that being of his, concerning which—by dint of sincere portraits which leave its idea no less incoherent, of rectifications that do not succeed in freeing its essence, of stays and defences that do not prevent his statue from tottering, of narcissistic embraces that become like a puff of air in animating it—he ends up by recognizing that this being has never been anything more than his construct in the imaginary and that this construct disappoints all his certainties? For in this labour which he undertakes to reconstruct *for another,* he rediscovers the fundamental alienation that made him construct it *like another,* and which has always destined it to be taken from him *by another.* This ego . . . is frustration in its essence . . . [pp. 41–42]

By questioning the place of the other (of the analyst in the discursive act of the analyzed subject), Lacanian theory has made a science of the study of the unconscious. It has done this by assigning to it the scientifically approachable bases of a discourse, through the formula that has since become famous: "The unconscious of the subject is the discourse of the other" [p. 55].

It is not at all a question here of blocking the discursive act in the

terms of a subject-addressee relation, as is commonly done in communications theory. Psychoanalysis notes "a resonance in the communicating networks of discourse" [p. 55] that indicates the existence of an
"omnipresence of human discourse" [p. 56] that will no doubt one day
be tackled in all its complexity by science. In this sense, psychoanalysis
is only taking the first step, by positing the dual structure of the subject
and his interlocutor. It does this by indicating that "this is the field that
our experience polarizes in a relation that is only apparently two-way,
for any positioning of its structure in merely dual terms is as inadequate to it in theory as it is ruinous for its technique" [p. 56].

In the structure thus outlined of the discursive act, the speaking
subject uses *la langue* to construct there the syntax or logic of his
discourse: a (subjective, personal) language in *la langue* (a neutral social
structure). "Language is thus used here as the act of speech {*parole*},
converted into that expression of instantaneous and elusive subjectivity
which forms the condition of dialogue. The subject's language {*la
langue*} provides the instrument of a discourse in which his personality
is released and creates itself, reaches out to the other and makes itself
be recognized by him," Benveniste stated ("Remarks on the Function
of Language in Freudian Theory").[5]

That amounts to saying that the language studied by psychoanalysis
can in no way be confused with the formal object-system that *la langue*
represents for modern linguistics. For psychoanalysis, language is, as it
were, a secondary signifying system, which relies upon *la langue* and
has an obvious relation to its categories but which superimposes its
own organization and specific logic. The signifying system of the unconscious, which is accessible in the signifying system of *la langue*
through the discourse of the subject, is, as Benveniste has remarked,
"supralinguistic in that it makes use of extremely condensed signs
which, in organized language, would correspond to large units of discourse rather than to minimal units" [p. 74].

The character of the extremely condensed signs of the symbolism of
dreams (and therefore of the unconscious) was first described by Freud.
He considered the system of dreams as analogous to that of a *rebus* or
a *hieroglyph:* ". . . it is fair to say that the productions of the dreamwork, which, it must be remarked, *are not made with the intention of
being understood,* present no greater difficulties to their translators than

do the ancient hieroglyphic scripts to those who seek to read them" ("The Dream-work").[6] Freud went on to say that the symbols of dreams

> frequently have more than one or even several meanings, and, as with Chinese script, the correct interpretation can only be arrived at on each occasion from the context. The ambiguity of the symbols links up with the characteristic of dreams for admitting of "overinterpretation"—for representing in a single piece of content thoughts and wishes *(Wunschregungen)*, which are often widely divergent in their nature. [pp. 388–89]

To illustrate this dream logic, Freud referred to an example of dream interpretation reported by Artemidorus that is based upon a play on words. "I think too that Aristander gave a most happy interpretation to Alexander of Macedon when he had surrounded Tyre and was besieging it but was feeling uneasy and disturbed because of the length of time the siege was taking. Alexander dreamt he saw a satyr dancing on his shield. Aristander happened to be in the neighbhorhood of Tyre, in attendance on the king during his Syrian campaign. By dividing the word for satyr into σά and τύρος he encouraged the king to press home the siege so that he became master of the city. (σα-τύρος = Tyre is thine)" [p. 99]. Freud added, "Indeed, dreams are so closely related to linguistic expression that Ferenczi has truly remarked that *every tongue has its own dream-language*" [p. 99; italics added].

We have formulated here the basic principle of the interpretation of discourse in psychoanalysis, which Freud elaborated and clarified in the course of his later writings. It can be summed up as a *relative autonomy of the signifier* under which slides a *signified,* which is not necessarily included in the morpho-phonological unit such as it appears in the communicated utterance. In the Greek language, *satyr* is a unit whose two syllables have no meaning by themselves. However, outside this unit, the signifiers *sa* and *tyr* that make up *satyr* can have another signified, namely, the village of Tyre whose imminent conquest *motivated* the subject's dream. In the logic of dreams, two signifying units are found condensed into a single one which can have a signified that is independent (from the signified of its components) and that can be represented by an image, the *satyr.*

By analyzing the dreamwork, Freud isolated three fundamental operations which indicate that the unconscious functions like a "language": *displacement, condensation,* and *considerations of representability.*

Freud remarked about *condensation* that "the first thing that becomes clear to anyone who compares the dream-content with the dream-thoughts is that a work of *condensation* on a large scale has been carried out. Dreams are brief, meagre and laconic in comparison with the range and wealth of the dream-thoughts" [279]. One might think that condensation operates by "omission: that is, that the dream is not a faithful translation or a point-for-point projection of the dream-thoughts but a highly incomplete and fragmentary version of them" [281]. But, more than an omission, it is a question of *nodal points* (as with *saytr*), "upon which a great number of the dream-thoughts converged, because they had several meanings in connection with the interpretation of the dream. The explanation of this fundamental fact can also be put in another way: each of the elements of the dream's content turns out to have been 'overdetermined'—to have been represented in the dream-thoughts many times over" [p. 283]. Freud was introducing there the concept of *overdetermination,* which has become indispensable for any analysis of the logic of dreams and the unconscious, or of any related signifying system.

The principle of *displacement* plays a no less important role in dream formation.

> What is clearly the essence of the dream-thoughts need not be represented in the dream at all. The dream is, as it were, differently centered from the dream-thoughts—its content has different elements as its central point. [p. 305]

> The consequence of the displacement is that the dream-content no longer resembles the core of the dream-thoughts and that the dream gives no more than a distortion of the dream-wish which exists in the unconscious. But we are already familiar with dream-distortion. We traced it back to the censorship which is exercised by one psychical agency in the mind over another. Dream-displacement is one of the chief methods by which that distortion is achieved. [p. 308]

After having established that "in the process of transforming the latent thoughts into the manifest content of a dream we have found two factors at work: dream-condensation and dream-displacement" [p. 344], Freud envisaged the "means of representation in dreams." He noted that "dreams take into account in a general way the connection which undeniably exists between all the portions of the dream-thoughts by combining the whole material into a single situation or event. They reproduce *logical connection* by *simultaneity in time.* Here they are acting like the painter who, in a picture of the school of Athens or of Parnassus, represents in one group all the philosophers or all the poets. It is true that they were never in fact assembled in a single hall or on a single mountaintop; but they certainly form a group in the conceptual sense" [p. 314]. The only *logical relation* used by the dream, just as with a hieroglyphic language like Chinese, is constructed by the mere *application* of symbols: as Freud has said, by "similarity, consonance, or approximation—the relation of 'just as' " [p. 320].

Elsewhere, Freud pointed out another peculiarity in the relations of the unconscious: it does not know contradiction, and the law of the excluded middle is foreign to it. The study Freud devoted to *negation (Verneinung)*[7] demonstrates the peculiar functioning of negation in the unconscious. On the one hand, Freud noticed that "the performance of the function of judgment is not made possible until the *creation of the symbol of negation"* [239; italics added]. But the negation of a statement can signify, starting from the unconscious, an explicit avowal of its repression, even though what is being repressed may not be admitted by the consciousness. "There is no stronger evidence that we have been successful in our effort to uncover the unconscious than when the patient reacts to it with the words, 'I didn't think that' or 'I didn't (even) think that' " [p. 239]. From that point, Freud was able to notice that negation is not considered a refusal by the unconscious, but instead as the constitution of what was given as denied; he concluded that "this view of negation fits in very well with the fact that in analysis we never discover a 'no' in the unconscious . . ." [p. 239].

We can easily see that for Freud a dream could not be reduced to symbolism; it was truly a *language,* that is, a system of signs, even a *structure* with its own syntax and logic. The *syntactic character* of Freud's vision of language must be emphasized, for it has often been passed over without comment in favor of an accentuation of the Freudian symbolic.

Now, when Freud spoke of language, he didn't just mean the discursive system in which the subject makes and unmakes himself. For psychoanalytic psychopathology, the body itself speaks. Remember that Freud founded psychoanalysis starting with hysterical symptoms which he saw as "talking bodies." The corporal symptom is overdetermined by a complex symbolic network, and by a language whose syntactic laws must be discerned in order to resolve the symptom. "If he taught us to follow the ascending ramification of the symbolic lineage in the text of the patient's free associations, in order to map it out at the points where its verbal points intersect with the nodal points of its structure, then it is already quite clear that the symptom resolves itself entirely in an analysis of language, because the symptom is itself structured like a language, because it is from language that speech must be delivered" (Lacan) [p. 59].

We have mentioned here only the schematic rules of the functioning of the language of dreams and the unconscious, such as they were discovered by Freud. Let us once again insist upon the fact that this language is not identical to *la langue* studied by linguistics; it is, however, made in this *langue*. Let us also emphasize that this language itself really exists only in discourse, whose laws Freud searched for, and that, consequently, Freudian research elucidates linguistic specificities that any science not taking *discourse* into account will never attain. At once ultralinguistic and supralinguistic, or *translinguistic,* the signifying system studied by Freud has a universality that "traverses" constituted national languages, for it is definitely a question of a *function of language* belonging to all languages. Freud supposed that what was common to the signifying system of the dream and the unconscious was genetic. Anthropological psychoanalysis has indeed demonstrated that the Freudian concept, and the operations of the unconscious that Freud isolated, are applicable to so-called primitive societies as well, as he himself indicated. "Things that are symbolically connected today were probably united in prehistoric times by conceptual and linguistic identity. The symbolic relation seems to be a relic and a mark of former identity. In this connection we may observe how in a number of cases the use of a common symbol extends further than the use of a common language. A number of symbols are as old as language itself . . ." [p. 387].

Without going so far as to advance a hypothesis claiming that "primitive language" conforms to the laws of the unconscious—a hypothesis that is not accepted by linguistics and that no ancient or primitive language seems to confirm, according to the current state of knowledge—it would be more pertinent to look for the logical rules discovered by Freud in the organization of *certain signifying systems* that are themselves types of languages. Freud noticed it himself. "This symbolism is not peculiar to dreams, but is characteristic of unconscious ideation, in particular among the people, and it is to be found in folklore, in popular myths, legends, linguistic idioms, proverbial wisdom and current jokes, to a more complete extent than in dreams" [p. 386].

We now understand that the import of psychoanalysis goes far beyond the zone of the troubled discourse of the subject. One could say that the major consequence of psychoanalytic intervention in the field of language is the prevention of the crushing of the signified by the signifier, which makes of language a compact surface that can be logically cut up. Psychoanalysis, in contrast, enables one to leaf through language, to separate the signifier from the signified, and requires us to think about each signified according to the signifier that produces it, and vice versa. That amounts to saying that the psychoanalytic intervention prevents the metaphysical gesture of identifying various language practices with One *Langue,* One Discourse, One Syntax, and that it encourages the search for differences in languages, in discourses in the plural, or rather of signifying systems constructed in what was taken for *La langue* [THE language] or THE discourse. As a consequence, an immense group of practices that signify through *la langue* is henceforth opened up for linguistics. Two discourses in the Greek language, for example, although they are both grammatical, do not necessarily have the same semiotic sequence. One could pertain to the logic of Aristotle, and the other could be close to that of hieroglyphs, if they had been constructed according to different syntactic rules, which could be qualified as translinguistic.

Freud was the first person to apply these conclusions, drawn from the syntax of dreams and the unconscious, to the study of complex signifying systems. By analyzing *Jokes and Their Relation to the Unconscious,* Freud discovered the procedures for the formation of what we have already observed in dreamwork: concision (or ellipsis), compression (condensation with the formation of substitutes), inversion, double meaning, etc. Moreover, the conclusions Freud drew from dream language enabled him to tackle complex and otherwise indecipherable symbolic systems, such as taboos, totems, and other prohibitions in primitive societies.

Freudian work today offers a new vision of language that psychoanalysis has been trying to systematize and clarify in the research of the last few years.

It is true that the analytical theory of language does not have the exemplary rigor specific to the formalized or mathematicized theories that are the crowning glory of modern linguistics. It is also true that linguists show little interest in what psychoanalysis is discovering about linguistic functioning. Moreover, it is hard to imagine how the formalizations of American structuralism and generative grammar, for example, could possibly be reconciled with the laws of linguistic functioning such as they have been formulated by modern psychoanalysis after Freud. It is clear that these approaches constitute two contradictory or at least *divergent* tendencies in the conception of language. Freud was not a linguist, and the object "language" that he studied does not coincide with the formal system tackled by linguistics, a system whose slow and laborious abstraction through history we have just outlined. But the difference between the psychoanalytic approach to language and that of modern linguistics is more profound than a change in the volume of the object. It is the *general conception* of language that differs radically between psychoanalysis and linguistics.

We shall try to sum up here the essential points of this divergence.

Psychoanalysis renders impossible the habit commonly accepted by current linguistics of considering language outside its *realization* in *discourse,* that is, by forgetting that language does not exist outside the *discourse of a subject,* or by considering this subject as *implicit,* as equal to himself, as a fixed unit coinciding with his discourse. This Cartesian postulate, which underlies the procedure of modern linguistics and which Chomsky brought to life, was shaken up by the Freudian discovery of the unconscious and its logic. From then on, it became difficult to talk about a subject without following the various configurations revealed by the different relations between subjects and their discourse. The subject *is* not; he makes and unmakes himself in a complex topology[8] where the other and his discourse are included. One cannot possibly talk about the *meaning* of a discourse without taking this topology into account. The subject and meaning are not; they are produced in the *discursive work* (Freud spoke of the dreamwork). In place of the flat structure that *la langue* and its transformational variations constitute for structural linguistics, the psychoanalyst substitutes the problematic of the production of meaning (of the subject that must be discerned theoretically). It is not a production as defined by generative grammar—which doesn't produce anything at all itself (for it doesn't question the subject and meaning) and is content to synthesize a structure in the course of a process that does not for one second question the foundations of that structure. The production of meaning is instead an actual production that traverses the surface of the *uttered* discourse, and that engenders in the *enunciation*[9]—a new stratum opened up in the analysis of language—a particular meaning with a particular subject.

Jakobson had already called attention to this distinction between the enunciation itself and its object (the uttered matter) in order to show that certain grammatical categories, called *shifters,*[10] can indicate that the process of the utterance and/or its protagonists refers to the process of the enunciation and/or its protagonists (for example, the pronoun "I," or "the particles and inflections fixing presence as the subject of the discourse, and with it the present tense of chronology"). Lacan used this distinction in order to grasp beyond the utterance, in the enunciation, an (unconscious) signified that remains hidden from linguistics: "In the utterance, 'I fear that he may come { *je crains qu'il ne vienne},'* I is the subject of the utterance, not the subject of true desire, but a *shifter* or index of the presence that utters." "The subject of the enunciation, to the extent his desire penetrates, is nowhere other than in this *may {ne}* whose value is to be found in a haste in logic. . . ."[11]

This enunciation/utterance distinction is only one example of the reshaping of the conception of language being done for the purpose of constructing a theory of language as *production.*

Linked to this problematic of the production of meaning and the subject is another one promised by psychoanalysis—that of the (synchronic) *supremacy of the signifier over the signified.* Here we are far from the mistrust toward the signified characteristic of Bloomfieldian and post-Bloomfieldian linguistics. On the contrary, the signified is present in each analysis, and it is to these logical relations between signifieds that the analyst listens in the condensed and displaced discourse of the dream. But this signified is not independent of the signifier; in fact, the signifier becomes autonomous, detaches from the signified to which it was clinging during the communication of the message, and is cut up into signifying units that are the vehicle of a new, unconscious signified that was not visible under the signified of the consciously communicated message (such as the case quoted above of the "satyr" or "I fear he may come"). Such an analysis of the signifier/signified relation in language shows "how in fact the signifier enters the signified, namely, in a form which, not being immaterial, raises the question of its place in reality," Lacan wrote.[12] He later clarified: "The supremacy of the signifier over the signified already appears to be impossible to elude in all discourse on language, not that it has disconcerted thinking so much that linguists in our day have not been able to tackle it." "Psychoanalysis alone is in a position to *impose* this supremacy *on thinking* by demonstrating that the signifier can do without all cogitation, even the least reflexive, in order to form non-doubtful regroupings in the significations that enslave the subject, or even more: in order to manifest itself in him by this alienating intrusion of which the notion of *symptom* in analysis takes on an emerging meaning—the meaning of the signifier which connotes the relation of the subject to the signifier."[13]

Finally, the principle of the supremacy of the signifier has instituted a *syntax* in analyzed language that explodes the linear meaning of the spoken chain, and reconnects the signifying units located in various morphemes of the text by following a combinatory logic. "Overdetermination must first be held to be a fact of syntax." This parceling out, ramification, and cross-checking of the signifying chain results in a complex signifying network in which the subject evokes the moving complexity of reality, without being able to fix a precise meaning (except on the level of the concept) to any name there, for "no signification can be sustained other than by reference to another signification" (Lacan).[14]

This schematic summary of several of the fundamental principles of the analytic conception of language, and their radical novelty with respect to the modern linguistic vision, inevitably raises the question of whether they can be introduced into linguistic knowledge. We are not able today to foresee the possibility, much less the result, of such a penetration. But it is obvious that an analytic attitude toward language will not spare the neutral systematicity of scientific language, and that it will force formal linguistics to change its discourse. What seems even more probable is that an analytical attitude will invade the field of study of signifying systems in general, the semiology Saussure dreamed of, and that, from that angle, it will modify the Cartesian conception of language and enable science to grasp the multiplicity of signifying systems elaborated in and from *la langue.*

21

THE PRACTICE OF LANGUAGE

The object of a particular science, the material where the subject and his knowledge are made, language is above all a *practice*. A daily practice that fills every second of our lives, including the time of our dreams, speaking and writing, it is a social function that is manifested and known through its exercise.

The practice of ordinary communication: conversation and information.

Oratory practice: political, theoretical, or scientific discourse.

Literary practice: oral folklore, written literature; prose, poetry, song, theater, etc.

The list could be lengthened: language invades the entire field of human activity. And while, in common communication, we practice language virtually automatically, as if we paid no attention to its rules, the *orator* and the *writer* are constantly confronted with this matter, and handle it with an implicit knowledge of its laws, which science has certainly not yet detected in their totality.

ORATORS AND RHETORS

History reports the example of famous Greek and Latin orators whose mastery dazzled and subjugated crowds. We know that it was not, or was not only, the "thinking" of the orators that exercised this hold on the masses, but instead the technique they used to make that thinking part of the national language.

Eloquence developed in Greece only at the end of the fifth century, under the influence of rhetors and sophists within the walls of the assembly, where every citizen participated in politics by speaking. It is believed, however, that rhetoric is of Sicilian origin, and owes its birth to the discourses spoken by citizens in their defense during trials. It was at Syracuse that Korax and Tisias wrote the first treatise on rhetoric, distinguishing as parts of the discourse the exordium, the narration, the discussion, and the peroration. But they also invented the vague but quite useful concept of likelihood *(vraisemblance)*, which played an important role in public affairs. If a weak man was accused of having struck a wounded person, that was considered unlikely; but if a strong man was accused of having struck a wounded person, that too was unlikely, for the man's strength automatically made him vulnerable to such an accusation. Such elasticity in the concept of likelihood is obviously useful to those in power.

The sophists, along with Protagoras (485–411), played a decisive role in the formation of oratory art. In his *Antilogiae* (Contradictions), Pythagoras professed that "there are two opposite theses for every subject," and that at times the orator had to know how to "make the weak thesis triumph over the strong one." Gorgias (485–380) was one of the greatest sophists. An impeccable stylist and dialectician, he was the inventor of the classical procedures for oratory art, such as the technique for making words with similar forms correspond in two clauses of consecutive sentences. We owe to his art a *Pythian Address,* an *Olympic,* a *Funeral Speech,* and *Eulogies* (Eulogy of Helen, Defense of Palamedes). Antiphon (480–411), and especially Andocides, Lysias, and Isaeus were logographers[1] and judiciary orators; the latter three left written discourses. Isocrates (b. 436) abandoned this style in order to cultivate a steady eloquence that was measured, perfect in its composition, and conversant with the resources of the language, the laws of logic, and the requirements of euphony, as is evident in his pane-gyric discourse on the glory of Athens. In the realm of political elo-quence, Demosthenes excelled (384–322). The legend surrounding him is too well known: it shows him as a sickly, stuttering child who practiced with his mouth full of stones in order to acquire perfect diction and an elegant stature. His famous *Philippics,* which were directed against the policy of Philip of Macedon, earned him a reputa-tion as a patriot. He fought against Philip and then against Alexander. After Alexander's death, he fled from Antipater's soldiers, who de-manded that he turn the principal orators over to them, and ended up poisoning himself in one of Poseidon's temples.

This illustrious school of orators was, of course, the product of an intense public life, and this school was bound to disappear with the decadence and fall of Athens.

Contact with this oratory practice, which made the great orators into great masters of the people, formed a science of discourse. It was not a study of *la langue*'s formal (grammatical) system and its (grammatical) categories, but instead a study of the large units constructed inside *la langue*'s system, which the orator used (while of course having a perfect knowledge of the grammar of this language) to build a signifying universe of proofs and demonstrations. The necessity of codifying the laws of this construction appeared in Greece in this way, and became known as *rhetoric.* Once constituted, as we have pointed out above, rhetoric split into two schools. On the one hand were the disciples of Isocrates, who distinguished four parts in a discourse (poem, narration, proof, and epilogue). On the other hand were the disciples of Aristotle, who, following their master's teaching, paid particular attention to the influence of discourse on the audience, and distinguished in discourses *proofs* (or the material content), *style,* and *arrangement.* The system of proofs is known to be the core of Aristotelian rhetoric. By that Aris-totle meant the functions of the discourse, and in fact the three-part theory: the theory of rhetorical *arguments* (with a logical basis, and an analysis of the syllogism), the theory of the *emotions,* and the theory of the author's *character.*

Rome had its own sober and measured oratory glory during the time of Cicero (106–43 B.C.) and Hortensius. The turbulent life of Marcus Tullius Cicero, who mingled closely in the political activity of Rome in the first century B.C., and who participated in the rise and fall of Sulla, Catiline, Pompey, and Caesar, is a perfect example of the power and vulnerability of the ancient orators. Proclaimed Father of the country, then exiled, then taken back once again by a Rome that welcomed him triumphantly, he composed a eulogy of Cato to which Caesar responded with an anti-Cato. Cicero wrote his famous *Philippics* in opposition to Antony, only to be put to death in the end by the triumvir's soldiers on Antony's order. Cicero created a new language. He brought Greek logic and philosophy to Rome, and, with an irresistible style, served a political ideal, a mixture of aristocracy and popular government. But above all he took to its height the exhilaration that comes of setting oneself up as owner and master of a way of speaking that guarantees domination over one's listeners, to whom is allotted the unique role of being the silence that supports the verb.

The fame of Seneca (55 B.C. to A.D. 39) was bound to eclipse Cicero's glory for a period of time, but only until the arrival of Quintilian. Born near the middle of the first century, Quintilian studied rhetoric with Domitius Afer, one of the most famous orators of his time. He presented the art of rhetoric in his *Institutio oratoria*. He taught for twenty years at Rome and had some famous students, among them Pliny, and Suetonius, who wrote a biography of the rhetors. Quintilian believed that a perfect orator had to be led from the cradle to the grave in order to be formed properly. He taught his students grammar, spelling, music, and geometry; he attached particular importance to education and to memory and declamation exercises, specifying the different parts and procedures of the perfect discourse. According to him, far from being a clever device, the perfect use of speaking could only be the attribute of a wise man.

> Let our ideal orator then be such as to have a genuine title to the name of philosopher: it is not sufficient that he should be blameless in point of character (for I cannot agree with those who hold this opinion): he must also be a thorough master of the science and art of speaking, to an extent that perhaps no orator has yet attained. Still we must none the less follow the ideal, as was done by not a few of the ancients, who, though they refused to admit that the perfect sage had yet been found,

none the less handed down precepts of wisdom for the use of posterity. Perfect eloquence is assuredly a reality, which is not beyond the reach of human intellect.[2]

The art of oratory that dominated antiquity seems nowadays to be dying out. Religion nourished it during the seventeenth century (with Bossuet, for example), but great orators are rare in daily life. Only revolutionary movements seem to offer an appropriate stage for the exercise of the power of speaking. In this last case, the rhetoric of antirhetoric is what is coming to light. A discourse transmits to the masses an impersonal, scientific way of speaking, which draws its strength from a rigorous analysis of economy and ideology, and which owes its influence to its capacity to conform to the (signified and signifying) desire of those whom it addresses.

Every dominant caste and class has known how to exploit the practice of language, and above all the practice of oratory, in order to consolidate its supremacy. For, while the language of a nation scarcely or only imperceptibly changes, the languages formed within it—the types of rhetoric, or style, the signifying systems—each constitute and impose a different ideology, conception of the world, and social position. The "manner of speaking," as is commonly said, is far from indifferent to the content of what is said, and every ideological content finds its specific form, its language, its rhetoric.

One can then understand why it is an objective law that every social transformation is accompanied by a rhetorical transformation, that every social transformation is in a certain and very profound sense a rhetorical change. The example of the French Revolution is striking in this respect.

Not only did the revolution rely upon the enormous innovative work that writers such as Voltaire, Diderot, Sade, etc., effected even on the level of language and French literature, not only did it advocate in its laws a change of vocabulary, but it was literally made, and not only heralded, by the discourses and writings of its leaders. One can follow the blossoming and course of the French Revolution through the blossoming and course of a new rhetoric, a new style that shook up the French language from the seventeenth to the eighteenth centuries, and that led to Robespierre's sentence.

While the Constituent Assembly was still dominated by traditional rhetoric inspired by Quintilian, with the Legislative Assembly one began to free oneself of academicism and ceremonial eloquence. But it was the Mountain (party of the insurgent people) that renewed the art of oratory, and Robespierre was its master. After his fall, the Directory was verbose, and the Consulate and the Empire were mute. Mirabeau, Barnave, Condorcet, Vergniaud, Danton, Robespierre, Saint-Just, who inherited Montesquieu's principles, Diderot, and Rousseau all manipulated a discourse that slowly and surely freed itself from the formalist, pompous rhetoric of the ancients, which still dominated the lawyers of the Constituent Assembly, and from the decadent classicism of the literary salons. The eloquence of the Republic took Tacitus and Titus-Livius [Livy] as its examples; the Republic resorted, in turn, to accents worthy of an aristocratic audience (Mirabeau), to the elegiac notes of a disappointed humanism and annoying individualism among the conquered (Vergniaud), to a legislating and incorruptible pathos (Robespierre) before becoming once again vainly declamatory under the Restoration in order to feed the nostalgia of the Romantics. Even though a concern for eloquence remained constant during this change, in which several social classes seized the opportunity to speak, each class marked it in its own way. "During that time, the language of Racine and Bossuet screamed for blood and carnage; it roared with Danton; it bellowed with Marat; it hissed like a serpent in the mouth of Robespierre. But it remained pure," wrote the royalist Desmarais.

Mirabeau

Necker had just proposed an exceptional contribution of one fourth of income.

". . . Gentlemen, amid so many tumultuous debates, may I not bring up for consideration today a small number of simple questions?

"Deign, gentlemen, deign to answer me!

"Isn't it true that the Chief Minister of Finances presented you with a most frightening portrait of our current state?

"Didn't he tell you that any delay would aggravate the peril? That a day, an hour, an instant could turn it into a mortal danger?

"Do we have a plan with which to replace his?

". . . My friends, listen to one word, one single word. Two centuries of degradation and banditry have hollowed out an abyss that is about to engulf the kingdom. This dreadful abyss must be filled! Very well, here is the list of French property owners. Choose the richest among them, so that fewer citizens will be sacrificed, but choose, for shouldn't a small number perish in order to save the mass of people? Come now, these two thousand notable people possess what is needed to fill the deficit. Bring order back to your finances, and peace and prosperity back to the kingdom. . . . Strike, immolate these sad victims without pity! Cast them into the abyss! It is going to close. . . . You draw back in horror. . . . Inconsequential men! Fainthearted men! Oh! Can you not see that by decreeing bankruptcy, or, what is even more odious, by making it inevitable by not decreeing it, you are soiling yourselves with an act that is a thousand times more criminal, for after all this horrible sacrifice would at least make the deficit disappear. But do you believe, because you haven't paid, that you don't owe anything? Do you believe that the thousands and millions of men who will lose in an instant, by the terrible explosion or its repercussions, all that consoles them in their lives, and perhaps their only means of sustenance, will allow you to enjoy your crime in peace?

"Stoic contemplators of the incalculable evils that this catastrophe will vomit on France, impassive egotists who think these paroxysms of despair and misery will pass as so many others have passed, and even more quickly because they are even more violent, are you really so sure that so many men without bread will let you tranquilly savor that dish, which you didn't want to diminish in quantity or delicacy? . . . No, you shall perish, and in the universal cataclysm that you did not shudder to ignite, the loss of your honor shall not save a single one of your pleasures or possessions. . . ."[3]

Vergniaud

After the routing of the armies of Dumouriez at Aix-la-Chapelle on March 1, 1793, and the reinforcement of the revolutionary Tribunal, the Mountain {party} had grown in importance.

During the course of the previous month, events had started to move quickly: on March 10, the Vendée uprising broke out; on April 4, Dumou-

riez joined the enemy; on April 5, the Committee on Public Health was created. Circumstances demanded firmer direction. Robespierre showed it. Vergniaud's defense was already desperate: it preceded by several weeks the arrest of the Girondist chiefs.

". . . Robespierre has accused us of having suddenly become 'moderates,' *'feulliants.'*[4]

"Us 'moderates'? I was not one on August 10, Robespierre, when you were hiding in your basement! 'Moderates'! No, I am not one in the sense that I wish to extinguish the national energy; I know that liberty is always active like a flame, that it is irreconcilable with perfect calm, which suits only slaves: if one had wished only to nourish this sacred fire, which burns in my heart just as ardently as it does in the hearts of the men who constantly speak of the impetuosity of their character, dissensions of this order would not have exploded here in this Assembly. I also know that in these revolutionary times, there is as much folly in claiming to calm at will the effervescence of the people as in commanding the ocean waves to be tranquil when they are battered about by the winds; but it is the legislator who must, to the extent he is able, prevent the disasters that come with the tempest, by offering wise advice; and if under the pretext of a revolution one must, in order to be patriotic, declare oneself the protector of murder and banditry, then yes, I am a 'moderate'!

"I have heard much talk of revolution since royalty was abolished. I said to myself: only two types of revolution are possible: that of properties, or agrarian law, and that which will lead us to despotism. I have made a firm resolution to combat one and the other of these, and all the indirect means which could lead to them. If that is what it means to be a moderate, then we are all moderates, for we all voted the death penalty for any citizen who proposed one or the other of these. . . ."[5]

Robespierre

". . . The government of the Revolution is the despotism of liberty against tyranny.

". . . How long will the furor of despots be called justice, and the justice of the People barbarism or rebellion?

". . . Indulgence for the royalists! some people cry: Mercy for the villains! No: mercy for innocence, mercy for the weak, mercy for the unhappy, mercy for mankind!

". . . The internal enemies of the French People are divided into two sections, like two army corps. They march under different-colored banners and take different routes, but they march toward the same goal.

"This goal is the disorganization of the popular government, the ruin of the Convention, that is, the triumph of tyranny. One of these two factions pushes us toward weakness, the other toward excess. One wants to change liberty into a bacchant, the other into a prostitute.

". . . The first were given the name moderates; there is more precision in the denomination of ultrarevolutionaries given to the others.

". . . The false revolutionary is perhaps more often short of rather than beyond the revolution. He is moderate, he is crazy with patriotism, according to the circumstances. Decisions are made in the Prussian, Austrian, English, and even Muscovite committees about what he will think tomorrow. He is opposed to energetic measures, and exaggerates them when he cannot stop them. Harsh when it comes to innocence but indulgent when it comes to crime, accusing even the guilty parties who are not rich enough to buy his silence or important enough to merit his zeal; but being very careful never to compromise himself to the point of defending virtue when it is slandered; at times uncovering plots that have been uncovered, tearing the mask off traitors who have been demasked and even decapitated; but extolling traitors who are still alive and in good standing; always in a hurry to entertain the opinion of the moment, and no less attentive to avoid ever clarifying this opinion or above all going up against it; always ready to adopt tough measures, provided they are very inconvienient; always slandering those that offer nothing but advantages, or adding amendments to them so that they become harmful; telling the truth sparingly, and only as much as necessary, in order to acquire the right to lie with impunity; dispensing good drop by drop, and pouring out evil in torrents, full of fire for great resolutions that mean nothing; more than indifferent to those capable of honoring the cause of the People and saving the Fatherland; giving generously to the forms of patriotism; very attached, like the pious who are his declared enemy, to external practices, he would rather use one hundred red bonnets than do one good deed.

".. . Is it necessary to act? They harangue. Is it necessary to deliberate? They want to begin by acting. Are the times peaceful? they are opposed to any useful change. Are they stormy? they talk of reforming everything in order to disrupt everything. Do you wish to contain the insurgents? they remind you of Caesar's clemency. Do you wish to rescue patriots from persecution? they suggest Brutus' severity as a model. They discover that so-and-so was a noble when he serves the Republic; they don't remember it as soon as he betrays it. Is peace useful? they spread the palms of victory before you. Is war necessary? they praise the sweetness of peace. Do we need to take back our fortresses? they want to take the churches by storm and scale the skies; they forget the Austrians in order to make war on the pious. . . ."[6]

A discourse bears and imposes an ideology, and every ideology finds its discourse. One can then understand why every dominant class pays particular attention to the practice of language and controls its forms and the means of its distribution: the news, the press, literature. One can understand why a dominant class has its favorite languages, its literature, its press, its orators, and why it tends to censor any other language.

LITERATURE

Literature is no doubt the privileged realm in which language is exercised, clarified, and modified. From myth to oral literature, from folklore and the epic to the realist novel and modern poetry, literary language offers a diversity whose many genres are studied by literary science, but literary language is nonetheless united by one and the same characteristic that differentiates it from the language of simple communication. While *stylistics* analyzes the different peculiarities of this or that text, and contributes in this way to the constitution of a theory of genres, *poetics* tries to define the function common to language in its various literary manifestations. The specificity of the function of language in literature has been called the *poetic function.* How can this poetic function be clarified?

Jakobson has given a schema for linguistic communication, set out in figure 21.1.

Figure 21.1

If the message is oriented toward the *context,* its function is *cognitive,* denotative, and referential. If a statement's aim is to express the addresser's attitude with respect to what he is speaking about, the function is *emotive.* If the statement emphasizes the *contact,* its function is *phatic.* If the discourse is centered on the *code,* it fills a *metalingual* role. However, "the set *(Einstellung)* toward the message as such, focus on the message for its own sake is the poetic function of language."[7] It is important to quote the entire definition Jakobson gives of the poetic function:

> This function cannot be productively studied out of touch with the general problems of language, and, on the other hand, the scrutiny of language requires a thorough consideration of its poetic function. Any attempt to reduce the sphere of poetic function to poetry or to confine poetry to poetic function would be a delusive oversimplification. Poetic function is not the sole function of verbal art, but only its dominant, determining function, whereas in all other verbal activities it acts as a subsidiary, accessory constituent. This function, *by promoting the palpability of signs,* deepens the fundamental dichotomy of signs and objects. Hence, when dealing with poetic function, linguistics cannot limit itself to the field of poetry. [p. 93; italics added]

This "poetic function" obviously does not belong just to one single kind of discourse, for example, to poetry or literature. Besides poetry, every exercise of language can partake of the poetic function.

As far as poetry strictly speaking is concerned, this emphasis on the message for its own sake, this dichotomy of signs and objects, is first indicated by the importance at work there of the *organization of the signifier,* or of the phonetic aspect of language. Similar sounds, rhymes, intonation, the rhythmics of different types of verses, etc. have a function which, far from being purely ornamental, is the vehicle of a new signified that is superimposed on the explicit signified. "An undercurrent of meaning," Poe said; "the sound must seem an echo of the sense," Pope declared; "a poem, that prolonged hesitation between sound and sense," Valéry noted. The modern science dealing with this signifying organization—prosody—talks about a symbolism of sounds.

In order to further clarify the poetic function, Jakobson introduced the terms *selection* and *combination.* Let us say, for example, that the topic of a message is the "child": the speaker can choose from a whole series of words (infant, child, kid, tot, brat, street urchin) to note this topic; and to comment upon this topic, he also has a choice of various words: *sleeps, dozes, nods,* and *naps.*

> Both chosen words combine in the speech chain. The selection is produced on the base of equivalence, similarity and dissimilarity, synonymity and antonymity, while the combination, the build up of the sequence, is based on contiguity. *The poetic function projects the principle of equivalence from the axis of selection into the axis of combination.* Equivalence is promoted to the constitutive device of the sequence. In poetry, one syllable is equalized with any other syllable of the same sequence; every word stress is assumed to equal word stress; as unstress equals unstress; prosodic long is matched with long, short with short, word boundary equals word boundary, no boundary equals no boundary, syntactic pause equals syntactic pause, no pause equals no pause. Syllables are converted into units of measure, and so are morae or stresses. [p. 95]

Let us recall that we have already run into this principle of the equivalence of contiguous sequences in the syntax of dreams.

To such peculiarities of literary language the science of literature, constituted on the basis of linguistics and on the experience of traditional literary descriptions, adds others in order to demonstrate that the poetic function is indeed "a total reevaluation of the discourse and of all its components, whatsoever" [p. 119]. As the Prague Linguistic Circle has already shown, this reevaluation generally consists "of the fact that all the planes of the linguistic system which have only a service role to play in the language of communication, take on in poetic language autonomous values that are more or less considerable. The means of expression grouped in these planes, as well as in the mutual relations that exist between them and that tend to become automatic in the language of communication, tend on the contrary to be actualized in poetic language." In certain cases, the search for the autonomy of the signifier, impregnated with a signified that seems superimposed on the signified of the explicit message, is taken so far that the poetic text constitutes a new language. It breaks the very rules of the language of communication of a given language, and presents itself as a supra- or infra-communicative *algebra,* such as in the poems of Browning and Mallarmé. Translating texts such as these, which seem to destroy the language of habitual communication in order to construct on it another language, is nearly impossible: they tend, through the material of a natural language, toward the establishment of signifying relations that are less obedient to the rules of a grammar than to the universal laws (common to all languages) of the unconscious.

Mallarmé wrote in order to create through French such an *other* language. While *Igitur* and *Un coup de dés* testify to this language, Mallarmé's theoretical conceptions reveal its principles. First of all, this language is not that of communication: "The best of what takes place between two people always escapes them as interlocutors." The new language, to be constructed, traverses the natural language and its structure, or transposes it: "This aim, I say Transposition—Structures another." It decenters the apparent structure of communication and produces a supplementary meaning—a chant: "The air or chant under the text, leading the divination from here to there. . . ." How can this *language* be constructed in *la langue?* First of all, in accordance with the comparative linguistics of his time (which had just discovered Sanskrit and was researching the genesis of language), Mallarmé set out to get to know the laws of the languages of all the peoples of the world in order to reach not an original language—that was the linguistic fantasy—but the engendering, universal, and because of that, anonymous principles of every language. "Doesn't it seem at first glance that in order to perceive an idiom well and embrace it in its entirety, all those that exist and even those that have existed must be known" *(Les Mots anglais)*. To read this text is to lend an ear to the generation of each element that makes up the present structure: "mais plutôt des naissances sombrèrent en l'anonymat et l'immense sommeil l'ouïe à la génératrice, les prostrant, cette fois, subit un accablement et un élargissement de tous les siècles. . . ."[8]

The language that writing is looking for is found in myths, religions, and rituals—in the unconscious memory of humanity that science will one day uncover by analyzing the various systems of meaning.

> Such a magisterial effort of Imagination, that desires not only to satisfy itself by the symbol exploding in the world's spectacles, but also to establish a link between these and the speech charged with expressing them, touches upon one of the sacred and perilous mysteries of Language. These mysteries can be prudently analyzed only when science, with the vast repertory of [all the] idioms ever spoken on earth in its possession, writes the history of the letters of the alphabet through the ages, and what was almost their absolute signification, which was sometimes guessed at, sometimes unrecognized by men, the creators of words. But by that time there will be no science left to sum this up, nor anyone to write it down. A chimera; let us be satisfied, for now, with the glimmer cast on this subject by magnificent writers.

The function of literature is to work at shedding light on the laws of this immemorable language, this unconscious algebra that traverses discourse, this basic logic that establishes *relations* (Jakobson would say a logic of equivalence): "how extraordinarily well the limpid structure of the language receives the primitive thunderbolts of Logic" ("Mystery in Literature").[9] Or instead: "But literature is more of an intellectual thing than that [Naturalism]; things already exist, we don't have to create them; we simply have to see their relationships. It is the thread of these relationships which go to make up poetry and music" ("The Evolution of Literature") [pp. 23–24].

For what purpose? In order to reach, through the present language, the laws of man's dreams, so that a theater of symbolicity recaptured at its source can be made of it: "I believe that Literature, recaptured at its source, which is Art and Science, will furnish us with a theater whose representations will be the true modern cult; a Book, the explanation of man, enough for our most beautiful dreams" *("Sur le théâtre")*.

In other literary texts, the autonomy of the sign that characterizes the poetic function is less emphasized, and literary language does not present particularities that are very different from those of the language of communication. Indeed, a superficial reading does not uncover striking differences between the language of a realist novel and that of common communication, except, of course, a difference in style. Indeed, certain genres such as the epic or the novel do not have as their primary function the disarticulation of the signifier, as is the case for poetry and especially for modern poetry. They borrow the common rules of the grammatical sentence from their national language, but they arrange the *whole of the literary space* as a particular system, let's call it a *language,* whose specific structure can be described. Let us recall the work of Croce, of Spitzer, etc., who devoted their attention to the study of the language of literature, or of literature as a language.

On a more positive level, and one rid of aestheticism and closely connected to linguistic research, Russian formalism and particularly OPOJAZ [St. Petersburg Society for the Study of Poetic Language] were able to detect the fundamental (and in all cases omnivalent) rules of such an organization in narrative. Propp analyzed the Russian folktale by distinguishing the general lines of its structure, its principal protagonists, and the logic of their action. Jakobson, Eichenbaum, Tomachevski, etc., were the first to consider literary texts as a structured signifying system. With much more precision, Lévi-Strauss described the structure of the language of myths *(The Raw and the Cooked, From Honey to Ashes).* Since that time, there has been a closer collaboration between linguists and literary scholars; the transfer of linguistic rules, applied to sentence analysis, to the vaster whole of myth, narrative, and the novel has been more frequent and more fruitful. Research of this type is today being devoted to modern literature as well, and the importance of this work, which adds to the most advanced practice of language an analysis inspired by the most recent science, cannot be overemphasized.

The studies of Saussure published in this realm are extremely important. By tackling the system of poetic language, Saussure in his *Anagrammes* (published in part by Starobinski, *Mercure de France,* 1964; *Tel Quel,* vol. 37, 1969)[10] indulged in demonstrations that seem to question even the notion of the linguistic sign. He studied Saturnian verse and Vedic poetry, and noticed that in each line there almost seemed to be hidden the name of a divinity, or a warrior chief, or some other character that could be reconstituted from the syllables dispersed in various words. It seemed that each message contained an underlying message that was at the same time a double code; each text was another text, each poetic unit had at least a double signification, no doubt unconscious, that was reconstituted through the play of the signifier. Saussure was probably mistaken about the regularity of this law requiring the existence of a name hidden under the manifest text, but the main point is that through this "error" he isolated a particularity of poetic functioning: that supplementary meanings slip into the verbal message, tear its opaque cloth, and rearrange another signifying scene. This is similar to phrascographic writing, which uses the material of verbal signs to write a transverbal message; it superimposes itself on the message transmitted by the line of the communication, and amplifies the line's volume. Such a conception refutes the thesis of the linearity of the poetic message, and substitutes for it one of poetic language as a complex network stratified by semantic levels.

Now parallel to the studies science is devoting to the organization of literary texts, literature itself is being practiced as a search for the laws of its own organization. The modern novel has become a disarticulation of the constants and rules of the traditional narrative, an exploration of narrative language, which brings its procedures to light before exploding them. The "nouveau roman" has become a veritable grammar of the narrative. *La Modification* by Michel Butor, *Le Voyeur* and *Les Gommes* by Alain Robbe-Grillet, and Nathalie Sarraute's *Tropismes* explore the units of the traditional narrative: the narrative situation (addresser-author/addressee-"you"); the characters, anonymous entities that become personal pronouns; their confrontation; the ascending, descending, or circular line of the action, etc. This is often done with the author's manifest consciousness of writing in order to lay bare the narrative *code* and with it, the rules of the discursive situation. Modern literature is thus becoming not only a science of narrative but also a science of discourse, of its subjects, its figures, and its representations, and thus of *representation* in and through language. This is an implicit science, sometimes even explicit, but one that positive science has not yet systematized.

Even more, by emphasizing what we have called "the poetic function of language," the modern novel is becoming an exploration not only of narrative structures but also of the specifically sentential, semantic, and syntactic structure of *la langue*. The example set by Mallarmé or Ezra Pound is currently being followed in the French novel as it is now being written, as in *Nombres* by Philippe Sollers (we will not here tackle the ideological aspect of this text), as a precise analysis of the phonic, lexical, semantic, and syntactic resources of the French language, on which is constructed a logic unknown to the speaker communicating in this language, a logic that reaches the degree of condensation of dreams, and approaches the laws of ideograms or of Chinese poetry—a logic whose hieroglyphs, traced in the French text, come to tear us away from what an entire "logocentric" science (the one we have followed during the course of the preceding analysis) wanted to make us accept as the image of our language.

22

SEMIOTICS

During the course of our exposition, and especially in the last two chapters, we have had the opportunity to treat several signifying systems (dreams, poetic language) as particular types of "language." It is apparent that the meaning of the term "language" as it is used here does not correspond to that of *langue* such as it is described by grammar, and has in common with it only the fact of being a system of signs. What are these signs? What are their relations? What is the difference between them and the *langue*-object of grammar?

These questions have been asked more or less insistently since the time of the Stoics, in the Middle Ages with its *modi significandi,* through the Solitaries and their logical theory of the sign, up until the first "semiologists" of the eighteenth century who worked their way toward a general theory of language and signification: Locke, Leibniz, Condillac, Diderot, etc. The *modi significandi* of the Middle Ages, however, reflected and demonstrated a transcendental theory that had to be founded on *la langue.* The Ideologues of the eighteenth century, in contrast, saw the sign as idealism's nerve center, which they wanted to recuperate in order to demonstrate its implantation in reality and its realization in the senses of the free subjects of an organized society. Today *semiotics* is again taking this path, which was interrupted after the bourgeois revolution and smothered by Hegelian historicism and logical-positivistic empiricism. By adding to it an *interrogation* of the very matrix of the sign, the types of signs, their limits and vacillation, semiotics has become the place where science questions itself about the fundamental conception of language, the sign, signifying systems, their organization, and their change.

By tackling these questions, linguistic science is thus induced today to profoundly revise its conception of language. For if several signifying systems are possible in *la langue,* then it no longer appears as *one* system, but instead as a plurality of signifying systems of which each is one layer of a vast whole. In other words, the language of direct communication described by linguistics seems more and more to be *one* of the signifying systems that are produced and practiced as *languages*—a word that from now on must be written in the plural.

On the other hand, some signifying systems seem able to exist even if they are not necessarily constructed with the help of *la langue* or by using it as a model. Thus, gesturality, the various visual signals, and even the image, photography, cinema, and painting are so many languages to the extent that they transmit a message between a subject and an addressee by using a specific code, even though they do not obey the rules for the construction of verbal language that have been codified by grammar.

The study of all these verbal or nonverbal systems as languages, that is, as systems in which signs are articulated by a syntax of differences, is the subject of a vast science that has barely begun to be formed called *semiotics* (from the Greek word σημειον, sign).

Two scholars almost simultaneously yet independently of one another fixed the necessity and the large frameworks of this science: Peirce (1839–1914) in the United States and Saussure in Europe.

Peirce, a logician and axiomatician, built the theory of signs in order to establish logic there. He wrote (1897) that logic in a general sense is the other name for semiotics: an almost necessary or formal doctrine of signs, founded on abstract observation, which should in its realizations approach the rigor of mathematical reasoning. Semiotics therefore had to embrace in a logical calculus the whole of signifying systems and had to become the "hair-splitting calculus" Leibniz had dreamed of. It would have three parts: *pragmatics,* which implicates the speaking subject, *semantics,* which studies the relation between the sign and what is signified *(designatum),* and *syntax,* the description of the formal relations between signs.

With Saussure, the semiotic project was oriented more toward natural languages.

> A science that studies the life of signs within society is conceivable; it would be a part of social psychology and consequently of general psychology; I shall call it *semiology* (from the Greek *sémêïon,* "sign"). Semiology would show what constitutes signs, what laws govern them. Since the science does not yet exist, no one can say what it would be; but it has a right to exist, a place staked out in advance. *Linguistics is only a part* of the general science of semiology; the laws discovered by semiology will be applicable to linguistics, and the latter will circumscribe a well-defined area within the mass of anthropological facts. To determine the exact place of semiology is the task of the psychologist. [p. 16; italics added]

Thus, to the extent that linguistics adopts the concept of the "arbitrary" sign and thinks of *la langue* as a system of differences, it will make semiology possible. Indeed, it is because of the possibility of reducing the verbal system to *autonomous marks* that Saussure was able to foresee linguistics as "the master-pattern for all semiology" [p. 68]. He wrote, "Signs that are wholly arbitrary realize better than the others the ideal of the semiological process; that is why *la langue,* the most complex and universal of all systems of expression, is also the most characteristic; in this sense linguistics can become the master-pattern for all branches of semiology although *la langue* is only one particular semiological system" [p. 68].

Nevertheless, Saussure pointed out that semiology could not be the neutral, purely formal, even abstractly mathematized science that logic and even linguistics are, for the semiotic universe is the vast realm of the social, and to explore it is to join in sociological, anthropological, psychological, etc., research. Semiotics thus would have to draw on all the sciences, and would first have to devise for itself a *theory* of signification before it could formalize the systems it wanted to tackle. The science of the sign would thus become inseparable from a theory of signification and knowledge, from *gnosiology.*

Circa 1920, the development of logic elicited a semiotic current that was clearly a formalizing one; we saw an example of this in the semiological theory of Hjelmslev, but it found its apogee in the work of the Vienna Circle, and more particularly, in R. Carnap's book *Logical Construction*. This tendency remains very much alive today, even though semiotics seems to be going off in another direction. Let us cite among the works proposing a formal theory of semiotics those of C. Morris. For him, as for Cassirer, man is less a "rational animal" than a "symbolic animal," caught in a general process of symbolization, or *semiosis*. Morris defined it in this way: "Semiosis (or sign process) is regarded as a five-term relation—*v, w, x, y, z*—in which *v* sets up in *w* the disposition to react in a certain kind of way, *x*, to a certain kind of object *y* (not then acting as a stimulus), under certain conditions *z*. The *v*'s, the cases where this relation obtains, are *signs*, the *w*'s are *interpreters*, the *x*'s are *interpretants*, the *y*'s are *significations*, and the *z*'s are the *contexts* in which the signs occur" (*Signification and Significance*, 1964).[1]

Semiotics, attentive to Saussure's teaching, took a decidedly different orientation.

First of all, in order to construct the systems of the languages it tackles, it takes as its model linguistics and the different ways linguistics arranges, structures, or explains the system of language. One is now aware, as incidentally Saussure had indicated, that *la langue* is only one particular system in the complex universe of semiotics, and research is continuing in an effort to systematize languages other than the language of direct communication (such as gestures, poetic language, painting, etc.), without necessarily mimicking the categories that are valid for the languages of ordinary communication. Moreover, as Saussure has already expressed, it is clear that this formalization of signifying systems cannot be a pure mathematicization, for formalism needs theory in order to assure the semantic value of its marks and their combination.

Here one touches upon the fundamental problem of the human sciences, such as they are being worked out today. While thinking in various realms of human activity is tending toward an unprecedented exactitude and rigor, it is trying to base itself on the most rationalized of these realms. It turns out that linguistics is the first of the sciences dealing with human practice to be constituted as an exact science, by limiting to the utmost, as we have seen, the object it intends to study. The human sciences therefore have only to transfer this method to other areas of human activity, by beginning to consider them as languages. One can see that every human science is thus more or less implicitly related to semiotics, or, in other words, that semiotics as the general science of signs and signifying systems impregnates all the human sciences: anthropology, psychoanalysis, the theory of art, etc. (see Roland Barthes, *Elements of Semiology,* 1966; English edition, 1968).

On the other hand, however, while it was at first believed that one could do without theory by proposing only a formal schema of the units, levels, and relations inside the system being studied—and this was done by keeping as close as possible to one or another schema borrowed from linguistics—it has become more and more obvious that if semiotics is not accompanied by a sociological, anthropological, psychoanalytic theory, it remains a naïve description without great explanatory force. Human sciences are not sciences in the sense that physics and chemistry are. In their case, it would be better to place the word *science* in quotation marks (by referring here to the theoretical operation that *establishes* the formalizations and places the quotation marks). Indeed, critical thinking about the formalization methods borrowed from linguistics and their basic principles (sign, system, etc.) can lead to a revision of these very categories and to a reformulation of the theory of signifying systems that is likely to change the orientation of the science of language in general. For one thing is at least certain, thanks to the arrival of semiotics: the thinning-out of the object language that modern linguistics has fashioned for itself appears in all its narrowness and all its inadequancies. And once again—as if one were returning to a time when language signified an ordered cosmogony— thinking is grasping complex reality through a full language. But this time science is present for the exploration.

STRUCTURAL ANTHROPOLOGY

After literature, which had been submitted to a quasi-structural analysis by the Russian formalists who were inspired by the development of linguistics during the middle of this century, *anthropology* became the principal realm to have a methodology close to that of linguistics applied to it. One can say consequently that, without presenting itself explicitly as a semiotics and without giving itself up to thinking and exploration about the nature of the sign, structural anthropology *is* a semiotics, to the extent that it considers various anthropological phenomena as languages and applies to them the descriptive procedure specific to linguistics.

Since Mauss, anthropologists have clearly been interested in linguistic methods in order to borrow from them information, especially etymological information, that could shed light on rituals and myths. It was, however, Trubetskoi's phonology that powerfully renewed this collaboration, as well as the conception of *la langue* as a system of *communication*.

Lévi-Strauss, the founder of structural anthropology based on phonological methodology, wrote in 1945 that "Structural linguistics will certainly play the same innovating role with respect to the social sciences that nuclear physics, for example, has played for the physical sciences."[2] The phonological procedure has indeed been applied to the kinship systems of so-called primitive societies.

Before this encounter between phonology and anthropology, details of terminology and rules of marriage were, each for their part, attributed to one custom or another, and no systematicity was discerned there. However, while resulting from the action of various heterogeneous, historical factors, kinship systems, considered as a synchronic whole, testified to a certain regularity. There were patrilineal or matrilineal systems in which women were exchanged in a certain order; marriages were permitted with one relative, or one member of the same tribe or of a close or distant tribe, and forbidden with another type of relative or with a member of a different type of tribe. Faced with this regularity, Lévi-Strauss posited the analogy between kinship systems and language systems.

> In the study of kinship problems (and, no doubt, the study of other problems as well), the anthropologist finds himself in a situation which formally resembles that of the structural linguist. Like phonemes, kinship terms are elements of meaning; like phonemes, they acquire meaning only if they are inte-

grated into systems. "Kinship systems," like "phonemic systems," are built by the mind on the level of unconscious thought. Finally, the recurrence of kinship patterns, marriage rules, and similar prescribed attitudes between certain types of relatives, and so forth, leads us to believe that, in the case of kinship as well as linguistics, the observable phenomena result from the action of laws which are general but implicit. The problem can therefore be formulated as follows: Although they belong to *another order of reality,* kinship phenomena are *of the same type* as linguistic phenomena. Can the anthropologist, using a method analogous *in form* (if not in content) to the method used in structural linguistics, achieve the same kind of progress in his own science as that which has taken place in linguistics? [p. 34]

It is obvious that starting from these basic principles, structural anthropology has had to define the *elements* of a kinship system, just as linguistics defined the basic units of a linguistic system, and at the same time the specific relations of these elements in the structure. Ethnological observations have shown that the *avunculate* (the primordial importance of the maternal uncle) is the simplest imaginable kinship structure. It is based on four terms: brother, sister, father, son, joined among themselves (as in phonology) into two couples of correlative oppositions (brother/sister, husband/wife, father/son, maternal uncle/sister's son) so that in each of the two generations in question there is always a positive and a negative relationship. The axis of the *brothers-in-law* is inevitable and central; the kinship structure is constructed around it.

Obviously, the establishment of rules that recall phonological ones is possible only if kinship is considered to be a *communication* system that is also related to language. This was indeed the case for Lévi-Strauss, who noted that the "message" of a kinship system is *"the women of the group* who are circulated between clans, lineages or families, in place of the *words of the group* which are circulated among individuals" [p. 60]. Starting with this conception of kinship rules as social communication rules, Lévi-Strauss contested the habit anthropologists had of classifying these rules in heterogenous categories designated by various terms such as the prohibition on incest, preferential types of marriages, etc. He felt that

> they can be interpreted as being so many ways of insuring the circulation of women within the social group or of substituting the mechanism of a sociologically determined affinity for that of a biologically determined consanguinity. Proceeding from this hypothesis, it would only be necessary to make a mathematical study of every possible type of exchange between *n* partners to enable one almost automatically to arrive at every type of marriage rule actually operating in living societies, and, eventually, to discover other rules that are merely possible; one would also understand their function and the relationships between each type and the others. [p. 60]

It is not our task here to analyze all the subtlety with which Lévi-Strauss established kinship systems during the course of his research and of which his book *The Elementary Structures of Kinship* (1949; English edition, 1969) is the masterful summary. We only want to emphasize how the problematic of language, even the problematic of phonology, a particular science of language, became the lever for a new science in a new realm, structural anthropology, and thus enabled it to discover the fundamental laws on which communication, that is, human communication, is based.

Is this to say that the order of language is absolutely analogous to that of culture? If there were no relation between the two, human activity would have been a disparate disorder without any rapport among its various manifestations. That is not what has been observed. If, on the contrary, the correspondence between the two orders were total and absolute, it would be accepted without raising any problems. Lévi-Strauss, having made this observation, opted for a middle position; those who work for the construction of a new science, semiotics, which is understood to be a science of the laws of symbolic functioning, cannot be reminded of this position too often:

> Some kind of correlation exists between certain things on certain levels, and our main task is to determine what these things and what these levels are. This can be done only through

a close cooperation between anthropologists and linguists. I should say that the most important results of such a cooperation will not be for linguists alone or for anthropology alone, or for both; they will most certainly be for an *anthropology* conceived in a broader way, that is, a knowledge of man that incorporates all the different approaches which can be used and that will provide a clue to the way our uninvited guest, the human mind, works. [pp. 79–80]

THE LANGUAGE OF GESTURES

When we tackled the problems of literary or poetic language, we pointed out that this language is considered a signifying system distinct from *la langue* in which it is produced—a system whose specific elements must be isolated and precise laws of articulation found—and is the object of part of the science of signs, *literary semiotics.* Since the work of the Russian formalists and the Prague Linguistic Circle, which was in large part devoted to the study of poetic language as the essential if not primary part of semiotics, studies have progressed appreciably. With structuralism, literary semiotics has become the most original way to tackle literary texts, and its methods pervade criticism as well as the teaching of literature.

The possibility of studying gestural practices, such as gesture, dance, etc., as languages may seem less obvious. While it is clear that gesturality is a communication system that transmits a message, and that consequently it can be considered a language or a signifying system, it is nevertheless still difficult to clarify certain elements of this language. For instance, what are the minimal units of this language (corresponding to the phonemes, morphemes, or syntagms of verbal language)? What is the nature of the gestural sign: does it have a signified that is attached in as strict a way as the signified is to the sign of verbal language? What is the relationship between the gesture and the verb when they coexist in a message? And so on.

Before sketching out the solution that today's gestural semiotics is proposing for these problems let us point out that the value of the gesture as a primordial act of signification, or rather as the process where signification is *engendered* before being *fixed* in the word, has always attracted the attention of different civilizations, religions, and philosophies. We have mentioned the importance attributed to the gesture in the study of the genesis of symbolism and of writing in particular. Let us add to these remarks the example of the Dogon god *Ama* who "created the word by *showing* it," or instead that of the Bambaras for whom "things were *designated* and named silently before they existed, and were called into being by their name and their sign." The indicative gesture, or the gesture alone, seems to be a primordial sketch of *signifiance* but is not *signification*.[3] It is no doubt the property of gestural practice of being the very space where signification *germinates,* that makes the gesture the privileged realm of religion, sacred dance, and ritual. Let us here recall the example of the secret traditions of Nō, Japanese theater, or instead Kathakali, Indian theater, or Balinese theater, which served as the basis for Antonin Artaud's proposition for a radical transformation of the West's theatrical conception *(Theater and Its Double).*

Describing this gestural practice, which opens up a zone of symbolic activity unknown to natural languages such as they are studied by grammar, Artaud (*Lettre sur le langage,* 1931) wrote: "alongside culture through words, there is culture through gestures. There are other languages in the world besides our Western language, which opted for a lack of ornamentation and a dessication of ideas, and where ideas are presented to us in an inert state without stirring up along the way a whole system of natural analogies known in oriental languages."

In the eighteenth century, when philosophy was looking for the mechanism of the sign, the *gesture* became an important object of thought. From Condillac to Diderot, from the original gesture to the gestural sign language of the deaf and dumb, the problems of gesturality were one of the most important terrains on which the Encyclopedists sketched out the materialist theory of signification.

For Condillac, gestural language was the original language. "Gestures, facial movements, and inarticulated stresses—these were the first means men had to communicate their thoughts to one other. The language formed with these signs was called *action language"* (*Principes généraux de grammaire,* 1775). Studying the evolution of language, Condillac (*Essai sur l'origine des connaissances humaines,* 1746) insisted upon the fact that the first human language, after the constitution of cries/signs of passions, was this action language, which he defined in the following way:

> It seems that above all this language was retained in order to instruct people about things that they were more interested in: such as the police and religion. That is because it made a more lasting impression, since it acted on the imagination with more liveliness. There was even something strong and great about this expression, something that languages, being still sterile, couldn't come close to. The ancients called this language by the name of *dance:* that is why it is said that David danced in front of the Ark [of the Covenant].
>
> Men, by perfecting their taste, gave this *dance* more variety, more grace, and more expression. Not only were arm movements and body attitudes subject to rules, but the steps to be formed by the feet were marked down. By that, dance naturally was divided into two arts that were subordianted to it. One, if I am permitted to use an expression in accordance with the language of antiquity, was the *dance of gestures:* it was preserved in order to concur when communicating men's thoughts. The other was principally the *dance of steps:* it was used to express certain situations of the soul, particularly joy; it was used for jubilant occasions, and its principal object was pleasure. . . .

A study of the relation between the gesture and the chant led Condillac to analyze *pantomime* among the ancients as a distinctive art, or rather, signifying system.

Such themes were frequent in the writings of the Ideologues and Materialists of the eighteenth century. While today they may seem abrupt or naïve, it is important to emphasize that, on the one hand, they represent the first attempt at a systematic glimpse of various signifying practices, something science is just barely starting to take on seriously now, and that, on the other hand, the study of gesturality and writing as a search for the origin of language, or rather of a preverbal symbolicity, seemed at the time to constitute a zone that rebelled against Cartesian teaching on the equivalence of the subject and its vcrb, and thus to introduce a subversive element, premeaning, into verbal reason. Wasn't the problematic of the production, change, and transformation of meaning thus infiltrating, through the gesture, the rationalism of the materialists?

When our century has once again taken up the problem of the gesture, this has either been within the framework of the constitution of a general doctrine of languages (see P. Kleinpaul, *Sprache ohne Worte. Idee einer Allgemeinen Wissenschaft der Sprache,* Leipzig, 1884), or within the framework of medicine and psychology (such as the studies of the behavior of deaf-mutes). In both cases the gesture has been envisaged as the opposite of verbal language and irreducible to it. Certain psychologists have demonstrated that grammatical, syntactic, and logical categories cannot be applied to gesturality because these categories cut up and partition the signifying whole and, in this way, do not take into account gestural specificity, which cannot be reduced to this partitioning. For "gesticulated language," P. Oléron (1952) wrote, "is not only language but also action and participation in action and even in things." It has been noted that the gesture translates the modalities of discourse (order, doubt, prayer) just as well as verbal language, but that it imperfectly translates grammatical categories (substantive, verb, adjective). Others have noted that the gestural sign is polysemic (endowed with several meanings) and that the usual "syntactic" order (subject-predicate-object) is not followed in the gestural message. It more closely resembles childlike discourse and "primitive" languages: for instance, it emphasizes the *concrete* and the *present,* it proceeds by antithesis, it puts negation and interrogation in the final position, etc. Finally, there has been a return to the intuition of the eighteenth century, which held that gestural language was the true means of authentic and original expression, and that verbal language was a late and limited manifestation of it.

We find ourselves faced here with the essential problem raised by the gesture: is it a communication system like others, or instead a *practice* in which the meaning transmitted during the course of the communication is engendered? To opt for the first solution signifies that one will study the gesture by applying to it the models elaborated by linguistics for the verbal message, and that the gesture will therefore be reduced to this message. To opt for the second solution means, on the contrary, to try, starting with the gesture, to renew the general view of language: if the gesture is not only a communication system but also the production of this system (of its subject and its meaning), then perhaps one could conceive of every language as something other than what is revealed by the now common schema of communication. Let us note right away that this second option is, for the moment, theoretical, and that the research—very recent, by the way—devoted to it is of a purely methodological nature. The conception that is currently dominating the study of gesturality is that of American *kinesics*.

It has been defined as a methodology that studies "the communicative aspects of the learned and structured behavior of the body in motion." It was born in America in close relation to ethnology, which was supposed to give an account of the general behavior, linguistic as well as gestural, of primitive societies. By what system does man structure his body space during the course of communication? What gestures characterize a tribe or social group? What is the meaning of gestures? How are they inserted into the complexity of social communication? Anthropology and sociology, made aware of the importance of language and communication by the study of the laws of society, were the first to outline a study of the gesture.

Since then, however, kinesics has declared itself a science and posits in a more direct manner the problem of knowing to what extent the gesture is a language.

Kinesics acknowledges first of all that gestural behavior is a particular and autonomous "stratum" in the communication network. To this stratum is applied an analysis that is inspired by, but does not literally imitate, phonological procedures, to the extent that phonetics is recognized as the most advanced human science in the systematization of its subject matter. The *minimal* element of the position or motion is therefore isolated, the axes of *opposition* are found, and these are used to establish the relations of the minimal elements in a structure of several tiers. What are these tiers? They can be thought of as analogous to linguistic levels: phonematic and morphematic. Other researchers, reticent about the analogy between verbal and gestural language, have proposed an autonomous analysis of the gestural code into *kine* (the smallest perceptible element of body motions; for example, the fact of raising or lowering one's eyebrows) and *kineme* (the same motion repeated in a single signal before stopping at the initial position). These are combined like prefixes, suffixes, and transfixes and form in this way units of a higher order: *kinemorphs* and *kinemorphemes*. For instance, the kine "eyebrow movement" can be an *allokine* of the kines "head-shaking," "hand movement," etc., or it can be used with stresses, and thus form *kinemorphs*. The combination of kinemorphs gives rise to complex kinemorphic constructions. One can clearly see the analogy between such an analysis and that of verbal discourse into sounds, words, clauses, etc.

A specialized part of kinesics, *parakinesics,* studies the individual and accessory phenomena of gesticulation, which are added to the current gestural code to characterize social or individual behavior. Here again, the analogy with linguistics is obvious: in the same way, *paralinguistics,* defined by Sapir, studies the accessory phenomena of vocalization and, in general, the articulation of discourse.

Such studies, while they are still far from grasping all the complexity of daily gesturality, and even less the complex universe of ritual gesturality or dance, are the first steps toward a science of complex practices, a science for which the name "the language of gestures" would not be a metaphorical expression.

MUSICAL LANGUAGE

The studies of musical language that are not content with just reproducing the habitual impressionism of music theory are rare and recent. These studies still limit themselves principally to dissociating themselves from the subjective and vague discourse that floods music treatises, as well as from precise but purely technical studies (acoustic, quantitative evaluation of lengths and frequencies, etc.), and to positing in a theoretical fashion the relation between music and language: to what extent is music a language, what radically distinguishes it from verbal language?

Among the first to have tackled music as a language, let us mention Pierre Boulez, *Notes of an Apprenticeship* (1966), who talked about "musical language," "semantics," "morphology," and the "syntax" of music. The semiotics of music, which has inherited works such as these, is trying to clarify the meaning of these terms, by including them in the specific system that the signifying system of music is.

Indeed, the similarities between the two systems are considerable. Verbal language and music are both realized by utilizing the same material (sound) and by acting on the same receptive organs. The systems both have *writing* systems that indicate their entities and their relations. But while the two signifying systems are organized according to the principle of the *difference* of their components, this difference is not of the same order in verbal language as it is in music. Binary phonematic differences are not pertinent in music. The musical code is organized by the *arbitrary* and *cultural* (imposed within the frameworks of a certain civilization) difference between various vocal values: *notes.*

This difference is only one consequence of a capital difference: while the fundamental function of language is the *communicative* function, and while it transmits a *meaning,* music is a departure from this principle of communication. It does transmit a "message" between a subject and an addressee, but it is hard to say that it *communicates* a precise *meaning.* It is a combinatory of differential elements, and evokes an algebraic system more than a discourse. If the addressee hears this combinatory as a sentimental, emotive, patriotic, etc., message, that is the result of a subjective interpretation given within the framework of a cultural system rather than the result of a "meaning" implicit in the "message." For while music is a system of *differences,* it is not a system of *signs.* Its constitutive elements do not have a signified. Referent/signified/signifier here seem to melt into a single mark that combines with others in a language that doesn't mean anything. Stravinsky wrote in this sense: "I consider music, in its essence, as powerless to *express* anything at all: a feeling, an attitude, a psychological state, a phenomenon of nature, etc. *Expression* has never been the immanent property of music. . . . The phenomenon of music is given to us for the sole purpose of instituting order in things. To be realized, therefore, it necessarily requires only a construction. Once the construction is finished, and order is achieved, everything has been said. It would be useless to search for or hear something else there."

Music thus takes us to the limit of the system of the sign. Here is a system of differences that is not a system that *means* [something], as is the case with most of the structures of verbal language. We noticed the same particularity in gestural language when we indicated the specific status of meaning in the gesture, that of a *production* of meaning which doesn't manage to fix itself in the signified product. But in gestural practice, the lack of ornamentation of the productive code, which is not laden with the produced signified, is less visible than in music, for the gesture accompanies verbal communication and has not yet been studied as autonomous (ritual, dance, etc.). Music, though, makes this problematic that stops semiotics evident, and questions the omnivalence of the sign and meaning. For music is indeed a differential system without semantics, a formalism that does not signify.

Since this has been established, what can semiotics possibly say about the musical system?

On the one hand, it can study the formal organization of different musical texts.

On the other hand, it can establish the common "code," the common musical "language" of an era or culture. The degree of communicability of a particular musical text (that is, its possibility of reaching the addressee) would depend upon its resemblance to or difference from the musical code of the time. In monolithic societies, like primitive societies, musical "creation" requires strict obedience to the rules of the musical code, which is considered as a given and as sacred. Conversely, the so-called *classical* type of music testifies to a tendency toward variation, so that each musical text invented its own laws and did not obey those of the common "language." This is the famous loss of "universality" that music history attributes principally to Beethoven. For such a musical text to break off ties with common musical language it had to be organized on the inside as a regulated system. Hence the reason for the exact repetition of certain parts of the melody, which traced the coordinates of a musical oeuvre as a particular system in and of itself, which were different, for example, in Bach and in succeeding composers. "Since the beginning of the nineteenth century," Boris de Schloezer wrote *(Introduction to Johann Sebastian Bach),* "style has been dead," style being "the somewhat collective product in which were crystallized certain modes of thinking, feeling, and acting of a century, a nation, or even a group, if it succeeded in imposing its mind on a society."

In the modern era the work of Schoenberg is, from what Boulez says,

> the very model of a search for language. Arriving during a period of dissolution, he pushed that breaking-up to its extreme result: "suspension" of the tonal language. . . . An important discovery, as important as any in the story of the morphological evolution of music. For the true measure of the Schoenberg phenomenon cannot be taken from the fact of his having instituted a rational organization of chromaticism by means of the twelve-tone series; rather, it seems to me, it must be taken from the fact of his institution of the serial principle itself, a principle that could, I should gladly be inclined to think, rule a sound-world of intervals more complex than the semitone. For just as the modes or the tonalities engender not only musical morphologies, but also—out of them—syntax and forms, so the serial principle also conceals new morphologies departing from that new distribution of the sound-space, in which the idea of sound itself comes to occupy the preponderant position—a new syntax and specific new forms. . . . With Webern, on the other hand, the SOUND-CLARITY is achieved by the birth of the structure out of the material. I am speaking of the fact that the architecture of the work derives directly from the ordering of the series. To say it another way, schematically, whereas Berg and Schoenberg in some manner limit the role of serial writing to the semantic level of the idiom *{language}*—the invention of elements that will be combined by a nonserial rhetoric—with Webern the role of that writing is understood as extending to the rhetoric itself.[4]

Finally, musical semiotics can establish the concrete organizational laws of a musical text of a precise period, in order to compare them to the respective laws of literary texts or of the pictorial language of the same period, and establish the differences, divergencies, delays, and advances of signifying systems with respect to one another.

VISIBLE LANGUAGE: PAINTING

In the classical conception of art, painting is considered a *representation* of reality, which it is placed before in the mirror position. It *tells* or *translates* an act or a story that really exists. For this translation it uses a particular language of forms and colors which, in each painting, are organized into a system founded on the pictorial *sign.*

It is clear that starting from such a conception, one can analyze a painting as a structure with its own entities and rules, according to which it is articulated. Among the research, very recent by the way, conducted in this realm, we must mention that of Meyer Schapiro. His research is concerned first of all with defining the pictorial sign, which is called the *iconic sign,* to the extent that it is an image ("icon") of a referent that exists outside the system of the painting. Several different problems, not yet resolved, have been raised by this perspective: what are the components of the iconic sign? Should we say that the iconic sign is the painted object with respect to the real object? But isn't the specificity of pictorial language then destroyed by reducing its components to the components of a spectacle outside the painting, whereas the language specific to the painting is a language of laws, forms, and colors?

It can thus be observed that before resolving such problems, which would lead us to the definition of the pictorial sign, the very concept of *representation,* on which representational painting is based, must be questioned.

If one takes a classical painting, that is, a painting whose iconic signs are analogous to the reality represented (for example, *The Checker Players* by Paris Bordone, as J.-C. Schefer has done in *Scénographie d'un tableau,* 1969) one can note that the reading of this painting's language passes through three poles: (1) the internal organization of a finite number of elements of the painting into a closed structure (the combination of elements in correlative oppositions: the human figures, the objects, forms, perspectives, etc.)—this is the *figurative code;* (2) the *real* to which this mode refers; (3) the discourse in which the figurative code and the real are uttered. The third element, the uttering *discourse,* reunites all the painting's components; in other words, the painting is nothing other than the *text that analyzes it.* This text becomes a cross-roads of signifiers, and its syntactic and semantic units refer back to other, different, texts that form the cultural space of the reading. One *deciphers* the painting's code by assigning each of its elements (the figures, forms, positions) one or several meanings that they could have been given by the texts (philosophical treatises, novels, poems, etc.) evoked in the process of the reading. The painting's code is joined to the history that surrounds it and in this way produces the text constituted by the painting.

In this "becoming-text" of the painting, one understands that the painting (and consequently the iconic sign) does not represent a real, but instead a "simulacrum-between-the-world-and-language," on which is based a whole constellation of texts that interect with and are added to each other in a reading of the said painting, a reading that is never finished. What one believed to be a mere representation turns out to be a destruction of the represented structure in the infinite play of the correlations of language.

Two consequences follow from such a conception of pictorial language.

First, the specifically pictorial code is in close relation to the language that constitutes it, and pictorial representation refers therefore to the network of *la langue,* which emanates from the simulacrum represented by the pictorial code, but dissolves it by surpassing it.

Second, the concept of structure truly seems to be applicable only to the pictorial code itself; it is moved off center in the text that the painting becomes by means of the reading. A painting, even a classical, representational one, is nothing other than a structured code. This code triggers a signifying process that arranges it. And the process in question is itself only the history of a culture that represents itself by passing itself through the filter of a given pictorial code.

One can see how such a conception of the iconic sign and its system leads us to explore the laws of symbolization, of which those of the linguistic sign seem more and more to be a particular case.

According to a sound observation by M. Pleynet, the intervention of Paul Cézanne (1839–1906) in European painting modified the conditions of pictorial language. Indeed, in Cezanne's oeuvre and in that of many who came after him, the process that "decenters" the painting's structure and goes beyond the pictorial code itself—a process that, in classical painting, took refuge in the painting's "text" (or in that of the subject looking at it)—penetrates the object itself. The object then ceases to be a painted object in order to become an infinite process that takes into consideration the whole of the forces that produce and transform it in all their diversity. Let us remember, to support this thesis, the quantity of unfinished and unsigned canvasses Cézanne left, the repetition of the same forms, the use of different types of perspective, and his famous statement, "I will not allow myself to get my claws on it." Let us also recall the passage from a vision with a monocular perspective to the splitting-up in depth of a binocular type of vision, and so on. After Cézanne, Pleynet noted, his revolution was interpreted in two ways: either as a purely formal search (the Cubists), or as a reshaping of the object/pictorial process relationship. The latter interpretation remains the most faithful to the Cézannian transformation of the object in process retracing its history (Duchamp, dada, anti-art).

As a result, a painting is no longer an object: the representation of a painting has been replaced by the process of its reproduction. *A painting*—a closed structure traversed by *la langue*—can therefore be contrasted with *painting*—a process that traverses the object (the sign, the structure) that it produces.

With Matisse, Pollock, Rothko, to mention just these names, modern painting and sculpture are illustrating the "productive-transforming relation of a practice with respect to its history." In other words, painting has become a process of production that does not represent any sign or any meaning, except the possibility, starting from a limited code (a few forms, some color oppositions, the relation of a certain form to a certain color) of elaborating a signifying process that analyzes the components of what was originally given as the foundations of representation. This is how (modern) *painting* silences verbal language, which was usually added to (classical) *paintings* claiming to be *representation*. Before painting, phantasies cease, speech stops.

VISIBLE LANGUAGE: PHOTOGRAPHY AND CINEMA

While the nature of photography and cinema has often been dealt with, the approach that consists of considering them languages is very recent.

The difference in structure between photography and cinema has been noted to be their different ways of grasping reality. Thus, Barthes saw in the temporality of photography a new space-time category: "spatial immediacy and temporal anteriority, the photograph being an illogical conjunction of the *here-now* and *there-then.*"[5] Photography shows us a prior reality, and even if it does give us an impression of ideality, it is never experienced as purely illusory: it is the *document* of a "reality from which we are sheltered" [p. 44].

In contrast, cinema calls for the subject to project himself into what he sees; it is not presented as an evoking of a past reality, but as a fiction the subject is in the process of living. The reason for the impression of imaginary reality that cinema elicits has been seen in the possibility of representing *movement, time, the narrative,* etc.

Moreover, independent of phenomenological criticism, directors themselves have been looking into the characteristics of cinema from its beginnings and have defined its laws. We are referring here to theoreticians such as Eisenstein and Vertov. We owe to Eisenstein, for example, the first authoritative treatises on form and signification in cinema in which he demonstrates the importance of *montage* in cinematographic production, and by that, in every signifying production. Cinema does not copy the reality proposed to it in an "objective," naturalistic, or continuous fashion. It cuts up sequences, isolates shots, and recombines them by means of further montage. Cinema does not reproduce things, it manipulates, organizes, and structures them. And it is only in the new structure obtained by editing these elements that they take on meaning. The principle of montage, or better, that of joining isolated, similar, or contradictory elements, whose collision provokes a signification they don't have by themselves, was found by Eisenstein in hieroglyphic writing. His interest in eastern art is known, as is the fact that he learned Japanese. According to him, a film must be a hieroglyphic text in which each isolated element has meaning only in the contextual combination and according to its place in the structure. Let us recall the example of the three different statues of a lion filmed by Eisenstein in the *Battleship Potemkin:* isolated in independent shots and arranged one after the other, they form a "cinematic utterance" whose meaning would supposedly be the identification of the lion's power with the Bolshevik Revolution.

Thus, from its beginnings, cinema has considered itself as a language and has looked for its syntax. One could even say that the search for the laws of cinematic enunciation was more marked during the period when cinema was being constructed outside speech: silent, cinema was looking for a language with a different structure from that of speech.

Another tendency, in contrast with that of montage, is oriented toward a cinematographic narrativity in which shots are not cut up and then organized, but instead in which the shot is a sequence, a free movement of the camera (a "pan"), as if film had given up showing the *syntax of its langue* (in and out tracking, horizontal and vertical panoramic shots, etc.) and was satisfied with speaking a *language.* Such is the case with Antonioni, and Visconti; with certain others (Orson Welles, Godard) both procedures seem to be used equally.

These brief remarks already show that not only can cinema be considered a language, with its own units and syntax, but that it already is one. We have even been able to detect a difference between the conception of cinema as *langue* and the conception of cinema as language. Today many studies are devoted to the internal rules of cinematographic language. Some are even going beyond the framework of films strictly speaking, and studying the language of comic strips: there the succession of sketches no doubt imitates the arrangement of cinematographic images, and by this means goes beyond the static nature of photos and sketches, and introduces time and movement into the narrative. The isolated image (or photograph) is an utterance; when arranged with others, it produces a narration. An interesting field of exploration can be seen opening up here: the relation between cinematographic language and that of comic stips, on the one hand, and the linguistic text (speech, the verb) that corresponds to this language, translates it, and serves as its support, on the other.

One quickly notices, however, that the term "language" used here is not understood in its linguistic sense. It is more a question of an analogy. Since cinema is a system of differences that transmits a message, it can be christened a language. The problem being posed is that of knowing, after the numerous psychological studies done about the cinematographic phenomenon, whether the linguistic conception of language is of use in the analysis of films, whether it can lead to a semiotics of cinema.

In his *Essai sur la signification du cinéma* (1968), Christian Metz noted that there is nothing in the cinematographic system that can be compared to the phonological level of language. Cinema has no unit on the order of the phoneme. Nor does it have "words." The image is often considered to be a word, and the sequence a sentence, but for Metz the image is equal to one or more sentences, and the sequence is a complex segment of *discourse*. That amounts to saying that the image is "always speech, never a unit of language." Consequently, if there is a syntax of cinema, it must be constructed on syntactic, not morphological bases.

The semiotics of cinema can be conceived of either as a semiotics of connotation or as a semiotics of denotation. In the second case the centering of the image, the camera movements, the effects of the camera lights, and so on, would be studied. In the first case it would be a question of detecting the different significations, "atmospheres," etc., that a denoted segment evokes. Moreover, it is obvious that cinematographic semiotics would be organized as a *syntagmatic* semiotics—the study of the organization of the elements inside a synchronic whole— rather than as a paradigmatic semiotics: the list of units likely to appear in a precise place in a cinematic chain is not always limited.

It is possible to envisage the way in which the semiotics of cinema can be presented as a study of its syntax, of the logic of the arrangement of its units. An example of this logic is the *alternating syntagm:* image of an Egyptian statue, image of a blast furnace, image of an Egyptian statue, image of a blast furnace, etc. The repeated collision of these images, seen from various angles and conveyed from different sides, can reconstruct in the language of cinema a whole narrative that literature would have introduced between the two polar syntagms (statue-furnace) to explain the reason for their arrangement. In such a narrative, the alternating syntagm outlines a story which, in this precise case, is that of Mediterranean civilization (*Mediterranée,* by Jean-Daniel Pollet).

The problem of the syntagmatic analysis of film, to grasp the mode of signification specific to cinema, is, as one can see, complex. What will the superior minimal unit of the filmed example be? How can the components image-sound-speech be articulated in a single unit or several units that are themselves combined? And so on. It is clear that the transposition of linguistic principles onto cinematographic analysis produces results only if they are completely reinterpreted and adapted to the film's specific system. It is less a question of *linguistic notions* than of linguistic *methods:* the signifier/signified distinction, cutting up, communication, pertinence, etc. Here as in other signifying systems, the importance of semiotic study consists of the fact that it reveals laws of the organization of signifying systems that were not observed in the study of verbal language. With these laws, language can probably be reconsidered one day to find there zones of "signifiance" that are being censored or repressed in the current state of linguistic science: zones appropriated by what has been called "art" in order for it to unfurl and explore them.

ZOOSEMIOTICS

The observation of animal behavior furnishes interesting data that testify to the existence of a communication system in the animal world that is often highly developed. Indeed, the variety of "expressions" of the animal body denoting a state or precise function (see the illustrations), the various animal noises and bird songs, seem at different levels to indicate that animals handle a specific code of signaling. Research to this effect has been undertaken by biologists and zoologists who have indeed furnished an abundant amount of material on everything from the communication of insects to that of primates. This data was published by Thomas A. Sebeok in the collection *Animal Communication,*[6] which appeared in 1968.

We will limit ourselves to two examples: the "gestural" communication of bees, and the "vocal" communication of dolphins.

Kircher's texts in *Misurgia Universalis* (1771) are among the earliest to deal with the problem of animal language. But particularly since the 1930s science has the precise investigative means needed to study the animal code.

Karl von Frisch, a professor in Munich, observed the dance of bees in 1923. A nectar-gathering bee, once back in its hive, performs before the other inhabitants of the hive a dance of which two essential components have been detected: horizontal circles and imitations of a figure 8. These dances seem to indicate to the other bees the exact location of the flower the nectar-gathering bee has just returned from. Indeed, within a short time, bees from the same hive can be found on this same flower. Von Frisch supposed that they were guided by the dancing language of the nectar-gathering bee; the horizontal circles would indicate the existence of nectar, and the figure 8 the pollen. Between 1948 and 1950, Von Frisch clarified the results of these observations. The dance indicated the distance between the hive and the nectar; the "rounddance" announced a maximum distance of one hundred meters, whereas the figure 8 could announce a distance of up to six kilometers. The number of figures in a given amount of time designated the distance, whereas the axis of the 8 revealed the direction with respect to the sun [p. 232].

We are faced here with a *subtle code* that strongly resembles human language. Bees can transmit messages composed of several pieces of data: the existence of food, position, distance. They have a memory, since they are capable of retaining the information to be transmitted. Finally, they *symbolize,* for here a gestural sequence indicates something other than itself: food, its position, its distance. Nonetheless, Benveniste has noted that it would be difficult to assimilate this system of communication, even though it is highly elaborate, to human language. Indeed, bee communication is gestural, and not vocal. It presupposes not a response on the part of the addressee but a reaction. In other words, there is no *dialogue* between bees. The bee receiving the message cannot transmit it to a third bee (therefore no message is constructed from the message). Finally, communication concerns only food. Benveniste concluded that bee communication is not a language, but a *code of signals* which, in order to develop and be used, needs a *society,* the group of bees and their common life.

On the other hand, observing dolphin communication has revealed supplementary facts about animal language. Certain dolphins give out vocal signals that carry either underwater or in the air. They can receive an answer from the addressee that enables the group to find them again. These signals are not just designed to indicate the location of food, or to connect the members of the group. Several of them seem to be a real song performed for the pleasure of listening to it:

Figure 22.1. The language of animals: various postures of the lynx (above) and the fox (below) corresponding to aggressivity and sociability. Adapted from T. Sebeok, *Animal Communication* (Bloomington: © Indiana University Press, 1968), pp. 372–73.

such is the case of certain dolphins, under the Arctic ice. The signals start at a frequency of seven KHz and are comprised of several pulsations, such as leaps of several hundred Hz, followed by a rapid decrease to below the preleap frequency. Some signals can last a minute and fall to a frequency of under a hundred Hz. The change in fre-

Figure 22.2. Attempts at a musical notation of various animal cries, done by A. Kircher, *Misargia Univeralis*. Adapted from T. Sebeok, *Animal Communication* (Bloomington: © Indiana University Press, 1968), p. 638.

quency of a signal cuts it into sequences that have a distinctive value in communication. Finally, the signals of submarine animals often serve to locate food or the enemy. The transmission and return of a signal reflected by an obstacle helps orient the animals.

With animal communication we are faced with a system of information that, while being a language, does not seem to be founded on the sign and meaning. The sign and meaning appear more and more as specific phenomena of a certain kind of human communication, and are far from being the universals of all signaling. A typology of signs and signals thus becomes necessary that would assign the correct place to the phenomenon of verbal communication.

Zoosemiotics enables us to discover *codes of information* in all living organisms. "This is because terrestrial organisms, from protozoans to man, are so similar in their biochemical details as to make it virtually certain that all of them have evolved from a single instance of the origin of life. A variety of observations support the hypothesis that the entire organic world has descended lineally from primordial life, the most impressive fact being the ubiquity of the molecule DNA. The genetic material of all known organisms on earth is composed largely of the nucleic acids DNA and RNA that contain in their structures information that is reproductively transmitted from generation to generation and that have, in addition, the capability for self-replication and mutation. In brief, the genetic code 'is universal, or nearly so' . . ." [p. 11].

Moreover, the Soviet mathematician Lapunov (1963) has emphasized that all living systems transmit, through strictly defined and constant channels, small quantities of material energy that contain an important quantity of information and that then control a series of organisms. Sebeok, for his part, has concluded that biological as well as cultural phenomena can be envisaged as aspects of the information process. Even reproduction can be considered as an information-answer or as a type of control that seems to be a universal property of earthly life, independent of its form or structure.

For the moment, given the relatively small number of research studies conducted in this area, any conclusion is premature, and the cybernetic vision of life could turn out to be a metaphysical presupposition that establishes [a type of] knowledge but limits it at the same time. Certain scholars remain convinced that the combined effort of genetics, information theory, linguistics, and semiotics can contribute to an understanding of "semiosis," which, according to Sebeok, can be considered the definition of life. Here we are faced with a phenomenological postulate that is given as empirically demonstrated: the order of *language* unites that of *life* and *ideality*. The element of signification, the substance of expression that makes up speech reunites in a parallelism (transcendental) *meaning* and *life*.

CONCLUSION

The representations and theories of language we have just summarily run through approach through the name "language" an object that is noticeably different each time. By shedding light on it from various points of view, by making it known in different ways, these theories testify especially to a type of knowledge that is specific to a society or a historical period. Throughout the history of linguistic knowledge, what appears is not so much the upward evolution of a knowledge of language: it is the story of thought tackling this unknown that constitutes it.

In what is commonly called prehistory, reflection on language was confused with a natural and sexual cosmogony from which it was inseparable and which it arranged by arranging itself as agent, actor, and spectator. Phraseographic writing—the basis of logography and morphography—heralded a type of functioning in which the message was absent from words and was transmitted in a transverbal articulation, which dreams, or modern poetry, or the hieroglyph of every aesthetic system commemorate.

Indian and Greek atomism tried to reconcile the act of signifying, perceived from then on in its difference, with what it signified by looking for an atomization, a powdering of the two series that had melted into one other or were reflected by each other. This was before the Greek Idea—that "transcendental signified" (see Derrida, *On Grammatology*)—came to light, and jointly constituted the birth certificate of *philosophy* and of *grammar* as the empirical support and subordinated reflection of a philosophical or logical theory. From its beginning until today, grammar was to be didactic and pedagogical, the first instrument to *teach* the art of thinking well to be ordained by philosophy.

The *object language*—a sonorous substance that bore meaning—was isolated from the cosmos in order to be studied for itself. The act of removing language from that which it wasn't, but which it named and arranged, was no doubt the first important jump in the current leading to the constitution of a *science* of language. This was offered and accomplished in Greek philosophy and grammar. Meaning became from then on the enormous and unknown region that grammar, logic, and every other approach to *la langue* would look for across epistemological avatars.

First language, isolated and delimited as a particular object, was considered a collection of elements whose relation to meaning and things was sought: the representation of language was *atomistic.* Later came a *classification* that distinguished linguistic categories: this was *morphology,* which preceded syntax by two centuries (at least as far as Greece and Europe are concerned), and which testified to *relational* thinking.

The Middle Ages understood language as the echo of a transcendental meaning, and studied *signification* in depth. During this period, language was less a collection of morphological and syntactic rules than a reply to ontology. It was the *sign: significans* and *significatum.*

With the Renaissance and the seventeenth century, the classifying knowledge of newly discovered languages did not, for all that, abolish the metaphysical goals: concrete languages were represented on the universal ground of a common logic, whose laws were later fixed by Port-Royal. The *structuralist* Renaissance gave way to the *science of reasoning:* the *General Grammar.*

The eighteenth century tried to separate itself from this logical ground, but it did not forget it. It attempted to organize the surface, *la langue,* into a specifically linguistic syntax. It did not, however, abandon the research intended to explain, through the intermediary of signs, the link between *la langue* and the lost order of the real, of the cosmos.

With comparativism, the search for the original place of *la langue* was no longer directed toward a *real,* which previously had somehow to be signified, but toward the mother tongue of which all current languages would be the historical descendants. The language-reality problem was replaced with the problem of an ideal history of languages. These languages were already formal systems with subsystems: phonetic, grammatical, inflectional, declensional, syntactic. With the neogrammarians the study of *la langue* became an operational study of transformations; the ideal history was systematized if not structured.

The structuralism of the twentieth century abandoned this vertical axis that had oriented the preceding linguistics either toward extralinguistic reality or toward history. Structuralism applied the method of relational composition within the same language. Thus, cut up and delimited in itself, *la langue* became a system with Saussure, a structure in the Prague Circle and with Hjelmslev. Stratified into more and more formal and autonomous layers, it is being presented in the most recent research as a system of mathematical relations among terms without names (without meaning). Having arrived at this extreme formalization, where the very notion of the *sign* is fading away after those of the *real* and *history,* and where *la langue* is no longer either a communication system or a production-expression of meaning, linguistics seems to have reached the summit of the trail it blazed when it was constituted as the science of an object, of a system in itself. From now on, on this path, it can only multiply the application of logico-mathematical formalisms to the systems of *la langue.* This demonstrates only its own skill in joining a rigorously formal system (mathematics) to another system *(la langue),* which had to be stripped in order to make it fit. One can say that this formalization, this arranging of the signifier bereft of the signified, represses the metaphysical foundation that the study of *la langue* relied upon in order to begin: the detachment and the link to the real, the sign, meaning, and communication. One can wonder if this repression, while consolidating these bases, doesn't facilitate—by a didactic game—the thought process that is already beginning, and that consists of *criticizing* the metaphysical foundations of a phenomeology that linguistics is subject to but wants to ignore.

For, outside linguistics, the psychoanalytic study of the relation between a subject and his discourse has indicated that language cannot be dealt with—no matter how systematic *la langue* appears to be—without taking the subject into account. The *langue*–formal system does not exist outside speech; *la langue* is above all a *discourse*.

Moreover, the expansion of the linguistic method to other fields of signifying practices, that is, semiotics, has the advantage of confronting this method with resisting objects. It shows more and more that the models found by formal linguistics are not omnivalent, and that the various modes of signification must be studied independent of the summit-limit reached by lingustics.

These two realms, psychoanalysis and semiotics, which in the beginning were founded on linguistics, demonstrate that the expansion of linguistics—the result of a totalizing gesture that wanted to architecturalize the universe into an ideal system—has forced it to confront its limits and to transform itself in order to provide a more complete vision of linguistic functioning, and, in general, of signifying function. It will retain, no doubt, the memory of the systematization and structuration our century imposed upon it. But it will take into account the subject, the diversity of modes of signification, and the historical transformation of these modes in order to refound itself in a *general theory of signification.*

For one cannot assign a place to linguistics, much less make a science of signification, without a theory of social history as the interaction of various signifying practices. Then the true value of the thinking that sees every realm organized as a language can be appreciated. Only then can the place of language, as well as that of meaning and the sign, find their exact coordinates. It is precisely toward this goal that semiotics can tend, a semiotics understood not as a mere extension of the linguistic model to every object that can be considered as having meaning but as a criticism of the very concept of *semiosis,* on the basis of an in-depth study of concrete historical practices.

The reign of language in the sciences and modern ideology has the effect of a general systematization of the social realm. But, under this appearance, a more profound symptom can be discerned, that of the complete change of the sciences and ideology of technocratic society. The West, reassured by the mastery it has acquired of the structures of language, can now confront these structures with a complex and constantly transforming reality. It can find itself face to face with all the forgotten and censored things that enabled it to erect this system—a system that was only a refuge, *la langue* without the real, a sign, even merely a signifier. Sent back to these very concepts, our culture is being forced to question once again its own philosophical mastery.

Hence the preponderance of linguistic studies, and, even more, the Babylonian diversity of linguistic doctrines—a diversity that has been christened with the name "crisis"—indicate that modern society and ideology are going through a phase of self-criticism. The agent of this fermentation will have been that still unknown object—language.

NOTES

TRANSLATOR'S NOTE: The translation of a book of encyclopedic scope such as this one poses certain problems, which I have addressed to the best of my knowledge and ability.

First, it is common publishing practice in France not to give detailed information on quoted material. Kristeva followed that practice in this book, often giving no more than the name of the author she quoted from. Although every effort was made to locate the sources of quotations and to locate English translations of non-French books, this was not always possible. The translations are my own unless otherwise indicated.

Titles of books cited by Kristeva in French that were translated from some other language have been given in English.

Kristeva used the French method for transliterating words not written in the Roman alphabet (Chinese, Arabic, etc.). These have been anglicized when possible.

Finally, I would like to thank the following people: Julia Kristeva, for her encouragement and patience; Sharon Shelly, for advice on linguistic terms; Per Nykrog, for assistance in translating Ramus; Dan Gunn, for carefully reading the first chapters; and Karen Mitchell, for outstanding editing. Special thanks to Patsy Baudoin and, above all, to Alice Jardine, for their expertise and unfailing moral support and friendship.

TN = Translator's note.

1. Language, *La Langue,* Speech, and Discourse

1. TN. Ferdinand de Saussure, in his *Course in General Linguistics* (Paris: Payot, 1922), established a distinction between *le langage* (language), *la langue, la parole* (speech), and *le discours* (discourse). Kristeva discusses these important concepts in this chapter. Wade Baskin, in his English version of Saussure's *Course* (New York: McGraw-Hill,

1966) translated these as human speech, language, speaking, and discourse, respectively. I have decided to use the less awkward "language" for *langage,* and "speech" for *parole.* The difference between language as a whole and the language system, *la langue,* that is studied by linguistics is of capital importance in this book. I have therefore decided to retain *la langue* in French whenever this system is referred to.

2. TN. Saussure, *Course,* p. 9. Further page numbers in Baskins' translation appear in the text.

3. TN. Jacques Lacan, "The Function and Field of Speech and Language in Psychoanalysis," *Ecrits: A Selection,* Alan Sheridan, tr. (New York: Norton, 1977), p. 49.

4. TN. The "real" is a term that was introduced by Lacan, and must be differentiated from reality, as well as from the imaginary and the symbolic. In his translator's note to *Ecrits: A Selection,* Alan Sheridan describes its difference in the following way: "The 'real' emerges as a third term, linked to the symbolic and the imaginary; it stands for what is neither symbolic nor imaginary, and remains foreclosed from the analytic experience, which is an experience of speech. What is prior to the assumption of the symbolic, the real in its 'raw' state (in the case of the subject, for instance, the organism and its biological needs), may only be supposed, it is an algebraic x. This Lacanian concept of the 'real' is not to be confused with reality, which is perfectly knowable: the subject of desire knows no more than that, since for it reality is entirely phantasmatic.

"The term 'real,' which was at first of only minor importance, acting as a kind of safety rail, has gradually been developed, and its significaiton has been considerably altered. It began, naturally enough, by presenting, in relation to symbolic substitutions and imaginary variations, a function of constancy: 'the real is that which always returns to the same place.' It then became that before which the imaginary faltered, that over which the symbolic stumbles, that which is refractory, resistant. Hence the formula: 'the real is the impossible.' It is in this sense that the term begins to appear regularly, as an adjective, to describe that which is lacking in the symbolic order, the ineliminable residue of all articulation, the foreclosed element, which may be approached, but never grasped: the umbilical cord of the symbolic" [pp. ix–x].

2. The Linguistic Sign

1. TN. See C. S. Peirce, *Collected Papers,* Charles Hartshorne and Paul Weiss, eds. (Cambridge: Harvard University Press, 1931), vol. 2, ch. 2.

2. TN. *Paiera* is the 3d person plural future of the French verb *payer,* "to pay."

3. TN. See A. Martinet, "The Word," *Diogenes* (1965), vol. 51.

4. For a more detailed analysis of the theses of N. Chomsky, see chapter 19 of this work.

5. The French philosopher Jacques Derrida has proposed the concept of writing {*écriture*}, which allows us to think about language, including its phonic manifestation, as a difference (which Derrida intentionally spells *differance,* in order to highlight the differentiation process). Already for Saussure *la langue* was a *system of differences.* In fact, no structure exists without the differences that constitute its various elements. But Derrida goes further. In his system, the "gramme" is at the same time a structure and a movement. It is, he says, "the systematic play of differences, of the traces of differences, and of the *spacing* which relates the elements to one another." Here is why, with the "gramme-differance," language is presented as a transformation and a generation, and

the place of the classic concept of "structure" is bracketed. By the same token, the Saussurian *linearity* of the spoken chain (which only imitates the sonorous process and its proclivity) is put into question.

Thus writing is inherent in language, and phonetic speech can be envisioned as writing. The dominance of the *sign/meaning/concept* system is therefore displaced; this opens up the possibility of thinking within language about what is not a sign/meaning/concept. The subject depends upon the system of differences; he constitutes himself only by being divided, by being spaced, by being differentiated. "Subjectivity—like objectivity—is an effect of difference, an effect inscribed in a system of differences," Derrida writes. One can thus understand how the concept of the *gramme* neutralizes the phonological hypostasis of the *sign* (the supremacy it accords to phonetics), and brings to considerations about the sign (about *la langue*) the graphic substance and all the philosophical problems that this poses, across all of history and in all writing systems, beyond the Western area of phonetic writing.

[TN. See Jacques Derrida, *Of Grammatology,* Gayatri Chakravorty Spivak, tr. (Baltimore: John Hopkins University Press, 1976).]

3. The Materiality of Language

1. TN. Edward Sapir, *Language: An Introduction to the Study of Speech* (New York: Harcourt, Brace, and World, 1921), pp. 8–9.

2. TN. *Herodotus,* Henry Cary, tr. (Freeport, N.Y.: Books for Libraries Press, 1847, reprint 1972), p. 281.

3. TN. See *The Incas: The Royal Commentaries of the Inca Garcilaso de la Vega, 1539–1616,* Maria Jolas, tr. (New York: Orion Press, 1961), pp. 158–60, for a discussion of *quipus.* The passage cited by Kristeva is not in the English edition.

4. TN. The source of this quotation is unclear—evidently a later work than Chomsky's *Syntactic Structures,* discussed in chapter 19.

5. TN. Emile Benveniste, "Subjectivity in Language" in *Problems in General Linguistics,* Mary Elizabeth Meek, tr. (Coral Gables, Fla.: University of Miami Press, 1971), p. 224. Further page numbers appear in the text.

6. Aorist: a past tense that in the Greek verbal system designated a finished action. [TN. Prospective: a future tense that designates a potential, likely, or expected action.]

7. TN. The French language makes use of two forms to express a past action, the *passé simple, il fit* [he did], and the *passé composé, il a fait* [he did]. In addition to the imperfect and the pluperfect, the text cited by Benveniste uses only the *passé simple,* or aorist, as Benveniste calls it. An English translation, such as the one given below, cannot differentiate between these two past tenses. Note also that *histoire* means both history and story in French; hence Benveniste's use of a text by Balzac to illustrate historical enunciation.

"After a tour of the gallery, the young man *looked* at the sky and his watch in turn, *made* an impatient gesture, *entered* a tobacco shop, *lit* his cigarette there, *sat down* in front of the mirror, and *cast* a glance at his outfit, which was a little richer than the laws of taste in France allow [here the *present* tense is due to the fact that the author is reflecting upon something that escapes the plane of the narrative]. He *readjusted* his collar and his black velvet vest over which was crossed several times one of those large gold chains made in Genoa; then, after having thrown his velvet-lined overcoat over his left shoulder in a single movement that draped it elegantly, he *resumed* his walk and resisted being distracted by the bourgeois winks he *kept getting.* When the boutiques *began* to light up and the night *appeared* dark enough, he *made his way* to the Calais-Royal square as a man who *feared* being recognized, for he *walked alongside* the square up to the fountain in order, sheltered from the carriages, to enter Froidmanteau Street. . . ."

8. Today, this distinction is less sharp, and sometimes contradicts the dichotomy established by M. V. von Wartburg. For example, I believe in *{en}* you; I believe *{à}* your stories.

Part Two: Language in History

1. Deictic: a term designating all the words that situate and indicate the act of enunciation and are intelligible only in relation to it (*here, now, today,* etc.). The deictic consequently plays an important role in the Saussurian theory of discourse, and corresponds to *indication* in the tradition of Peirce.

4. Anthropology and Linguistics

1. TN. Franz Boas, *Introduction to the Handbook of American Indian Languages* (Lincoln: University of Nebraska Press, 1966), p. 69. Further page numbers appear in the text.

2. As we shall see later, "primitive man" is far from being "unconscious" of the system through which and in which he orders the real, his own body, and his social functions: language. The term "unconscious" cannot be allowed here unless it claims to indicate an incapacity in certain civilizations to separate the differentiating and systematizing (signifying linguistic) activity from what it systematizes, and consequently the incapacity to elaborate a science of the laws of language as a separate science.

3. TN. James Frazer, *The Golden Bough: A Study in Magic and Religion* (New York: Macmillan, 1951), p. 284. Further page numbers appear in the text.

4. TN. Sigmund Freud, *Totem and Taboo* in *The Standard Edition of the Complete Psychological Works,* James Strachey, ed. (London: Hogarth Press, 1953–74), 13:28–29. Further page numbers appear in the text.

5. TN. Geneviève Calame-Griaule, *Words and the Dogon World,* Deirdre LaPin, tr. (Philadelphia: Institute for the Study of Human Issues, 1986). Page numbers appear in the text.

6. TN. Maurice Leenhardt, *Do Kamo: Person and Myth in the Melanesian World,* Basia Miller Gulati, tr. (Chicago: University of Chicago Press, 1979). Page numbers appear in the text.

5. The Egyptians: Their Writing.

1. Neolithic civilization: Copper is already known but little used. An alloy of this metal with tin was not known. J.-G. Février, *Histoire de l'écriture* (Paris: Payot, 1958), p. 120.

7. China: Writing as Science

1. TN. This is Kristeva's questioning and correction.

2. We are following here the description given by Joseph Needham in *Science and Civilisation in China* (Cambridge: Cambridge University Press, 1965), vol. 1. [TN. pp. 27–28. Further page numbers appear in the text. When the source of Kristeva's information is Needham, I have given his spelling of Chinese words; otherwise I have retained the spelling as it appears in Kristeva's text.]

3. TN. This passage is from *The Kung-Sun Lung Tzu*, a short treatise in six chapters, much of which is in a very corrupt state. According to Wing-Tsit Chan, "the word *chih* has so many meanings that scholars have found it easy and even tempting to read their own philosophies into Kung-sun Lung. Those who affirm universals would interpret *chih* to mean universal concepts, while nominalists would insist on its common meaning of finger or designation." The following excerpts are from his translation in *A Source Book in Chinese Philosophy* (Princeton: Princeton University Press, 1963), ch. 3, "On Marks *(chih)* and Things," pp. 237–38: "All things are marks. But marks are no marks [for themselves]. If there were no marks of things in the world, nothing could be called a thing. . . . If there were no marks of things in the world, who could say that [x] are not marks? If there were nothing in the world, who could say that [x] are marks? If there were marks in the world but no marks of things, who could say that [x] are not marks, or that all things are not marks?"

8. Indian Linguistics

1. TN. K. Raghavan Pillai, *The Vakyapadiya* [of Bhartrhari] (Delhi: Motilal Banarsidass, 1971), 1:78–81. Further passage numbers appear in the text.

2. TN. Kristeva's French text for the *Vakyapadiya* reads: "This energy called speech has the nature of an egg (at first undifferentiated and [later] giving birth to a peacock of varied colors). Its development unfolds progressively, bit by bit, like an action."

10. The Hebrews: The Bible and the Cabala

1. TN. The translations given are those of the King James version of the Bible.

2. TN. In the French Bible, the text in question appears in verse 20, and reads "[the rod] would make God's strength shine forth."

3. TN. The French biblical text continues, "He Himself wrote His Ten Commandments, and wrote them twice to emphasize their importance, so that the necessity of observing them would be more keenly felt." This passage is not in the King James version.

4. TN. Related to a phantasy. According to Jean Laplanche and J.-B. Pontalis in *Vocabulaire de la psychanalyse* (Paris: PUF, 1967), p. 313, "this spelling was proposed by Susan Isaacs . . . to designate an unconscious fantasy, and to emphasize the difference between it and conscious fantasy."

11. Logical Greece

1. TN. Homer, *The Iliad*, W.H.D. Rouse, tr. (New York: Mentor, 1938), p. 16. Further page numbers appear in the text.

2. TN. Plato, *The Cratylus* in *The Works of Plato*, George Burges, tr. (London: Henry G. Bohn, 1859), vol. 3. Page numbers appear in the text in brackets. The numbers in parentheses correspond to passages; the English translation used did not indicate passage numbers. When the translation of certain words is important to Kristeva's argument, the term she used appears in brackets.

3. TN. Aristotle, *The Metaphysics*, Hugh Tredennick, tr. (Cambridge: Harvard University Press, 1975). Passage references appear in the text.

4. TN. Aristotle, *Poetics*, W. Hamilton Fyfe, tr. (Cambridge: Harvard University Press, 1946). Passage references appear in the text.

12. Rome: The Transmission of Greek Grammar

1. TN. Varro, *On the Latin Language*, Roland G. Kent, tr. (Cambridge: Harvard University Press, 1958), 6:37. Further passage references appear in the text.

2. TN. This passage is not from *On the Latin Language;* perhaps it is from one of the 450 fragments.

3. TN. Lucretius, *De natura rerum*, W. H. D. Rouse, tr. (New York: Putnam's, 1931). Passage references appear in the text.

4. TN. "It remains, therefore, that the earth deserves the name of mother which she possesses, since from the earth all things have been produced" (5:795). "Wherefore again and again the earth deserves the name of mother which she has gotten, since of herself she created the human race" (5:821). Italics added.

5. TN. I could not locate an English translation of Priscian's *Institutiones grammaticae.*

6. TN. R. H. Robins, *Ancient and Mediaeval Grammatical Theory in Europe* (London: Bell, 1951), p. 64.

14. Medieval Speculations

1. TN. Holger Pederson, *The Discovery of Language*, John Webster Spargo, tr. (Bloomington: Indiana University Press, 1962), p. 5.

2. TN. See note 3 to chapter 22 for a discussion of the difference between signification and "signifiance."

3. TN. *Dante's Treatise "De Vulgari Eloquentia,"* A. G. Ferrers Howell, tr. (London: Kegan Paul, Trench, Trubner, 1890), pp. 2 and 6.

15. Humanists and Grammarians of the Renaissance

1. TN. *Sorbonnard* is a familiar and pejorative name for a student or professor of the Sorbonne University.

2. We would like to thank M. J. Stefanini for having acquired for us the unpublished French translation of J. C. Scaliger's difficult text.

3. TN. The passage Ramus is referring to is from Aristotle's *Metaphysics* 9:8:1050a20. Ramus states that, according to Alexander, Pauson's statue of Mercury [Hermes] was such that it was difficult to tell whether the form was inside or outside the stone, since the outside was smooth, and the inside showed no evidence of joinings or roughness. See Pierre de la Ramée [Ramus], *Dialectique*, 2:136 (Geneva: Droz, 1964), p. 154.

4. TN. The game of *blanque* was an Italian lottery in vogue during the sixteenth century. If one drew a white *{blanque}* tablet, one lost.

5. *Monoplata* refers to nouns having only one case.

6. TN. Francis Bacon, *Advancement of Learning* (New York: Colonial Press, 1900), p. 165. Further page references appear in the text.

16. The Grammar of Port-Royal

1. TN. Francis Bacon, *Advancement of Learning* (New York: Colonial Press, 1900), book 6, pp. 165–66.

2. TN. Claude Lancelot and Antoine Arnauld, *A General and Rational Grammar*, tr. (of the seventeenth century) unknown (Menston, Eng.: Scolar Press, 1968). Page numbers appear in the text.

3. TN. *The Philosophical Works of Descartes*, Elizabeth S. Haldane and G. R. T. Ross, trs. (Cambridge: Dover, 1955), p. 252.

4. TN. Antoine Arnauld and Pierre Nicole, *The Port-Royal Logic*, Thomas Spencer Baynes, tr. (Edinburgh: Murray and Gibb, 1861). Page numbers appear in the text.

17. The *Encyclopédie: La Langue* and Nature

1. In what precedes and follows, we are sketching out this effort while referring especially to the work already mentioned several times of J.-Cl. Chevalier, *La Notion de complément chez les grammariens* (Geneva: Droz, 1968).

2. TN. *The New Science of Giambattista Vico*, Thomas Goddard Bergin and Max Harold Fish, trs. (Ithaca, N.Y.: Cornell University Press, 1968), p. 127. Further page numbers appear in the text.

3. TN. John Locke, *An Essay Concerning Human Understanding*, 2 vols. (New York: Dover, 1959), vol. 2, book 3, "Of Words," p. 10. Further page numbers appear in the text.

4. TN. G. H. Leibniz, *New Essays Concerning Human Understanding*, Alfred Gideon Langley, tr. (New York: Macmillan, 1896). Page numbers appear in the text.

5. TN. Denis Diderot, "Letter on the Deaf and Dumb for the Use of Those Who Hear and Speak" in *Diderot's Early Philosophical Works*, Margaret Jourdain, tr. (Chicago: Open Court, 1916), pp. 160–61. Further page numbers appear in the text.

6. TN. The translations here are my own; p. 208 in Jourdain's translation.

18. Language as History

1. TN. Johann Gottfried v. Herder, *Outlines of a Philosophy of the History of Man*, T. Churchill, tr. (New York: Bergman [1966?]), p. vii. Further page numbers appear in the text.

2. TN. See *The Aesthetic and Miscellaneous Works of Frederick von Schlegel*, E. J. Millington, tr. (London: Bohn, 1849).

3. TN. Holger Pederson, *The Discovery of Language*, John Webster Spargo, tr. (Bloomington: Indiana University Press, 1962), pp. 256–57. Further page numbers appear in the text.

4. The text of F. Hegel, excerpted from *Science of Logic*, is reproduced here in the Aubier edition version. [TN. G. W. F. Hegel, *Science of Logic*, W. H. Johnston and L. G. Struthers, trs. (New York: Macmillan, 1929). These remarks are from Hegel's "Preface to the Second Edition" (1831), 1:39–40.]

19. Structural Linguistics

1. TN. Emile Benveniste, "Recent Trends in General Linguistics" in *Problems in General Linguistics*, Mary Elizabeth Meek, tr. (Coral Gables, Fla.: University of Miami Press, 1971), pp. 4–5. Further page numbers appear in the text.

2. TN. Jacques Derrida, *Speech and Phenomena*, David B. Allison, tr. (Evanston, Ill.: Northwestern University Press, 1973), p. 5.

3. TN. Edmund Husserl, *Logical Investigations*, 2 vols., J. N. Findlay, tr. (New York: Humanities Press, 1970), 2:527.

4. TN. Peter Steiner, ed., *The Prague School: Selected Writings, 1929–1946* (Austin: University of Texas Press, 1982), p. 5. Further page numbers appear in the text.

5. TN. Louis Hjelmslev, *Prolegomena to a Theory of Language*, Francis J. Whitfield, tr. (Baltimore: Waverly Press, 1953). Page numbers appear in the text.

6. TN. Edward Sapir, *Language: An Introduction to the Study of Speech* (New York: Harcourt, Brace, and World, 1921), p. 8. Further page numbers appear in the text.

7. TN. Leonard Bloomfield, *Language* (New York: Henry Holt, 1933). Page numbers appear in the text.

8. TN. Bloomfield used the term "meaning" for what Kristeva is calling the signified.

9. TN. John B. Carroll, *The Study of Language: A Survey of Linguistics and Related Disciplines in America* (Cambridge: Harvard University Press, 1953), p. 21. Further page numbers appear in the text.

10. TN. Bernard Bloch and George L. Trager, *Outline of Linguistic Analysis* (Baltimore: Linguistic Society of America, 1942), p. 54.

11. TN. Carroll, *The Study of Language*, p. 37.

12. TN. Zellig S. Harris, *Structural Linguistics* (Chicago: University of Chicago Press, 1951); see ch. 13, "Morpheme Alternates."

13. TN. Zellig S. Harris, *String Analysis of Sentence Structure* (The Hague: Mouton, 1964). Page numbers appear in the text.

14. TN. A corpus (plural corpora) is a collection of recorded utterances used as the basis for a descriptive analysis of a language.

15. TN. Noam Chomsky, *Syntactic Structures* (The Hague: Mouton, 1957), p. 13. Further page numbers appear in the text.

16. TN. See *Syntactic Structures* "Phase Structure", pp. 26–32 for a definition and discussion of terminal versus "finite state" languages.

20. Psychoanalysis and Language

1. Let us mention among these linguists J. Van Ginneken and his *Principles of Psychological Linguistics* (1907).

2. See on this subject, J.-C. Sempé, J.-L. Donnet, J. Say, G. Lascault, and C. Backès, *La Psychanalyse,* a SGPP publication from "Le point de la question" collection.

3. TN. Sigmund Freud, *The Interpretation of Dreams* in *The Standard Edition of the Complete Psychological Works,* James Strachey, ed. (London: Hogarth Press, 1953–74), vols. 4 and 5, 5:651.

4. TN. Lacan, "The Function and Field of speech" in *Ecrits: A Selection,* Alan Sheridan, tr. (New York: Norton, 1977), p. 40. Further page numbers appear in the text.

5. TN. Benveniste, "Remarks on the Function of Language in Freudian Theory," in *Problems in General Linguistics,* Mary Elizabeth Meek, tr. (Coral Gables, Fla.: University of Miami Press, 1971), p. 67. Further page numbers appear in the text.

6. TN. Freud, *The Interpretation of Dreams,* p. 341. Further page numbers appear in the text.

7. TN. Freud, *Negation {Die Verneinung}* in *Standard Edition,* vol. 19. Page numbers appear in the text.

8. Topology: a mathematical study of spaces and forms. By extension, the study of the configuration of the discursive space of the subject with respect to the other and discourse.

9. TN. The term "utterance" *{énoncé}* refers to the actual words spoken, whereas "enunciation" [*énonciation*] refers to the act or *process* of speaking them. This distinction leads to a very important one for psychoanalysis, that of the difference or discontinuity between the subject of the utterance and the subject of the enunciation. See Benveniste's chapter "Subjectivity" in *Problems,* and "The Ego, The Subject" heading in the index to Lacan's *Ecrits: A Selection.* For a discussion of this difference and its importance in film theory, see Kaja Silverman's *The Subject of Semiotics* (New York: Oxford University Press, 1983), especially ch. 5, "Suture."

10. TN. See Roman Jakobson, *Shifters, Verbal Categories, and the Russian Verb,* Russian Language Project, Department of Slavic Languages and Literatures, Harvard University, 1957.

11. TN. Lacan, "Remarque sur le rapport de Daniel Lagache: Psychanalyse et structure de la personnalité" in *Ecrits* (Paris: Seuil, 1966), p. 664. My translation.

12. TN. Lacan, "The Agency of the Letter in the Unconsicous or Reason Since Freud" in *Écrits: A Selection,* p. 151.

13. Saussure, in his *Anagrammes,* was the first linguist to have understood that this "supremacy of the signifier" formulates a theory of signification called "poetic" [TN. I was unable to locate the source of these two Lacan quotations.]

14. TN. Lacan, "The Agency of the Letter. . . , p. 150.

21. The Practice of Language

1. TN. The first Greek prose writers were called "logographers," as were rhetors who wrote discourses and defense speeches for clients.

2. TN. *Institutio Oratorio of Quintilian,* H. E. Butler, tr. (New York: Putnam, 1920), 1:18–20.

3. Mirabeau, "Sur la banqueroute" discourse, September 26, 1789, in *Les Orateurs de la Révolution française* (Paris: Larousse, 1939).

4. TN. "Feuillants" was the name given in 1791 to the moderates or constitutionals whose club was located in an old *feuillant* convent; *feuillants* were members of the Cîteaux order of priests and nuns.

5. Vergniaud, in *Les Orateurs*.

6. Robespierre, "Réponse aux accusations de despotisme," in *Les Orateurs*.

7. TN. Roman Jakobson, "Linguistics and Poetics" in *The Structuralists from Marx to Lévi-Strauss,* Richard and Fernande DeGeorge, eds. (Garden City, N.Y.: Doubleday, 1972), p. 93. Further page numbers appear in the text.

8. TN. I must agree with Kristeva here: "translating texts such as these is nearly impossible."

9. TN. *Mallarmé: Selected Prose Poems, Essays, and Letters,* Bradford Cook, tr. (Baltimore: Johns Hopkins University Press, 1956), p. 32. Further page numbers appear in the text.

10. TN. For the full text see *Les Mots sous les mots: Les Anagrammes de Ferdinand de Saussure* (Paris: Starobinski, 1971); English version: Jean Starobinski, *Words Upon Words,* Olivia Emmet, tr. (New Haven: Yale University Press, 1979).

22. Semiotics

1. TN. Charles Morris, *Signification and Significance: A Study of the Relatons of Signs and Values* (Cambridge: MIT Press, 1964), p. 2.

2. TN. Claude Lévi-Strauss, *Structural Anthropology,* Claire Jacobson and Brooke Grundfest Schoepf, trs. (New York: Basic Books, 1963), p. 33. Further page numbers appear in the text.

3. TN. As Kristeva explained in chapter 3 of this book, signification is the psychological *process* that results in meaning, which is static. Kristeva introduced the concept of *signifiance* in her book *Semeiotiké: Recherches pour une sémanalyse* (Paris: Seuil, 1969). It is "the *work* of differentiation, stratification, and confrontation that is practiced in *la langue,* and deposits on the line of the speaking subject a communicative and grammatically structured signifying chain" [p. 11]. Signifiance exceeds the language of communication, which is the realm of signification. "Signifiance becomes a differentiated infinity whose unlimited combinatory knows no bounds, 'literature'/ the text removes the subject from his identification with communicated discourse, and in the same movement breaks his disposition as a mirror reflecting the 'structures' of an outside" [pp. 12–13]. Signifiance is also discussed by Kristeva in "The Semiotic Activity," *Screen* (Spring/Summer 1973), vol. 14, nos. 1–2.

4. TN. Pierre Boulez, *Notes of an Apprenticeship,* Herbert Weinstock, tr. (New York: Knopf, 1968), pp. 11–12.

5. TN. Roland Barthes, "Rhetoric of the Image" in *Image, Music, Text,* Stephen Heath, tr. (New York: Hill and Wang, 1977), p. 44. Further page references appear in the text.

6. TN. Thomas A. Sebeok, *Animal Communication: Techniques of Study and Results of Research* (Bloomington: Indiana University Press, 1968). Page numbers appear in the text.

WORKS PRINCIPALLY RELIED ON

Carroll, John B. *The Study of Language: A Survey of Linguistics and Related Disciplines in America*. Cambridge: Harvard University Press, 1959.

Gernet, Jacques. *L'Ecriture et la Psychologie des peuples*. Paris: Armand Colin.

Février, J.-G. *Histoire de l'écriture*. Paris: Payot, 1958.

Lepschy, G.-C. *La Linguistique structurale*. Paris: Payot, 1968.

Kukenheim, L. *Esquisse historique de la linguistique française*. Leiden, 1966.

Leroy, M. *Les Grands Courants de la linguistique moderne*. Paris: PUF, 1967.

Mounin, G. *Histoire de la linguistique des origines au XXᵉ siècle*. Paris: PUF, 1967.

Pedersen, Holger. *The Discovery of Language: Linguistic Science in the Nineteenth Century*. Bloomington: Indiana University Press, 1962. 1st English edition 1931; original edition, 1924.

Robins, R. M. *Ancient and Medieval Grammatical Theory in Europe*. London: G. Bell, 1951.

Zvegintsev, V. A. *Istoiya Iazikoznaniya XIX–XX vekov*. Moscow, 1960.

INDEX

343

Universality of language, Sapir's idea, 239

Utterance, 275, 339*n*9; Indian concepts, 91; phonemes and, 22; separation of levels, 253

Vachek, J., 224

Valla, G., 146; *De elegantia,* 159

Van Ginneken, Jacques, 23, 45

Vargas, 85

*Variation de la langue française depuis le XII*ᵉ *siècle,* Génin, 206

Varro, 117, 118-21

Vaugelas: *Dictionnaire de l'Académie,* 170; *Remarques sur la langue française,* 159

Vedic texts, and speech, 83

Velarized consonants, 22

Vendryes, J., 224

Verbal language: and gestures, 306; and music, 308-9

Verb complements, 32-33

Verb phrase, 33; Arab concept, 133

Verbs: Aristotelian view, 113, 114; Greek, 111; Latin, 120; medieval concepts, 138-39; Port-Royal concepts, 166, 167; Renaissance concepts, 150, 151; Stoic views, 115

Verginaud, Pierre, 284-85

Vergleichende Grammatik, Bopp, 200

Vergleichende Zergliederung des Sanscrits und der mit ihm verwandten Sprachen, Bopp, 200

Vernacular languages, Renaissance studies, 144-45

Verner, Karl, 211

Vertov, Dziga, 315

Vibrants, liquid sounds, 21

Vico, G., *Scienza Nuova,* 173-74

Vienna Circle, 298

Villedieu, Alexandre de, *Doctrinale puerorum,* 137-38

Visconti, Lucino, 316

Visible language: painting, 312-14; photography, 315-18

Vives, *De disciplinis libri XII,* 146

Vocal apparatus, 20; study of, 215

Vocal communication of dolphins, 320-22

Vocalized phonetic writings, 29

Voice: in ancient Egyptian writing, 67; Stoic concepts, 115

Voiced sounds, 20

Voiceless sounds, 20

Voltaire, François Marie Arouet, 183

Von Frisch, Karl, 319

Vosseler, K., *Positivism and Idealism in Linguistics,* 211

Vowels, 106; in ancient Egyptian writing, 68-67; Arab concepts, 130; Aristotelian view, 113; in cuneiform writing, 70; Saussure's views, 214

Vowel sounds, 21

Le Voyeur, Robbe-Grillet, 293

Wackernagel, Jacob, 115

Wartburg, M. W. von, *Problems and Methods in Linguistics,* 37

Watson, J. B., 240

Weaver, Warren, 252

Webb, John, 81

Webern, Anton von, 311

Weil, R., 66

Weiner, Norbert, 10

Weingart, M., 224

Weisgerber, L., 47, 232

Weiss, A. P., 240

Wey, F., *Histoire des révolutions du langage en France,* 206

Whitney, W. D., 216

Whorf, Benjamin Lee, 47

William of Occam, 141

Winter-count writing system, 24, 27

Words, 12, 31; Aristotelian view, 113; Chinese, 74; as conceptual symbols, 109; Greek theories, 109; Indian concepts, 87-88, 90; Liebniz' ideas, 176-77; Locke's idea, 176; Lucretius' views, 123, 124; medieval theories, 141; in non-Indo-European languages, 246-47, Port-Royal concepts, 162-64; Priscian's view, 125; psychological theories, 213; Renaissance concepts, 150; in sign theory, 15

EUROPEAN PERSPECTIVES: A SERIES OF COLUMBIA UNIVERSITY PRESS

Daniel Roche, editor, *Journal of My Life: The Autobiography
of Jean-Louis Menetra*   1986
Franco Basaglia, *Psychiatry Inside Out*   1987
Arnold Gehlen, *Man*   1987
Volker Meja, Dieter Misgeld, and Nico Stehr, *Modern Ger-
man Sociology*   1987
Gilles Deleuze and Claire Parnet, *Dialogues*   1988
Michel de Certeau, *The Writing of History*   1988
Julia Kristeva, *In the Beginning Was Love*   1988
Sarah Kofman, *The Childhood of Art*   1988